Praise for *James Dean*
A BookSense 76 Selection

"*James Dean Died Here* is an addictively irresistible tour through pop culture past and present."
— *Chicago Tribune*

"The whereabouts of 600-plus places that have helped shape national identity, from the momentous (site of the world's first A-bomb explosion) to the ridiculous (where Zsa Zsa slapped that hunky Beverly Hills cop)."
— *USA Today*

"Who says Americans don't know much about history? . . . Epting's quirky factoids are most appealing."
— *Publishers Weekly*

"Chris Epting has written a guidebook to a broad range of historic and often hysterical American landmarks — more than 700 in all. *James Dean Died Here* includes the spot where the young movie icon perished in a car accident, the location of the *Brady Bunch* house, and the hangar where the final scene of *Casablanca* may have been shot."
— *National Public Radio's "All Things Considered"*

"Chris Epting's omnibus picks up where standard guidebooks leave off, directing couch potatoes to the spots they've always imagined but never seen . . . . 49 states are represented, the 600-plus locations are almost entirely free to visit, and you'll never again lose $40 to take a stupid 'star tour.' "
— *Arthur Frommer's Budget Travel*

"Just in time for summer road trips comes a cool new book that lists the location of about 650 pilgrimage-worthy pop culture sites across the United States. *James Dean Died Here: The Locations of America's Pop Culture Landmarks* is a guide to sites morbid, trashy and profound. Epting has assembled a treasure trove of pop landmarks!"
— *Albuquerque Journal*

"Want to know where Zsa Zsa Gabor was arrested? The house that was built on the Indian burial ground in Poltergeist? Where Elvis recorded 'Heartbreak Hotel'? It's all in here, Baby!"
— BookSense 76

"This book bulges with facts!"
— *Los Angeles Times*

"With sweep both noble and tacky, Chris Epting's book, *James Dean Died Here: The Locations of America's Pop Culture Landmarks,* is the complete package for those who like their American history unadulterated by the usual cultural distinctions . . . . Whether you are sticking to that armchair or planning a road trip this summer, *James Dean Died Here* is a spirited companion, one that will steer you off the interstate to some of the country's most exalted, tragically charged and hopelessly hokey landmarks."
— *Baltimore Sun*

Praise for *Marilyn Monroe Dyed Here*

"Tabloid readers and tourists on the fringe will love Chris Epting's *Marilyn Monroe Dyed Here*, a *Hollywood Babylon* meets Fodor's guide to the historic, tragic and scandalous."
                    —*Los Angeles Magazine*

"There's something intriguing about visiting a place where a historical moment occurred. Of course, one's definition of history varies. If you're Chris Epting, you're obsessed with uncovering the strange, weird and wonderful moments that constitute American pop culture history. Epting has unearthed a ton of information here, dividing this fun and irresistible guide into palatable pop culture chunks: history and tragedy, crime, murder and assassination, celebrity deaths, movies, music and literary stuff. This book will keep you entertained for hours."
                    —*Chicago Tribune*

"Makes the random, unusual and weird cool again."
                    —Knight-Ridder

"Chris Epting has done it again!. . . .From Christopher Columbus and Johnny Appleseed to Michael Jackson and Elizabeth Smart, *Marilyn Monroe Dyed Here* spans American history. I just wish my high school history text had been half as compelling a read."
                    —Roadtripusa.com

"A compendium of pop culture locations that range from Al Capone's house on Star Island to the spot where Jackson Pollock died in a car crash to the street near Fresno where Anne Heche was found dazed and confused after her breakup with Ellen DeGeneres. As in his first book, Chris Epting does an amazing job of compressed research."
                    —*Palm Beach Post*

"A virtual roadmap of Hollywood and pop culture history."
                    —ABC News

"You could call these books magical for their power to transform your car or reading nook into a time machine. They add the dimension of nostalgia to armchair traveling while planting seeds of wanderlust for future road trips. . . . Whether you'd like to check out Woody Allen's New York, a Bob Dylan Walking Tour or simply explore an unexpected side of more than 1,000 stories you thought you knew, these extraordinary photo and fact-filled repositories will put you there."
                    —*Car and Travel Monthly* (AAA NY)

"Author Chris Epting identifies pop-culture landmarks that have yet to be turned into official attractions, including the Army barracks where Elvis got his hair cut and the beauty salon where Marilyn first became a blonde."
                    —*Wall Street Journal*

Elvis Presley Passed Here

Even *More* Locations of America's Pop Culture Landmarks

Chris Epting

SANTA
MONICA
PRESS

ELVIS PRESLEY

PASSED HERE

DEPARTMENT OF RECREATION AND PARKS
CITY OF LOS ANGELES

Even *More* Locations of America's Pop Culture Landmarks

Chris Epting

Author of *James Dean Died Here*
and *Marilyn Monroe Dyed Here*

S A N T A

M O N I C A

P R E S S

Published by:
Santa Monica Press LLC
P.O. Box 1076
Santa Monica, CA 90406-1076
1-800-784-9553
www.santamonicapress.com
books@santamonicapress.com

Printed in the United States

Santa Monica Press books are available at special quantity discounts when purchased in bulk by corporations, organizations, or groups. Please call our Special Sales department at 1-800-784-9553.

ISBN 1-59580-001-8

Library of Congress Cataloging-in-Publication Data

Epting, Chris, 1961-
  Elvis Presley passed here : even more locations of America's pop culture landmarks / Chris Epting.
      p. cm.
  ISBN 1-59580-001-8
  1. Historic sites--United States--Guidebooks. 2. Popular culture--United States--History. 3. United States--Guidebooks. 4. United States--History, Local. I. Title.
  E159.E675 2005
  306'.0973--dc22
                              2005003982

Book and cover design by Ohmontherange
Interior production by Future Studio

Table of Contents

"The past does not repeat itself, but it rhymes."
—Mark Twain

"One's destination is never a place, but a new way of seeing things."
—Henry Miller

"The journey, not the arrival matters."
—T. S. Eliot

Hello, once again, fellow fans of pop culture travel. In the year or so since writing the introduction to my last book, we've had some wonderful adventures. I can speak for myself and my family when I say we've logged some of the best miles in our lives; meeting people and standing where spectacular things happened. And I know from the communiqués I've received from many of you that you've also been out exploring. To that end, I'd like to first thank you for all of the great ideas, suggestions, critiques and support. It makes this process much more fun and memorable.

If you've been with me through the books leading up to this one (*James Dean Died Here* and/or *Marilyn Monroe Dyed Here*), welcome back. If you're new to the adventure, welcome aboard. Here, in what I'll refer to as Volume III, the same rule applies: pinpoint the exact places where things happened. Just what *things* am I referring to? Pop culture landmarks, of course. Events that have shaped our memories and public perceptions, thrilled us, mystified us, horrified us and everything in between. Historic events. Not-so-historic events. Events that, for some reason, have gotten stuck in our collective consciousness (or that maybe should have gotten stuck if they haven't already).

What makes this book different than the last two? One thing I've done more of this time out is to trace as many origins as I could think of—the exact spots where things like Memorial Day, Flag Day and "America the Beautiful" were inspired. Birthplaces of famous corporations and classic American brands where our foremost captains of industry changed the world, from Coca-Cola to Kool-Aid to Hilton. (Though I came up short locating exact site of the first Denny's, then called Danny's, back in 1953 in Lakewood, California. Anyone?) Places that inspired such famous paintings as Grant Wood's *American Gothic* or Georgia O'Keeffe's *The Lawrence Tree*.

With this collection I've included other little-known origin spots such as where Alcoholics Anonymous was created, a section of where certain religions were formed and a collection of sites related to children's literature.

Couple that with the inclusion of more exact sites from rock and roll, jazz, film, crime, TV, Americana and the just plain weird and you've got, well, the next book I always wanted to write. You'll discover hundreds of places and events, arranged in clear order, loaded with the facts, figures and trivia that I hope helps bring it all to life.

So there you go. In case you're interested, from here I will continue mining this concept of travel related to pop culture history. I have begun to outline the book that will result in the European version of this idea. I'm also currently working on *The Ruby Slippers, Madonna's Bra, and Einstein's Brain*—a book which locates specific cultural artifacts, as opposed to sites where events took place. And a few other projects I'll save as surprises.

I would once again like to thank you most sincerely for being a part of this ongoing adventure. Without your support and interest, this would be a much different kind of project, and so I am indebted to you. Also, I want to acknowledge the many people I have met in researching these books, who have helped piece the places and events together. Historians, librarians, townsfolk and others, from all around the country—thank you for the stories and good remembrances. You help bring these events back to life so others can experience them.

Until our roads cross again, remember to appreciate and cherish that ground you walk upon every day. After all, something interesting may have happened on that very spot.

Chris Epting

Comments, questions, or suggestions for upcoming editions? Write the author at: Chris@chrisepting.com and visit www.chrisepting.com for even more pop culture history.

This book is dedicated with love and devotion to my family and to the lasting memory of my grandmother, Margaret Gallo.

Americana:
The Weird and the Wonderful

America's Stonehenge

105 Haverhill Road
Salem, New Hampshire
603-893-8300
Directions: From I-93, take Exit 3. Then take Route 111 East (stay to the left of U.S. Gas). Follow 111 East about 4½ miles. When you see a blue marker sign that says "America's Stonehenge," take the next right. There is a traffic light and a Mobil station at that intersection.

This is weird! Located about 40 miles north of Boston in Salem, New Hampshire, you'll discover and explore 30 acres of strange cave-like dwellings, astronomically aligned rock formations and other cryptic structures left behind by an unknown people. "America's Stonehenge," as it is now called, opened to the public in 1958 under the name Mystery Hill Caves. The site baffles visitors and archeologists alike, an unnatural riddle out in the woods.

Just like the more famous Stonehenge in England, it is believed that America's Stonehenge was built by ancient people well versed in astronomy and stone con- struction. It has been determined that the site is an accurate astronomical cal- endar. It was, and still can be, used to determine specific solar and lunar events of the year.

"America the Beautiful"

Pikes Peak
Colorado Springs, Colorado

The lyrics to "America the Beautiful" were written by a woman named Katharine Lee Bates (1859-1929), an instructor at Wellesley College in Massachusetts. She wrote the poem when she visited Pikes Peak in 1893. It appeared in print in *The Congregationalist*, a weekly journal, on July 4, 1895. Over the course of several years Bates revised the lyrics, and it's interesting to note that the poem was not always sung to the now-familiar melody. (The tune, called "Materna," was composed by Samuel A. Ward in 1882, near-

ly a decade before the poem was written.) Interestingly, for the first couple of years the poem was written, it was sung by many to virtually any popular tune that let the lyrics fit ("Auld Lang Syne" being the most notable of those). The words of the poem were not fused with "Materna" until 1910, which is how we know the song today.

Archie Comics

Haverhill High School
137 Monument Street
Haverhill, Massachusetts

In 1941, Bob Montana created the "Archie Comic Strip" depicting his days as a student at Haverhill High School (Montana graduated in 1939). Haverhill is most likely called Riverdale High in the comics because of the influence of the Merrimack River. "The Thinker" statue stills sits outside the school's front entrance, just like it did in the famous comic strip. The main characters—Archie, Jughead, Betty, Veronica and Reggie—are all based on Montana's real-life friends at Haverill. Montana first sketched them on a napkin in 1941 while sitting at the Chocolate Shop on Merrimack Street in Haverhill. The shop is gone, but Archie fans know that it lives forever as the "Choklit Shoppe" on Riverdale's Main Street.

Automat

1557 Broadway
New York City, New York

The impetus of the legendary Horn & Hardart Automat restaurant chain was a 15-stool lunchroom at 3739 South 13th Street in Philadelphia, Pennsylvania. It was opened on December 22, 1888 by Joseph Horn and Frank Hardart. They were inspired to create automats after Frank Hardart visited Berlin and experienced the Quisiana Company Automat (a "waiterless" restaurant) in 1900.

The first Horn & Hardart Automat opened June 12, 1902 at 818 Chestnut Street in Philadelphia. This building was the site of the famous first Horn and Hardart Automat in New York. It opened on July 7, 1912. These places were called "automats" because, besides a cafeteria line, they featured low-priced prepared food and drinks behind small glass windows that had coin-operated slots. These automats were especially popular dining establishments during the Depression Era given the value they provided.

Horn & Hardart Automats encouraged the concept of prepared foods to take out and eat at home with their advertising motto "Less work for Mother." Although automats flourished during the first half of the 20th century, they eventually faded as competition in the restaurant category grew and people wanted "less automation" in their dining experience. A portion of the original automat machines is currently housed in the Smithsonian.

Baseball Hall of Fame

25 Main Street
Cooperstown, New York
888-425-5633

Today the induction ceremonies each summer to the National Baseball Hall of Fame are held at a nearby facility, but back in 1939, at the very first induction ceremony, the legends stood right here on the front steps of what was then the main building of the hall. A plaque marks the spot where Eddie Collins, Babe Ruth, Connie Mack, Cy Young, Honus Wagner, Grover Cleveland Alexander, Tris Speaker, Napoleon Lajoie, George Sisler, Ty Cobb and Walter Johnson all gathered together.

Beard, Daniel

322 East 3rd Street
Covington, Kentucky

This is the boyhood home of Daniel Beard, the man who is credited with helping to start the Boy Scouts of America. A plaque here reads: "Daniel Carter Beard (1850-1941). Boyhood home of 'Uncle Dan,' youth leader, outdoorsman, artist and author. Born in Cincinnati and later came to Covington to live. Inaugurated Boy Scout movement in America, 1905, and was one of the first national commissioners of the Boy Scouts of America. He was awarded the first medal for outstanding citizenship of state of Kentucky."

Big Duck

Route 24 (located off I-65 North on the route to the Hamptons)
Flanders, New York

Who doesn't like Long Island Duckling? The Big Duck, a 20-foot-tall, 40-foot-wide gift shop, was built in 1931 to lure travelers to purchase Peking ducks. This Route 24 roadside treasure nests comfortably in Flanders, New York, and greets road warriors traveling to and from the Hamptons on Long Island. Known familiarly as the "world's largest duck," the beloved piece of Americana is also listed on the National Register of Historic Places, since it actually represents a form of unique architecture (being a gift shop you can enter).

Biggest Parking Lot in the World

Blackwell's Corner
17191 Highway 46
Lost Hills, California
661-797-2905

Many pop culture aficionados know this roadside fruit-and-nut general store as the last place James Dean stopped just about 20 minutes before getting killed in a car accident. But it holds another odd distinction, as evidenced by the sign in the parking lot, which

reads "World's Biggest Parking Lot." The origin of the claim is this: In the early part of World War II, the army used to practice formations just behind the site of the store in a giant field (which is still there). One day, General George Patton arrived to survey the troops. Upon seeing all of the military vehicles gathered at this site he said something to the effect of, "This looks like the biggest damned parking lot in the world!" And so the title stuck.

Bowling Green Fence

**Broadway and Beaver Street
New York City, New York**

A gilded lead statue of George III, commissioned by grateful New York City merchants after the repeal of the Stamp Act, was the first statue in a city park when it was erected in the center of Bowling Green Park In 1770. In 1771, a wrought iron fence was built

around the irregular oval of the Bowling Green to protect the park and its royal monument. The famous fence survives to this day and is a designated New York City Landmark. It surrounds Bowling Green—New York's earliest park.

Bubblegum Alley

**700 block of Higuera Street
San Luis Obispo, California**

Bubblegum Alley started in 1960 when a few pieces of gum were stuck against the wall in an alley here in the quaint Central California town of San Luis Obispo. Over the years it became a local tradition and today, tens of thousands of pieces, some crafted into art, cover the walls. This is one of America's most bizarre public statements.

Cabazon

50900 Seminole Drive (Along I-10)
Cabazon, California
909-849-7012

The dinosaurs of Cabazon have been seen in movies and commercials for years. They were built by Claude Bell, who ran the Wheel Inn restaurant here on Interstate 10 right alongside the beasts. Supposedly, Claude had been inspired as a boy after visiting the famous Lucy the Margate Elephant in Margate, New Jersey. The kitschy, elephant-shaped building later gave Claude the idea to start constructing enormous sculptures. He began his career making figures of gold miners and a minuteman at Knott's Berry Farm in Buena Park, California.

He later bought 76 acres here in the desert to create these prehistoric masterpieces. Claude took 11 years to build Dinny, a giant Apatosaurus (arguably the largest dinosaur in America), and a small museum in Dinny's belly still sells souvenirs. A giant Tyrannosaurus was started as the next project, but was still not completed when Claude died.

Since the 1980s, the famous statues have been seen by millions—not just in person, but as featured images in commercials, music videos and such films as *Pee Wee's Big Adventure.*

"Camptown Races"

Junction of US 706 and PA 409
4.2 miles north of Wyalusing
Camptown, Pennsylvania

We all remember the lyrics, "Camptown ladies sing this song, do da, do da." Well, the popular sing-along (that cartoon rooster Foghorn Leghorn used to bellow) originated out of a little town in Bradford County appropriately named Camptown. Apparently, this Stephen Foster song was inspired by the horse races that ran from this village to Wyalusing. A historical marker acknowledging Camptown and its famous race is located at the junction of routes 706 and 409 in Camptown.

The Cereal Bowl of America

Capital Avenue NE, Bailey Park Entrance
Battle Creek, Michigan

Battle Creek is an important place to many all around the world—after all, it's where the leading producers of ready-to-eat cereals are located. Battle Creek is where some of the first attempts to process grains into appetizing new foods occurred, thus revolutionizing the eating habits of people everywhere. "Made in Battle Creek" was the iconic catchphrase used by over 40 cereal manufactures here in the early 1900s. Today, millions of people all over the world enjoy packaged breakfast foods that emanated from Battle Creek, Michigan, a.k.a. "Foodtown U.S.A."

Chess

Fairmont Miramar Hotel
101 Wilshire Boulevard
Santa Monica, California
310-576-7777

In July 1966, chess legend Bobby Fischer took second place to his arch nemesis Boris Spassky at the prestigious Piatigorsky Cup in Santa Monica. Over one thousand people watched his game with Boris Spassky, making it the largest audience ever for a chess game in the U.S.

Classic Hollywood

Chez Jay

1657 Ocean Avenue
Santa Monica, California
310-395-1741

The dark and cozy Chez Jay restaurant is a true Hollywood haunt—a place where the likes of Marlon Brando, Johnny Carson, Julia Roberts, Kevin Spacey, Cher, and Madonna have sought refuge. It's where Lee Marvin once rode a motorcycle through the front door and ordered a drink, where Quentin Tarantino has rehearsed actors in the back room, where Ben Affleck and Matt Damon have worked on scripts in the front, where Michelle Pfeiffer and David E. Kelly had their first date, where Angie Dickinson once waited tables, and where Frank Sinatra, Dean Martin, and Sammy Davis, Jr. were regulars back in the sixties. (In fact, Sinatra inspired the name of the place in the 1957 film *Pal Joey*. Sinatra's character Joey Evans runs a joint called "Chez Joey." Owner Jay Fiondella was a huge Sinatra fan and in a nod to the name in the movie called his joint "Chez Jay" and it stuck.)

It was also where the Pentagon Papers were leaked to the press in the always-dim environs of the bar. And then there's table 10, the infamous tryst table where Warren Beatty got his under-the-table idea for the movie *Shampoo* and where Linda Ronstadt would steal away with then-Governor Jerry Brown, (among many other private arrangements that took place here). Chez Jay is also home to a cocktail peanut that astronaut Alan Shepherd took to the moon (a nut that Steve McQueen nearly ate in the 1970s).

Ciro's

8433 Sunset Boulevard
Hollywood, California

Ciro's was opened in 1939, and for nearly 20 years it was a true Hollywood hotspot. Actress Lana Turner said it was her favorite place, and other regulars included Gary Cooper, Lucille Ball, Desi Arnaz, Betty Grable and Dean Martin. Ciro's may have been the most famous nightclub in the nation back then, where stars were not only in the audience but on the stage as well. Actor/bandleader Desi Arnaz and his band played there on occasion. Frank Sinatra famously punched out a photographer here, and

buxom screen legend Mae West even took the stage at one time to judge a bodybuilder's contest. Today, the building still stands as the famous Comedy Store.

Classic Hollywood

The Formosa Café

7156 Santa Monica Boulevard
Los Angeles, California
323-850-9050

This café to the stars opened in 1934, convenient-ly located right next door to what was then the Warner Hollywood Studios, thus securing it as a major Hollywood hangout. The walls of the low-key Formosa are lined with over 250 black and white shots of the stars who dined here in the past, autographed and hand-delivered by the stars themselves. (Look for James Dean, Frank Sinatra, Paul Newman, Humphrey Bogart, Elvis Presley, Marilyn Monroe, Clark Gable, Marlon Brando, Jack Benny, Elizabeth Taylor, Jack Webb, Martin & Lewis, and Grace Kelly to name a few.)

The highlights here over the years include Frank Sinatra eating chow mein the day after he won an Oscar for his performance in the film *From Here to Eternity,* Marilyn Monroe and Clark Gable dining here together while making *The Misfits* and Shannen Doherty smashing a bottle against a man's car in the restaurant's parking lot (she received two years probation for the incident).

Janes House

6541 Hollywood Boulevard
Hollywood, California
323-469-8311

This pretty Victorian cottage, built in 1903, was once (starting in 1911) a family-run school called "The Misses Janes School of Hollywood." What makes it notable is that it was where the children of Hollywood's elite attended school back in Hollywood's Golden Age. Classes were taught in the home's shady backyard to the children of Charlie Chaplin, Douglas Fairbanks, Cecil B. DeMille, Noah Beery, Jesse Lasky, and many others.

The school closed in 1926, but incredibly the building survived the modernization of Hollywood Boulevard. Today, the cottage still sits here, stuck in the back of a mini-mall that's called "Janes Square." Fittingly, the shopping center's design is based on the shin-gled Victorian look and feel of the Janes House. The house is where the Visitors Information Center for Hollywood is located today, so you can stop by to pick up a free map or ask questions about the area.

Classic Hollywood

The Mocambo

8588 Sunset Boulevard
Hollywood, California

The Mexican-themed nightclub Mocambo opened in 1941 and featured big bands, big singers and an exotic aviary of macaws and parrots. Errol Flynn, Frank Sinatra, Janet Leigh and Judy Garland frequented this much-talked-about establishment, which today is long gone with no trace of the original building.

Montmarte Café

6753 Hollywood Boulevard
Hollywood, California

Long considered to be Hollywood's first nightclub, this is actually where actress Joan Crawford was discovered. Located on the second floor of a financial institution, the Montmarte virtually sparked the nightlife of the Hollywood community in the early 1920s and was regularly frequented by fans and stars alike. The building stands virtually unchanged today, though the Montmarte is long gone.

Classic Hollywood

NBC Studios

1500 Vine Street
Hollywood, California

This was the site of one of the first studios in Hollywood, and also, later, the home of the NBC radio network, whose radio and TV studios went up in 1938. Until 1964, many famous radio shows were produced and aired from here, including The Jack Benny Show. The building was razed in 1964, outmoded in the new age of color television.

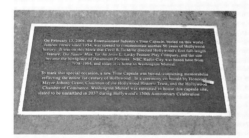

Today, a bank sits on the site and a plaque in the sidewalk reads: "On this corner in December 1913 Hollywood was born with the filming of the first full-length feature movie, The Squaw Man. For 26 years this famous corner was the symbol of another entertainment medium, as NBC broadcast to the world from radio and television studios located here.

On February 15, 1954, the Hollywood Chamber of Commerce and the Hollywood Radio and Television Society recognized the importance of Sunset and Vine by choosing this site for the entertainment industry's time capsule, to be removed from beneath this plaque and opened February 15, 2004." The capsule was in fact removed then, but then replaced with even more artifacts.

Today, a mural depicting the many great entertainers who worked at NBC adorns the front of the bank building that now stands here. Look for Jack Benny and George Burns among many others.

Classic Hollywood

Player's Club

8225 Sunset Boulevard
Hollywood, California

In the 1940s, writer/director Preston Sturgess opened a restaurant here on Sunset Boulevard called The Player's Club. It became a highly sophisticated meeting spot for the great literati of the day, including Dorothy Parker, George S. Kauffman, F. Scott Fitzgerald and many others. Today, it's a restaurant of another name, but the original structure is fully intact.

The Trocadero

8610 Sunset Boulevard
Hollywood, California

During Hollywood's Golden Age, the world-famous Trocadero became synonymous with starlets, movie producers and big-time nightlife. It was a posh, black-tie, French-inspired supper club as well as the setting for many famous movie premiere parties, notably Gone with the Wind. Among the celebrities who were regulars here were Bing Crosby, Myrna Loy, Cary Grant, Fred Astaire and Norma Shearer. The Trocadero was even featured in the film A Star is Born. The building was razed in the 1980s and no trace of it remains today.

Cobe Cup Race

Crown Point courthouse
Crown Point, Indiana

On June 19, 1909, the first major auto race in the U. S. was held south of this courthouse, over an approximate 25-mile track known as the Cobe Cup Race. This grueling contest was the forerunner of the famous Indianapolis 500 race. The winner's cup was presented here on the east steps of the courthouse to Louis Chevrolet, a Swiss-born master mechanic who later became the famous engineer and designer of the Chevrolet Motor Company.

Cocktail

Fairmont Hotel
123 Baronne Street
New Orleans, Louisiana
504-529-4764

America's first cocktail, the Sazerac, was actually created here in the Big Easy. It happened in the early 1800s thanks to a man named Antoine Peychaud. The Sazerac was named for his favorite French brandy, Sazerac-de-Forge et fils. In 1870, the drink was changed when American Rye whiskey was substituted for cognac and a dash of absinthe was added by local bartender Leon Lamothe (who today is regarded as the Father of the Sazerac).

Absinthe was banned in 1912, so Peychaud substituted his special bitters in its place. In 1893, the Grunewald Hotel was built in New Orleans, and the hotel earned the exclusive rights to serve the Sazerac (in 1965 the hotel was renamed the Fairmont Hotel). Today, the Sazerac is enjoyed in many of New Orleans's finest restaurants and bars, most notably the Sazerac Bar in the Fairmont Hotel, where celebrities, locals, and tourists enjoy the drink.

To make a Sazerac: 3-4 dashes of Herbsaint (120 proof)
2 oz. Rye of Bourbon blended whiskey
3-4 hearty dashes of Peychaud bitters
one long, thin twist of lemon
optional: a sugar cube, water, club soda

Place Herbsaint in a well-chilled Old Fashion glass. Tilt glass to coat sides completely and pour off excess Herbsaint. Place Rye and Peychaud bitters into cocktail shaker with ice cubes. Shake for 30 seconds and strain into prepared glass. Twist lemon peel over drink and drop in gently.

Dean, James

In the previous books *James Dean Died Here* and *Marilyn Monroe Dyed Here,* I documented many sites related to James Dean, from where he was born to where he died. Here are a few more:

Fairmount Historical Museum

203 East Washington Street
Fairmount, Indiana
765-948-4555

This local museum also provides the visitor with a chance to experience the life of James Dean traced through hundreds of rare photographs, his motorcycles, bongo drums, movie costumes, and many rare keepsakes donated by family and friends.

Friends Church

124 West First Street
Fairmount, Indiana

On October 8, 1955, James Dean's funeral was held at this church. Hundreds of fans sobbed as they waited outside, and Liz Taylor sent flowers.

Iroquois Hotel

49 West 44th Street
New York City, New York

Back in the 1950s, room 82 at this boutique hotel was the home of up-and-coming actor James Dean (and today the suite bares his name).

Dean, James

The James Dean Gallery

425 North Main Street
Fairmount, Indiana
765-998-2080

The James Dean Gallery features the world's largest private collection of memorabilia and archives dealing with the short life and career of the bigger-than-life actor. It traces his entire life, from his local accomplishments in sports and drama to his days growing up at Fairmount High School to his acting years in New York and Hollywood. Some of the items on display include clothing worn by Dean in his films, original movie posters, books, magazines and novelty items from over 20 different countries from around the world. There is also a screening room that shows a 30-minute video of rare television appearances and screen tests.

The Winslow Farm

County Road 150 East
Fairmont, Indiana

This was the boyhood home of James Dean. While it is not open to the public, photos can be taken from road and driveway.

Dinosaur State Park

400 West Street
Rocky Hill, Connecticut
860-529-8423

Dinosaur State Park officially opened in 1968, two years after 2,000 dinosaur tracks were accidentally uncovered during excavation for a new state building. Five-hundred of the tracks are now enclosed within the Exhibit Center's geodesic dome. The remaining 1,500 are buried for preservation. The park's 200-million-year-old sandstone track way is a Registered Natural Landmark.

Disney, Walt

Located near the Northern City Limit sign of Marceline on Missouri 5, just a few miles (several kilometers) south of U.S. 36.
Marceline, Missouri
660-376-2332

Walt Disney lived here from ages five to 11 and it was in this home that he created doodlings that became prototypes for many of the wonderful things he'd create later on in life. The home is privately owned and not open for tours, but visitors are welcome to walk down a path to a Cottonwood tree under which Disney used to draw, and encouraged to scrawl messages in a barn. No admission is charged.

"Dude"

270 Eatons Ranch Road
Wolf, Wyoming
800-210-1049

This was the first Dude Ranch in Wyoming, and also where the term "dude" was creat-ed. In 1879, three brothers, Howard, Willis, and Alden established their horse-and-cattle ranch near Medora, North Dakota. Almost immediately friends from the East began to visit. Some stayed for months at a time in the early days.

In 1882, one of the guests, or "dudes" as the Eatons called them, recognizing the expense these extended visits entailed, prevailed upon the Eatons to charge for room and board so "folks could stay as long as they like." Thus, the dude ranch business was born and an industry started. The Eatons moved to the present location in 1904. The ranch is currently managed by the fourth and fifth generation of Eatons and remains as popular today as it was then.

Espresso Cart

520 Pike Street
Seattle, Washington
206-625-0449

The world's first espresso cart was established below the Seattle Monorail terminal at Westlake Center in 1980. It's called Monorail Espresso, and it's still in business today.

First Pizzeria in North America

Lombardi's
53⅓ Spring Street
New York City, New York

The first known pizza shop was the Port 'Alba in Naples, Italy which opened in 1830 (and is still open today!). But, the first pizzeria in North America was opened in 1905 by Gennaro Lombardi at 53⅓ Spring Street in New York City. Lombardi's is still going strong today, but at a new address: 32 Spring Street in New York's Little Italy. Some more pizza geography: A Neapolitan man named Totonno Pero came to New York from Naples and as a teenager worked for Lombardi. In 1924 he opened Totonno's, a coal-oven pizzeria in Brooklyn, originally located on West 15th Street in Coney Island (now they're on West 16th Street). Today, Totonno's holds the record for the oldest continuous pizze-ria in business in the U.S. run by the same family.

First Traffic Light

105th Street and Euclid Avenue
Cleveland, Ohio

Did you know that Cleveland boasted America's first traffic light? It happened on August 5, 1914, when the American Traffic Signal Company installed red and green traffic lights at each corner of the intersection of 105th Street and Euclid Avenue. They were very primitive—in fact, they were "railroad switch stand" types of signals that had to be rotated manually by a policeman 90 degrees to show the indication "STOP" or "GO." The first "actuated" signals to be used (not requiring manpower) were installed on February 22, 1928 at the corner of Falls Road and Belvedere Avenue in Baltimore, Maryland.

Flying Saucers

Mount Rainier
Washington

It's considered the first modern sighting of UFOs and the birth of the term "flying saucer." On June 24, 1947, Seattle pilot Kenneth Arnold described nine brilliant, boomerang-shaped "discs" he saw flying above Mount Rainier. (The term "flying saucer" was coined by a reporter writing about the sighting.)

Arnold was piloting a single-engine Cessna in search of a missing military transport plane. At about 3:00 P.M. he spotted the objects zooming in and out of formation. He claimed to have clocked them as they flew between Mount Rainier and Mount Adams. He estimated their speed at 1,200 m.p.h. Arnold described the objects as each as big as a DC-4 passenger plane, "flat like a pie pan," and so shiny that they reflected the sun like a mirror.

The public was interested in the story, which was dismissed by the military. An Army spokesman in Washington, D.C. commented at the time: "As far as we know, nothing flies that fast except a V-2 rocket, which travels at about 3,500 miles an hour—and that's too fast to be seen." Despite this, accounts of Arnold's sighting spread all around the world and spawned a whole new interest in the subject of "flying saucers."

Another local UFO note: On the afternoon of July 4, 1947, Frank Ryman, an off-duty U.S. Coast Guard Yeoman, shot what is believed to be the first photograph of a flying saucer from the yard of his home in Lake City, north of Seattle.

Fuller, Buckminster

407 South Forest Avenue
Carbondale, Illinois
618-967-9679

"Think of it. We are blessed with technology that would be indescribable to our forefathers. We have the wherewithal, the know-it-all to feed everybody, clothe everybody, and give every human on Earth a chance. We know now what we could never have known before—that we now have the option for all humanity to *make it* successfully on this planet in this lifetime. Whether it is to be Utopia or Oblivion will be a touch-and-go relay race right up to the final moment."

Some words of wisdom from the great Buckminster Fuller. Fuller, known as "Bucky," was an inventor, architect, engineer, mathematician and poet. He is best known for his invention of the geodesic dome, a light, strong and cost-effective structure. This particular dome, where Fuller and his wife Anne lived from 1960–1971, is the only one the genius ever called home. Efforts are currently underway to restore the incredible home. For information on the worthwhile project visit www.buckysdome.org.

Geodetic Center of the United States

Marker is located on US 281 at the intersection of US 24 and 281
Rural Osbourne County, Kansas

On a ranch 18 miles southeast of this marker, a bronze plate marks the most important spot on this continent to surveyors and mapmakers. Engraved in the bronze is a cross-mark. On the tiny point where the lines cross depend the surveys of one-sixth of the world's surface. This is the Geodetic Center of the United States, the "Primary Station" for all North American surveys.

It was located in 1901 by the U.S. Coast and Geodetic Survey. Later, Canada and Mexico adopted the point and its supporting system as the base for their surveys and it is now known as the "North American Datum." What Greenwich is to the longitude of the world, therefore, a Kansas pasture is to the lines and boundaries of this continent. (Don't confuse this with the Geographic Center of the United States, which is 42 miles north, in Smith County.)

Gingerbread Castle

50 Gingerbread Castle Road
Hamburg, New Jersey

After being inspired by the famous "Hansel and Gretel" story, the Gingerbread Castle was constructed in 1930 by F. H. Bennett in conjunction with famous set designer and artist Joe Urban. The castle is the only structure of its kind in the U.S. and only one of

two in the entire world. This magnificent attraction recaptures the spirit of childhood and provides all visitors with a momentary glimpse back into almost forgotten memories. It is currently being restored to its original grandeur with plans to soon be open once again (as part of a bigger family theme park). In the summer of 2004, the Castle was partially restored by Hampton Inn hotels as part of their award-winning Save-A-Landmark program.

Girl Scouts

Andrew Low House

329 Abercorn Street
Savannah, Georgia
912-233-6854

After her marriage, Juliette Low lived in this 1848 house, and it was here where she actually founded the Girl Scouts. After her husband had died (they were already separated), Low met Sir Robert Baden-Powell in 1911. He was a great war hero and the founder of the Boy Scouts. The two quickly became friends and her admiration for the scouting movement led her to begin working with the Girl Guides, the Boy Scouts' sister organization in Great Britain. With Baden-Powell's help and advice, she then made plans to start a similar association for American girls. In 1912, she returned home to Georgia and formed several troops in Savannah in March of that year.

Juliette Low died on the premises in 1927. This home/museum is operated by the Colonial Dames as the Andrew Low House. The Carriage House that became the first headquarters of Girl Scouting is directly behind the Andrew Low House and works as the council shop for the Girl Scouts Council of Savannah. Tours are offered.

Girl Scouts

Girl Scout Cookies

1401 Arch Street
Philadelphia, Pennsylvania

A marker here reads: "On November 11, 1932, Girl Scouts baked & sold cookies for the first time in the windows of the Philadelphia Gas & Electric Co. here. This endeavor soon became a Philadelphia tradition. In 1936 the Girl Scouts of the U.S.A. adopted the annual cookie sale as a national program."

The background is as follows: On November 11, 1932, Philadelphia Girl Scouts demonstrated their baking skills in the windows here at the Philadelphia Gas Works headquarters. They were baking cookies for day nurseries as a community service project. As the freshly baked cookies piled up, people walking by asked if they could buy them. The girls agreed to sell the extras and used the money to support troop activities and camping equipment. The next year, a similar sale was held, attracting the public's interest and the attention of the press.

In 1934, then-Philadelphia based Keebler Baking Company was approached about baking and packaging a vanilla cookie in the shape of the Girl Scout emblem, called the "Trefoil." An agreement was made and the first commercial sale in Philadelphia took place from December 8–15, 1934. Cookies sold for 23 cents per box or six boxes for $1.35. The proceeds benefited Girl Scouts of Greater Philadelphia and individual troop projects.

News soon spread of the Philadelphia Girl Scouts enterprise and the national Girl Scouts office, Girl Scouts of the U.S.A., took notice. In 1936, the cookie idea went national when GSUSA contracted with Keebler as the national supplier for their Trefoil cookie. The first national sale was held October 24–November 7, 1936.

Girl Scouts

Low, Juliette Gordon

10 East Oglethorpe Avenue
Savannah, Georgia
912-233-4501

This is the birthplace of Juliette Gordon Low, founder of Girl Scouts of the U.S.A., who was affectionately known by her family and friends as "Daisy." The Girl Scouts organization was born a few blocks away at the Andrew Low House, but this historic home was where the Girl Scouts founder entered the world.

Dating back to 1821, the house is an interesting blend of Regency architecture and Victorian-style additions. The tour includes a memorial to Julliette Gordon Low, a Girl Scouts museum, and a chance for scouts to pop in at the home office, as the national headquarters are housed here.

The birthplace of Juliette Low was purchased by National Girl Scouts in 1953 and was restored to a late-1880's décor. It opened to the public in October 1956, and it was the first Registered National Historic Landmark in Savannah. Girl Scouts and Girl Guides from all over the world come to visit.

Juliette Low was laid to rest in the family plot at Laurel Grove North Cemetery. She was buried in her full Girl Scout uniform, her Silver Fish award (a high honor from the Girl Guides), her special jeweled Thanks Badge and a telegram in her pocket from Sir Baden-Powell: *You are not only the first Girl Scout, you are the best Girl Scout of them all.*

Golf

Jones, Bobby

Forest Hills Golf Club
1500 Comfort Road
Augusta, Georgia
706-733-0001

On April 7, 1999, the Georgia Historical Society dedicated a historical marker here in Augusta, Georgia commemorating Bobby Jones and the beginning of the Grand Slam. (The event was held at Augusta State University.) The marker, located at the entrance of the club, reads: "Bobby Jones and the Beginning of the Grand Slam. On the golf links of the Forrest Hills–Ricker Hotel, Bobby Jones won the Southeastern Open of 1930. He went on to victory that year in the British Amateur, British Open, U.S. Open, and U.S. Amateur—golf's Grand Slam and a feat yet unmatched. A lifelong amateur, Jones won four U.S. Opens, five U.S. Amateurs, three British Opens, and one British Amateur, but called his 13-shot victory in the 1930 Southeastern Open, "The best-played tournament I ever turned out in my life." Thirteen of the original Donald Ross-designed holes and the 1926 Golf House survive from Jones era.

Palmer, Arnold

Rancho Park
10460 West Pico Boulevard
Los Angeles, California
310-838-7373

During the first round of the 1961 Los Angeles Open at Rancho Park, legendary golfer Arnold Palmer went out of bounds five times on the par-five ninth (now the 18th) hole to shoot a 12. A plaque right at the hole commemorates the event.

Sarazen, Gene

940 Wynnewood Road
Pelham Manor, New York
914-738-5074

A plaque here, located to the left of the driveway near the putting green by the 1st hole of the course reads: "Sarazen's Victory in the 1923 PGA Championship at Pelham Country Club. On September 29, 1923 at Pelham Country Club, Gene Sarazen defeated Walter Hagen in the final of the P.G.A. Championship. The 38-hole match is considered the most dramatic match play final in the history of the P.G.A. Championship."

Hatfield-McCoy Feud

Pikeville, Kentucky—Various sites in West Virginia along Routes 319, 1056 and 292.

It's the most famous mountain feud in our country's history, the metaphor for all bitter rivalries, an Appalachian Capulet-Montague fight to the finish. The famous Hatfield-McCoy feud ran off and on in the West Virginia-Kentucky back-country from the mid-1860s until 1891. In that time, the hillbilly feud (that grew out of their being on opposite sides during the Civil War) claimed more than a dozen members of both these families.

On Monday, June 16, 2003, descendants of the Hatfield and McCoy families signed a symbolic truce in Pikeville. Today, the feud can be experienced throughout Pikeville, Kentucky

and into West Virginia as the Pikeville-Pike County Tourism Commission has laid markers out at 12 sites related to the feud as part of an interpretive driving tour. These sites include family homes, murder sites and gravesites. For information and a free map of the area call 800-844-7453 (Pikeville also stages a festival dedicated to the feud).

"Home on the Range"

Location: From the juncture of Highway K-8 and Highway US 36 near Athol go north 8 miles on Highway K-8 then 1 mile west at the marked turn-off.
Nearest Towns: Athol, Smith Center, Kensington.
North of Smith Center, Kansas.

Dr. Brewster Higley sat down on the banks of Kansas's Beaver Creek by his cabin here in 1872 and jotted down the lines that would become "Home on the Range." Little did he know how impactful his little poem would be. Dr. Higley moved to Kansas in 1871, settling on this small plot of land. In the fall of 1872, the beauty and peace of the environment inspired him to write his poem, originally called "My Western Home."

Oh, give me a home,
Where the buffalo roam,
And the deer and the antelope play,
Where never is heard a discouraging word,
And the sky is not clouded all day.

One day, a man who was visiting Higley named Trube Reese found the poem and was so moved by it he convinced Higley to set it to music. Higley hired fiddler Dan Kelley to create a melody (which quickly caught on). Texas singer Vernon Dalhardt recorded the first commercial version of the tune, and in 1932 President Franklin Roosevelt named it his favorite song. A plaque can be found just outside the cabin.

Hughes, Howard

L&L Motel
US Highway 95
Tonopah, Nevada

On January 12, 1957, a secret wedding took place in a forgotten roadside motel. It was here In room 33 of the L&L Motel that reclusive billionaire married actress Jean Peters. The place has long been closed but locals are currently working to turn the exact room and office below into a Howard Hughes Museum and Wedding Chapel to lure visitors to the town that once thrived as a center of political and financial influence in Nevada, but today is little more than a pit stop on U.S. Highway 95. It is believed Hughes married here because it was quiet, out of the way and would not attract undue attention.

Jackalopes

Douglas, Wyoming

Douglas has declared itself to be the Jackalope capital of America because, according to legend, the first jackalope was spotted here around 1829. Just what is a jackalope? A fictitious antlered species of rabbit, though try telling the people in Douglas that they never really existed. The legend describes that the jackalope is an aggressive species, willing to use its antlers to fight. Thus, it is also sometimes called the "warrior rabbit."

A large statue of a jackalope stands in the town center, and every year the town plays host to Jackalope Day, usually held in June. Jackalope hunting licenses can be obtained from the Douglas Chamber of Commerce, though hunting of jackalopes is restricted to the hours of midnight to 2:00 A.M. on June 31. Only in America!

Johnny Tocco's Ringside Gym

11 West Charleston Boulevard
Las Vegas, Nevada
702-383-8651

Johnny Tocco's is a sports history Mecca located right in the middle of Las Vegas. And it's only fitting since Vegas has been professional boxing's heartland for decades. This is the famous gym that has trained Ali, Spinks, Tyson and many more famous fighters. Johnny Tocco opened the Ringside Gym in the early 1950s and ran it until his death in 1997.

Kennedy, John F.

Hyannis Memorial

Ocean Street
Hyannis, Massachusetts

Overlooking Lewis Bay, a spot J.F.K. used to frequent during his years here, the J.F.K. Memorial attracts some 575,000 visitors from May through October. Money thrown into the memorial's wishing well is used to fund scholarships, sailing lessons for young people and upkeep of the memorial.

To see the famous Kennedy compound on Irving Avenue in Hyannis, it is best to take one of the several boat tours in the area. Also nearby is the family parish, Saint Francis Xavier Roman Catholic Church, located at 347 South Street. This is where J.F.K. attended Sunday school, and the main alter at the church is dedicated to Lieutenant Joseph P. Kennedy, J.F.K's older brother who was killed during World War II. Lastly, the Hyannis National Guard Armory on South Street is where J.F.K. made his victory speech after the 1960 presidential election.

Marriage

St. Mary's Church
Corner of Spring Street and Memorial Boulevard
Newport, Rhode Island
401-847-0475

Established on April 8, 1828, St. Mary's is the oldest Roman Catholic parish in Rhode Island. It was designated a National Historic Shrine on November 24, 1968 and is most famous as the wedding location of Jacqueline Bouvier to John Fitzgerald Kennedy on Septem-ber 12, 1953. More than 750 guests attended the wedding, which was presided over by Archbishop Richard Cushing. Following the 40-minute ceremony at which a papal blessing was read, the new couple emerged into a throng of 3,000 well-wishers as they made their way by motorcycle escort to Hammersmith Farm, the Auchincloss estate overlooking Narragansett Bay.

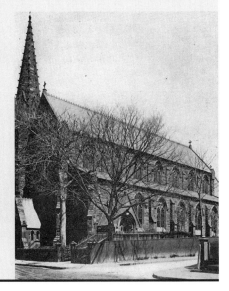

Kennedy, John F.

Reilly Stadium

1200 East 6th Street
Salem, Ohio

A plaque in one of the urinals here in the men's room commemorates where John F. Kennedy once relieved himself during a 1960 campaign stop.

Winthrop House

Harvard University
Cambridge, Massachusetts

J.F.K. spent his Harvard years in Gore Hall in the Winthrop House. Today, the rooms are called the Kennedy Suite and are used by the John F. Kennedy School of Government to house guest speakers.

Liberty Bell Slot Machine

406 Market Street (at Battery)
San Francisco, California

A plaque here reads: "Charles August Fey began inventing and manufacturing slot machines in 1894. Fey pioneered many innovations of coin operated gaming devices in his San Francisco workshop at 406 Market Street, including the original three-reel bell slot machine in 1898. The international popularity of the bell slot machines attests to Fey's ingenuity as an enterprising inventor whose basic design of the three-reel slot machine continues to be used in mechanical gaming devices today." (The plaque stands almost hidden under a tree at the eastern end of the Crown Zellerbach building in a little triangle.)

Lindbergh, Charles A.

Easy Street
Canaan, Maine
207-474-9841
Directions: From Route 2 in Canaan, Maine turn on Easy Street, directly across from Canaan Town Hall and Post Office. Go 1.1 miles until you see a black mailbox on the right side of road that says "Ross.")

After Lucky Lindy famously made history's first nonstop transatlantic flight, he was brought home by boat, not plane. Incredibly, the crate that carried home his plane, the *Spirit of St. Louis,* has been converted into a museum. The box, which is the size of a small house, contains Lindbergh artifacts among other aviation treasures. Visits are by appointment only.

Loch Murray Monster

Lake Murray
Irmo, South Carolina

Like Loch Ness and Lake Champlain, Lake Murray has its "monster." It first surfaced in 1973 and was described by locals in the paper back then as "A cross between a snake and something prehistoric." Of course, one has never been captured. Lake Murray is a man-made lake that's popular for motor-boating, jet-skiing, water-skiing, swimming and fishing.

Mastodon State Historic Site

1050 Museum Drive
Imperial, Missouri
800-334-6946

Mastodon State Historic Site contains an important archaeological and paleontological site—the Kimmswick Bone Bed. Bones of mastodons and other now-extinct animals were first found here in the early 1800s. The area gained fame as one of the most extensive Pleistocene Ice Age deposits in the country and attracted scientific interest worldwide. In 1979, archaeological history was made here when scientists excavated a stone spear point made by hunters of the Clovis culture (14,000–10,000 years ago) in direct association with mastodon bones. This was the first hard evidence of the coexistence of people and these giant prehistoric beasts.

Today, the 425-acre property preserves this National Register of Historic Places site and provides recreational opportunities. A museum tells the natural and cultural story of the oldest American Indian site one can visit in the state's park system. A full-size replica of a mastodon skeleton highlights the exhibits. A picnic area, several trails and a special-use campground offer chances to explore the land.

Mickey Mouse

1681 Broadway
New York City, New York

It was during a cross-county train ride in 1928 that 26-year-old cartoonist Walt Disney dreamed up a character named Mickey Mouse. There would later be two silent films featuring Mickey. Eventually, Disney decided to create one with synchronized sound. Walt Disney came back to New York to record the sound track to the film *Steamboat Willie,* and it premiered right here at the Colony Theater at Broadway and 53rd Street in Manhattan on November 18, 1928.

Because of this event, this is the date considered to be the famous mouse's birthday. The public response was so overwhelmingly positive that two weeks later *Steamboat Willie* was re-released at the world's largest theater, New York's Roxy. In 1932, Walt Disney was given a special Academy Award for creating Mickey Mouse, who today remains one of the world's most popular animated characters.

Moon Tree

Mission Plaza
751 Palm Street
San Luis Obispo, California

Apollo 14 launched in the late afternoon of January 31, 1971 on what was to be the third trip to the lunar surface. Five days later, Alan Shepard and Edgar Mitchell walked on the Moon while Stuart Roosa, a former U.S. Forest Service smoke jumper, orbited above in the command module. Packed in small containers in Roosa's personal kit were hundreds of tree seeds, part of a joint NASA/USFS project.

Upon return to Earth, the seeds were germinated by the Forest Service. Known as the "Moon Trees," the resulting seedlings were planted throughout the U. S. (often as part of the nation's bicentennial in 1976) and the world. Seeds were chosen from five different types of trees: Loblolly Pine, Sycamore, Sweetgum, Redwood, and Douglas Fir. The seeds were classified and sorted, and control seeds were kept on Earth for later comparison. Many of the Moon Trees planted around the U. S. still stand, including the Coast Redwood (sequoia sempervirens) Moon Tree in San Luis Obispo (which was planted as a 55-inch tall seedling on July 30, 1976).

The Most Crooked Street in the World

Snake Alley
At the 600 block of Washington Street
Burlington, Iowa

Ripley's Believe It or Not has dubbed Burlington's Snake Alley the most crooked street in the world. Snake Alley was constructed in 1894 as an experimental street design. The intention was to provide a more direct link between the downtown business district and the neighborhood shopping area located on North Sixth Street. It is made of tooled, curved limestone curbing and locally fired blue clay bricks. The constantly changing slant from one curve to the next necessitated a complicated construction technique to keep the high grade to the outside. Snake Alley consists of five half-curves and two quarter-curves over a distance of 275 feet, rising 58.3 feet from Washington Street to Columbia.

Most Haunted House in America

Whaley House
2482 San Diego Avenue
San Diego, California
619-297-9327

Is this America's most haunted house? Many believe so. Built by Thomas Whaley in 1857, it's the oldest brick structure in Southern California and over the years has housed a granary, a store, a school, a theater and the county courthouse. It's now a historical museum and many employees and visitors have seen ghosts throughout the house, including a figure of a woman in the courtroom, a man at the top of the stairs, a ghost-dog running down a hallway, a rocking chair moving, and a baby. People have also smelled perfume and cigars when no one else has been in the house. Some say they have even heard footsteps.

Whaley House is located on San Diego Avenue in the heart of Old Town, San Diego, California. More spookiness: To find the historic Campo Santo cemetery, go slightly south on San Diego Avenue. It is located behind an adobe mud wall, and is always open.

Most Powerful Earthquake

New Madrid, Missouri

The most powerful earthquake to strike the United States occurred here in 1811, centered in New Madrid, Missouri. The quake shook more than one million square miles, and was felt as far as one-thousand miles away.

Murphy's Law

Edward's Air Force Base
Rosamond, California

Murphy's Law ("If anything can go wrong, it will") was born here in 1949. The law was named after Captain Edward A. Murphy, an engineer working on Air Force Project MX981, which was designed to see how much sudden deceleration a person can stand in a crash. One day, after finding that a transducer was wired wrong, he cursed the technician responsible and said, "If there is any way to do it wrong, he'll find it." The contractor's project manager kept a list of "laws" and added this one, which he called "Murphy's Law."

National Monument to the Forefathers

Allerton Street
Plymouth, Massachusetts

The National Monument to the Forefathers was erected in 1889 and is the largest solid granite monument in the U. S. (81-feet tall). It was dedicated to honor the virtues of the Pilgrims: Faith, Liberty, Law, Education, and Morality. Forefathers Monument is also the original prototype for the Statue of Liberty.

The central figure of Faith is 180 tons and stands 36 feet tall atop a 45-foot pedestal. The circumference of the head at her forehead is nearly 14 feet, and her uplifted finger is over two-feet long.

Newton, Sir Isaac

Babson College
Babson Park, Massachusetts
781-235-1200

Here on the campus of this college you'll find a tree actually grown from a branch of Sir Isaac Newton's famous apple tree. Newton's tree, of course, became renowned in 1665 when an apple fell from it, hit Newton in the head, and thus led to his theories on gravity. In addition, Newton's study can be found here at the school. It seems when the legendary physicist's home in London was torn down in 1913, the head of this school had the idea to have it moved and reassembled here in the school's Horn Library.

The man responsible for this, Roger Babson, was so impressed by Newton's discoveries, especially his third law of motion ("For every action there is an equal and opposite reaction"), that he eventually incorporated Newton's theory into many of his personal and business endeavors.

Oldest Saloon in America

The White Horse Inn
Corner of Farewell and Marlborough Street
Newport, Rhode Island
401-849-3600

Originally constructed as the residence of Frances Brinley, this building was purchased in 1673 by William Mayes, Sr. who obtained a tavern license in 1687. Ownership of this building can be traced through the Mayes family for over 200 years, including one family member who was a pirate. In the early 1900s, after various owners had used it in a variety of ways, it began a steady decline into disrepair.

In 1957, through local philanthropic efforts, it was meticulously restored and is now privately owned and once again operated as a place to meet, eat and quench thirst. No other building is more typical of colonial Newport than the Tavern, with its clapboard walls, gambrel roof and plain pedimented doors bordering the sidewalk. Inside, you'll discover giant beams, a small stairway hard against the chimney, a tiny front hall and cavernous fireplaces—the very essence of 17th-century American architecture.

Oldest Street in America I

Huguenot Street
New Paltz, New York
914-255-1889

Here on Huguenot Street, houses date to the 1680s, thus making it the oldest continuously Inhablted street In the country. The entire slte Is a collection of hlstorlcal houses and museums furnished with antiques from the families' time. Included in the site are the Jean Hasbrouck house, Deyo house, Freer house, Grimm Gallery and Museum.

Also included here are the French church and cemetery, library, carriage museum, gallery, gift shop, and picnic facilities. Originally the home of a group of French Protestants who fled northern France because of political and religious persecution, New Paltz was founded in 1677 after the purchase of nearly 40,000 acres along the Wallkill River from the native Esopus Indians.

Oldest Street in America II

Elfreth's Alley
On 2nd Street, between Race and Arch
Philadelphia, Pennsylvania
215-574-0560

Located in the heart of Philadelphia's history-rich Old City neighborhood, Elfreth's Alley is a National Historic Landmark and considered by many to be America's oldest residential street. Many of the Alley's 33 houses were built prior to our nation's birth. In those 300-plus-years, the Alley has been the home to thousands, from Ben Franklin's colleagues to families of four, from immigrants to esquires, reflecting the rich diversity of Philadelphia itself. Each year the Alley welcomes thousands of visitors to stroll along the cobblestones and experience the 18th century homes—still private residences today—and to encourage their support of this American treasure.

Pony Express

69 Moonlite Road
Carson City, Nevada

It was recently discovered that the legendary 1860's mail route from St. Joseph, Missouri, to California passed right through the middle of the property now home to the Moonlite Bunnyranch brothel. A marker was placed to commemorate the fact, and a warning sign near the marker alerts would-be sightseers to the location of the brothel. Back then, an ad in California newspaper read: "Wanted. Young, skinny, wiry fellows. Not over 18. Must be expert riders. Willing to risk death daily. Orphans preferred."

Randy's Donuts

805 West Manchester Avenue
Inglewood, California
310-645-4707

Built in 1952 as part of the Big Donut Drive-In chain, Randy's Donuts has become one of America's most classic pop culture structures. Aside from being a place that serves great donuts, Randy's Donuts has been featured in many movies, including *Earth Girls Are Easy*, *Mars Attacks!*, *Golden Child*, *Into the Night*, *Coming to America*, *Breathless* and many more.

Roadside Table

Grand River (east of Morrison Lake Road)
Saranac, Michigan

In 1929, a county engineer named Allen Williams had an idea: to place a picnic table along a highway right-of-way along old U.S. 16. Little did he know his simple gesture intended as a pause-place for the road traveler would become a Michigan icon. The idea was a hit and soon the State Highway Department adopted the idea, resulting in many other tables being placed along the highways. Today, the roadside table has become an emblem of Michigan's hospitality, and the practice has been adopted by many other states. A marker identifying this first table was placed here in 1964.

Shortest Street in the World

McKinley Street
Bellefontaine, Ohio

McKinley Street, named after President McKinley, is the world's shortest street. It's just 17-feet long, and it's located right near the first concrete street in America, here in the small town of Bellefontaine.

Skiing

Located at the junction of NH 117 and Lover's Lane Road, about .5 miles south of the junction of NH 117 and NH 18.
Sugar Hill, New Hampshire

In 1929, on the slopes of the hill to the east, Austrian-born Sig Buchmayr established the first organized ski school in the United States. Sponsored by Peckett's-on-Sugar Hill, one of the earliest resorts to promote the joys of winter vacationing in the snow, the school provided an initial impetus to the ski sport America knows today. A marker on Route 117 marks the approximate spot.

Snakehead Fish

Anne Arundel County strip mall, just north of Route 50
Crofton, Maryland

In 2002, panic ensued when it was discovered that the notorious snakehead fish, those voracious predators from China that threaten native fish species, were thriving here in this Maryland pond. Though the containment efforts here were successful, a year later two other snakeheads turned up in other ponds where they wreaked havoc almost instantly.

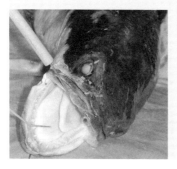

Snakeheads were thought by many to be able to walk on land, making them much scarier and threatening. But, in reality, they are not physically adapted to walk. However, they can wriggle through mud or wet grass. When snakeheads are spotted, efforts are aggressive to get them. Sandbags, electroshock equipment, traps, and hordes of anglers get recruited to capture the alien fish. Wanted posters alert anglers to cut and bleed the fish if they catch it, since it can live on land for several days at least.

Subliminal Advertising

Linwood Theater
Fort Lee, New Jersey

Back in the 1950s, a man named James Vicary coined the term "subliminal advertising." Vicary had conducted some unique studies of female shopping habits, allegedly discovering that women's eye-blink rates dropped significantly in supermarkets, that "psychological spring" lasts more than twice as long as "psychological winter," and that "the experience of a woman baking a cake could be likened to a woman giving birth."

Vicary's peculiar studies were largely dismissible, except for one that he conducted at the movie theater that once sat on this site. During the summer of 1957, Vicary claimed that an experiment he conducted in which moviegoers were repeatedly shown 0.003-second advertisements for Coca-Cola and popcorn significantly increased the moviegoers' tendency to purchase Coca-Cola and popcorn over a period of time. No detailed study of his findings was released, however, and no independent evidence turned up to support his claim. Eventually, in 1962, Vicary admitted that the entire original study was fabricated, thus debunking the entire myth of subliminal advertising. The building is today a CVS drug store.

Tail o' the Pup

329 North San Vicente Boulevard
Los Angeles, California

Hot dog! This iconic hot-dog-shaped restaurant was designed by architect Milton J. Black in 1938 and built in 1945. The Tail o' the Pup was actually declared a cultural landmark in 1987. (This saved it from demolition by a hotel developer and it was relocated to its present address in 1987.)

Located just north of the Beverly Center at the junction of Beverly Boulevard and San Vicente, it's been seen in many productions including the 1984 Brian De Palma thriller *Body Double* and Steve Martin's 1991 comedy *L.A. Story.*

"Taps"

Berkeley Plantation
Virginia Route 5
12602 Harrison Landing Road
Charles City, Virginia
888-466-6018

Berkeley is Virginia's most historic plantation. On December 4, 1619, early settlers from England came ashore at Berkeley Plantation and observed the first official Thanksgiving in America. It is also the birthplace of Benjamin Harrison, signer of the Declaration of Independence, and President William Henry Harrison. In addition, the haunting military bugle call "Taps" was composed here at Berkeley when General McClellan headquartered 140,000 Union troops in 1862. The music for "Taps" was adapted by Union General Daniel Butterfield, and it was played for the first time here in July of that year by bugler Oliver W. Norton.

Today, visitors can tour the house here, a 1726 Georgian mansion furnished with rare period antiques. Berkeley's grounds feature five terraces of restored boxwood and flower gardens that offer breathtaking vistas of the James River. Lunch can be enjoyed in the Coach House Tavern and the gift shop offers a unique collection of historical mementos.

Three-Pointer

Boston Garden
One FleetCenter Place
Boston, Massachusetts

On October 12, 1979, Boston Celtic Chris Ford entered the record books as the first player in the NBA to ever sink a three-point shot (in that game, the season opener, the Celtics defeated the Rockets 114-108). The shot came with three minutes and 48 seconds left in the first quarter. The game also marked the debut of Boston Celtic rookie Larry Bird. That season, Ford was second in the league in three-point percentage at .427. Larry Bird was third with .406. (The three point shot is 23' 9" from the basket.) Today, the FleetCenter sits at the place where the venerable Boston Garden once stood.

Tickertape Parades

Lower Broadway
New York City, New York

The tickertape parades in New York are some of the most famous parades in the world, having honored many of the world's greatest heroes. Today, granite markers commemorating each of the 176 tickertape parades are embedded in the sidewalk every 20 to 30 feet leading from Battery Park to City Hall. Called the "Canyon of Heroes," the historic route traces each event, depicting the name and date of each parade beginning with the very first, which was held on October 26, 1886, when an impromptu celebration of the Statue of Liberty dedication commenced downtown using leftover stock market tickertape as confetti.

Other parades were held in honor of President Theodore Roosevelt; General Dwight Eisenhower; Queen Elizabeth II; Astronaut John Glenn; Gertrude Ederle, the first woman to swim the English Channel; Charles Lindbergh, in honor of the first solo trans-Atlantic flight; and most recently, the New York Yankees.

Tony Packo's Café

1902 Front Street
Toledo, Ohio
419-691-6054

MASH fans take note: In the legendary CBS TV series, this was the supposed favorite restaurant of Corporal Max Klinger (Jamie Farr), who was Lebanese-American and a Toledo resident stationed in Korea in the 1950s. Whenever Klinger became homesick for stateside food, this is the restaurant he talked about in the show. In fact, Tony Packo's is mentioned six times on the program and once, the interior of the café was recreated for a scene in which Klinger dreamed of being home.

The restaurant, which was built in 1932, features Hungarian specialties (meat-filled cabbage rolls) and spicy, chili-topped hot dogs. And Tony's is famous for something else: In June, 1972 when Burt Reynolds was playing *The Rainmaker*
at a local auditorium, Nancy (Tony Packo Sr.'s daughter) invited him to the restaurant. He showed up about two nights later. Reynolds was the first big name to eat at Packo's and sign a hot dog bun, a precedent followed by scores of celebrities, including presidential candidates, whose autographed hot dog buns are now enshrined on Packo's walls.

"T'was the Night Before Christmas"

225 River Street
Troy, New York

Troy is where the famous Christmas poem, "A Visit from Saint Nicholas" was first published in the *Troy Sentinel* on December 23, 1823. There is some controversy about the poem since it was published anonymously, and later was attributed to Clement C. Moore. Some claim that Henry Livingston was the original author but he had died by the time that Moore was given the credit. But no matter, on December 23, 1823, the *Troy Sentinel*, a small newspaper on River Street, published for the first time ever an anonymous poem titled "Account of a Visit from St. Nicholas, or Santa Claus." Known today by its more popular "Twas the Night Before Christmas," this poem ranks as one of the most popular poems ever written. It probably is the most parodied poem of all times as well.

"23 Skidoo"

Flatiron building
Fifth Avenue between East 22nd and 23rd Streets
New York City, New York

The phrase "23 Skidoo" supposedly originated at this unique building with a police officer chasing off loiterers at the 23rd Street corner. The loiterers were hoping to catch a glimpse of a lady's stocking under a skirt blown up by the freakish Flatiron winds. Why the weird winds? The aerodynamic shape of the building led to a wind-tunnel effect up the streets on which it was situated. So as men lined up to watch women walk past, cops would shoo them from the site saying "23 skidoo!" The Flatiron was recently seen in the *Spiderman* movies as The Daily Bugle building.

The Flatiron was New York's first skyscraper and today it is the city's oldest. Officially named the "Fuller Building" (for the company that had commissioned it), the structure was instantly renamed by the public for its striking resemblance to a traditional flat iron.

Uncle Sam

Troy, New York

Most Americans think of "Uncle Sam" as a nickname for the U.S. government. But residents of Troy, New York, know otherwise—they know that Uncle Sam was an actual person named Samuel Wilson. Wilson worked as a meat-packer in Troy during the War of 1812 and many believe that Wilson's nickname, "Uncle Sam," was the original inspiration for the red, white and blue character that now symbolizes the U. S.

During the War of 1812, Wilson provided large shipments of meat to the U.S. Army in barrels that were stamped with the initials "U.S.." Supposedly, someone who saw the "U.S." stamp suggested, perhaps facetiously, that the initials stood for "Uncle Sam" Wilson. The suggestion that the meat shipments came from "Uncle Sam" led to the idea that Uncle Sam symbolized the federal government.

Samuel Wilson died in 1854, and he is buried in the Oakwood Cemetery in Troy. Uncle Sam's popular appearance, with a white goatee and star-spangled suit, is an invention of artists and political cartoonists. (In reality, Samuel Wilson was clean-shaven.) The best known Uncle Sam image originated over 50 years ago as part of a wartime recruitment poster, encouraging qualified citizens to join the armed forces. Today the town wraps itself in his heritage.

One of the bigger monuments to Uncle Sam Wilson is a statue at the corner of River Street and 3rd Street in downtown Troy. In 1989, this statue was featured on a postage stamp. Oddly, the stamp was issued not by the U.S., but by the island of St. Vincent, as part of a series of stamps that feature cartoon characters visiting American monuments.

More Uncle Sam: In the small town of Mason, New Hampshire, Samuel Wilson's boyhood home has also become a landmark. It's located on Route 123, about 1/2 mile south of Mason village.

The Wave

University of Washington–Husky Stadium
3800 Montlake Boulevard
Seattle, Washington
206-628-0888

The earliest recorded human wave (whereby fans respond, domino-like, by standing up and sitting down in progressive order around a stadium), was created at the University of Washington, Seattle, by cheerleader Rob Weller and UW Band Director Bill Bissell at a UW Husky football game on October 31, 1981 in Seattle at Husky Stadium. (And yes, the Rob Weller is the same one who co-hosted the TV show *Entertainment Tonight*.) The Wave is believed to have started in the third quarter as the Huskies successively scored 28 points in route to a 42–31 win over a John Elway-led Stanford team.

Winchester Mystery House

525 South Winchester Boulevard
San Jose, California
408-247-2101

It's one of the strangest, most interesting landmarks in the country. In 1884, a wealthy widow named Sarah L. Winchester undertook a project so vast that it took up the lives of carpenters and craftsmen until her death 38 years later. The final product, a classic Victorian mansion created by the Winchester Rifle heiress, is filled with so many unexplained oddities that it has come to be known as the Winchester Mystery House.

It features a mind-boggling 160-rooms, three working elevators, and 47 fireplaces. One of the first to see the place when it opened to the public was Robert L. Ripley, who featured the house in his popular column, "Believe It or Not." Visitors are puzzled by staircases leading to the ceiling, startled by windows in the floor and stunned by a door opening onto an eight-foot drop into a kitchen sink. (And the place is supposedly haunted, to boot.)

Born in the USA

Air Conditioning

Air Conditioning
490 Broadway Street
Buffalo, New York

On July 17, 1902, the first "air conditioner" began working at a printing company called Sackett-Wilhelms in Brooklyn, New York. It was designed and built here in Buffalo by a man named Willis Carrier who conceived of air conditioning one year after he went to work at the Buffalo Forge Company. His first major task was figuring out how to help Sackett-Wilhelms, who was having trouble with the four-color printing of a magazine (paper shrank or expanded as the humidity changed, and colored inks, applied in layers, failed to register properly—consequently, pictures printed fuzzy).

The problem, Carrier found, was not the heat, but the humidity. To that end, Carrier created a device that moved air over cooled pipes, sucking out moisture much as an iced drink collects dew on the outside of a glass. On July 17, 1902, he finished drawings for the world's first scientific air conditioning system. Although the old Buffalo Forge plant is no longer in use, the invention it produced affects millions of us around the world (and the building still stands today).

When World War I arrived, Buffalo Forge was forced to cut back and, amazingly, eliminated their air conditioning division. Carrier, with six colleagues, invested $32,600 in their own company, Carrier Engineering Corporation. Carrier moved his company to Syracuse, New York in the 1930s, and the company became one of the largest employers in central New York (and today remains the world leader in air conditioners).

Alcoholic's Anonymous

Alcoholic's Anonymous

Mayflower Hotel
263 South Main Street
Akron, Ohio

On May 11, 1935, Bill W. found himself at a crossroads. An alcoholic who had nearly drunk himself to death after four detox hospital stays, he'd managed to finally begin a sober life. His newfound sobriety was being threatened during a business trip here in Ohio. He found himself standing in the lobby of the Mayflower Hotel, desperate for a drink. With growing anxiety he weighed his options and decided he could do one of two things: he could order a cocktail in the hotel bar, or, he could call someone and ask for help in his fight to stay sober.

He gathered his strength, passed by the bar in the hotel, found a telephone directory, and minutes later he was on the phone with a woman named Henrietta Seiberling, an Oxford Group adherent. (The Oxford Group was a precursor of what we think of today as a self-help group.) She arranged a meeting with a Dr. Bob Smith to take place the next day at the Gate Lodge, the three-bedroom house located on the Stan Hywet Hall and Gardens estate where she lived. (The doctor was also an alcoholic at that time and she felt the meeting would benefit both men.) Today the Mayflower is called Mayflower Manor Apartments.

Dr. Bob's House

855 Ardmore Avenue
Akron, Ohio
330-864-1935

This is where Dr. Bob Smith lived. When he arranged to meet Bill W. at the Gate Lodge, he initially agreed to see Bill for only 15 minutes. However, their meeting lasted for hours. Bill W. told the Doctor of his drinking history and Bob identified with it immediately. Bill thanked Bob for hearing him out—and for his fellowship. "I know now that I'm not going to take another drink," Bill said, "and I'm grateful to you."
But the relationship did not end there. Bill stayed with Dr. Bob for the next three weeks.

Through their friendship, Dr. Bob also gained sobriety. The surgeon never took another drink after June 10, 1935. That day—Dr. Bob's "dry date"—is officially counted as the start of Alcoholics Anonymous. The white clapboard house, restored to reflect Dr. Bob's tenure, is open for tours.

Alcoholic's Anonymous

The Gate Lodge

**Stan Hywet Gate and Gardens
714 North Portage Path
Akron, Ohio
330-836-5533**

One of the finest examples of Tudor Revival architecture in America, this 65-room mansion is decorated with treasures from all over the globe, and is located on 70 artfully landscaped acres that include a fully-restored English garden, a Japanese garden, a lagoon, vistas, scenic alleys and more. But it holds even more signifi-cance for millions of Americans.

It was here on Mother's Day of 1939 that Alcoholics Anonymous was born. It was in the estate's Gate Lodge, the small, three-bedroom home originally designed to accommodate the estate's pri-mary caretaker at the entrance to the property, that Henrietta Sieberling brought Bill W. and Dr. Bob Smith together. They then went on to develop the founding principals of AA (the 12-step program). Their common goal was to provide support for recovering alcoholics, their family and friends. As we all know, they have made a huge impact on the world. The house is open for tours.

ATM

**10 North Village Avenue
Rockville Centre, New York**

It was here at a Chemical Bank in 1969 that the first modern Automatic Teller Machine (ATM) was installed. Don Wetzel, Vice President of Product Planning at a company that made automated baggage-handling equipment, got the idea in 1968 to develop a machine that dispensed cash (he and his partners also created the first ATM card with a magnetic strip). In 1969, Chemical Bank revolutionized banking by installing the first modern ATM in this Rockville Centre branch. Today, the bank is the Long Island regional headquarters for JP Morgan Chase.

Baseball

Pittsfield, Massachusetts

In May 2004, historians in the western Massachusetts city of Pittsfield rocked the baseball world by releasing a 213-year-old document that they think might contain the earliest written reference to baseball. The evidence exists in a bylaw from 1791 that aims to protect the windows in Pittsfield's brand new meeting house by prohibiting anyone from playing baseball within 80 yards of the building. In Cooperstown, New York (home of the Baseball Hall of Fame) it is believed (some argue through legend) that Abner Doubleday wrote the rules for the game in 1839, so Pittsfield's claim would trump Cooperstown by some 48 years.

The long-accepted story of baseball's origins centers on Cooperstown, New York, where Doubleday is said to have come up with the rules for the modern game. That presumption long legitimized the Baseball Hall of Fame's presence in Cooperstown, although later it became clear that a game with modern rules was played in Hoboken, New Jersey, in 1846. Currently, the debate rages as to whether Pittsfield is actually baseball's true Garden of Eden.

Boone, Daniel

500 Daniel Boone Road
Birdsboro, Pennsylvania
610-582-4900

The great American frontiersman, the legendary Daniel Boone, was born here in 1734. Today the Daniel Boone Homestead interprets the life of early English and German settlers in eastern Berks County. Visitors to the site will discover the Boone house, blacksmith shop, barn, Bertolet log house, sawmill, visitor center, picnic area and trails.

Business Computer

33 Highland Avenue
Rowayton, Connecticut
203-838-5038

In 1947, the first business computer starting taking shape, designed by a team of engineers under General McArthur right here at the Rowayton Library. The Remington Rand 409 plugboard programmed punch card calculator, first introduced in 1949, was sold in two models: the UNIVAC 60 and the UNIVAC 120. (The model number referred to the number of memory storage locations provided for data.) The machine was designed in "The Barn," a building that currently houses the Rowayton Public Library and Community Center.

Cohan, George Michael

90 Ives Street
Providence, Rhode Island

George M. Cohan, the world famous theatrical director, singer, playwright (*Seven Keys to Baldpate, The Song and Dance Man*), and composer ("Give My Regards to Broadway," "Over There," "You're a Grand Old Flag," "I'm a Yankee Doodle Dandy") was born on this site on July 3, 1878. A plaque marks the spot where the house in which he was born once stood; today this is the site of the Fox Point Boys and Girls Club. In 1942, a musical film biography of Cohan, *Yankee Doodle Dandy*, was released, with James Cagney playing the role of Cohan. Cohan enjoyed attending a screening of the film a few weeks before his death.

College Football

Rutgers University
New Brunswick, New Jersey

New Brunswick was the site of the first intercollegiate football game on November 6, 1869. Rutgers University beat Princeton by a score of six to four. The stadium where the game was played was called College Field, which is now the site of the College Avenue Gymnasium and its parking lot.

Commercial Radio

KDKA
1 Gateway Center
Pittsburgh, Pennsylvania

On November 2, 1920, KDKA, a small radio station in Pittsburgh began broadcasting and thus became the world's first commercial radio station. Broadcasting began at 8:00 P.M. and continued until midnight with reports of the Harding–Cox presidential election returns. The news that Warren Harding had won the race marked a dramatic end to a historic day in America's broadcasting as well as political history.

Though this is not the exact site where the broadcast took place (KDKA moved here in the 1950s), a marker does acknowledge the station's illustrious past. It reads: "RADIO STATION KDKA—World's first commercial station began operating November 2, 1920, when KDKA reported Harding–Cox election returns from a makeshift studio at the East Pittsburgh Works of Westinghouse. Music, sports, talks, and special events were soon being regularly aired."

Country Music

State Street
Bristol, Tennessee
423-989-4850

In 1998, the United States Congress passed a resolution recognizing Bristol, Tennessee, as the "Birthplace of County Music." It was in 1927 that the "big bang" of country music took place. Victor Records talent scout Ralph Peer traveled to Bristol and discovered Jimmie Rodgers and the Carter family, country music's first two stars. The Bristol Recording Sessions, by virtue of Rodgers and Carter's impact, laid the groundwork for what became the "country music industry." The building in which those sessions occurred

is no longer standing, but a monument marks the spot (on State Street). Bristol has also created a must-visit mural and monument downtown to commemorate this history.

Crockett, Davy

Davy Crockett Birthplace State Park
1245 Davy Crockett Park Road
Limestone, Tennessee
423-257-4500

The legendary Davy Crockett was born here in East Tennessee in 1786. Today, his birthplace has been preserved by the State of Tennessee Department of Environment and Conservation as a historic site within the state park system. The museum at the park tells of the different aspects of the life of the heroic (and somewhat mythical) frontiersman. You'll learn about Crockett the hunter, the politician, the businessman and the legendary hero as portrayed in the Walt Disney movie of the 1950s. A replica cabin depicts a typical frontier scenario much like the one in which Davy Crockett was born in 1786. (Located in front of the cabin is the engraved footstone to the original cabin.)

Drive-In Filling Station

Baum and St. Clair Streets
Pittsburgh, Pennsylvania

At this site in December 1913, Gulf Refining Co. opened the first drive-in facility designed and built to provide gasoline, oils, and lubricants to the motoring public (the East Liberty Station). Its success led to construction of thousands of gas stations by different oil companies across the nation. The East Liberty station was the first to offer free road maps produced by Gulf. They also made the employee restroom available to motorists, which greatly contributed to the concept of public restrooms at stations elsewhere. A recently placed marker commemorates the history.

Drive-In Movies

Camden Drive-In
Crescent Boulevard
Camden, New Jersey

New Jersey gave birth to the phenomenon of drive-in movies on June 6, 1933. The Camden Drive-In, in Pennsauken, showed *Wife Beware,* starring Adolphe Menjou. In 1933, a man named Richard Hollingshead received the first patent for the Drive-In Theater (United States Patent# 1,909,537) and it was issued on May 16, 1933. With an investment of $30,000, the inventor opened this first drive-in. The price of admission was 25 cents per car and 25 cents per person. The drive-in did not include the in-car speaker system we are familiar with today. Three main speakers were mounted next to the screen that provided sound. The sound quality was not good for cars in the rear of the theater.

ENIAC Computer

Chancellor Street between 33rd and 34th Streets
Philadelphia, Pennsylvania

A plaque here reads: "ENIAC, the Electronic Numerical Integrator and Computer, was invented by J. Presper Eckert and John Mauchly. It was built here at the University of Pennsylvania in 1946. The invention of this first all-purpose digital computer signaled the birth of the Information Age.

While the first fully automatic calculator (the Mark I or Automatic Sequence Controlled Calculator) was realized in 1939 at Harvard by Howard Aiken, the ENIAC (Electronic Numerical Integrator And Calculator), was the first all-purpose electronic digital computer. ENIAC, which used thousands of vacuum tubes, became (1951) the first computer to handle both numeric and alphabetic data with equal facility and was the first commercially available computer."

Food and Drink

Banana Split

805 Ligonier Street
Latrobe, Pennsylvania

In 1904, Dr. David Strickler, a pharmacist at Tassell's Drug Store, invented the banana split here (back then, pharmacists were forever coming up with "sweet" ideas to make people feel better). Strickler's recipe for a banana split 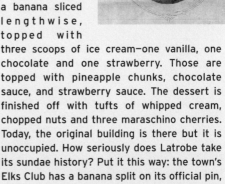 starts off with a banana sliced lengthwise, topped with  three scoops of ice cream—one vanilla, one chocolate and one strawberry. Those are topped with pineapple chunks, chocolate sauce, and strawberry sauce. The dessert is finished off with tufts of whipped cream, chopped nuts and three maraschino cherries. Today, the original building is there but it is unoccupied. How seriously does Latrobe take its sundae history? Put it this way: the town's Elks Club has a banana split on its official pin, and St. Vincent College uses the banana split story in its school recruiting material.

Food and Drink

Ben & Jerry's

Southwest corner of St. Paul and College Streets
Burlington, Vermont

In 1963, Bennett Cohen and Jerry Greenfield met in their seventh-grade gym class at Merrick Avenue Junior High School in Merrick (Long Island, New York). Both kids were

overweight, and both loved ice cream. While going to Calhoun High School in Merrick, Cohen hawked ice cream from a truck. As a student at Oberlin College in Ohio, Greenfield got a job as an ice cream scooper.

After moving to Vermont, the pals decided to embark on their ice cream dreams in May 1978 by opening Ben & Jerry's Homemade here in a renovated gas station. Soon, word of the unique ice cream place with the wildly creative flavors and community-minded business style spread like crazy. By 1985, Ben & Jerry's annual sales exceeded $9 million and in 1998, they topped over $200 million worldwide. A plaque in the sidewalk marks the spot of the first store, which is now a vacant lot. Note: Nearby, in Waterbury, Vermont, visitors can take a tour of the Ben & Jerry's ice cream factory. Take exit 10 off of I-89 in Waterbury, go north on route 100 towards Stowe. The ice cream factory is about one mile up the road on the left. Phone: 866-BJTOURS.

Big Mac

Uniontown Shopping Center
942 Morgantown Street
Uniontown, Pennsylvania

The famous Big Mac sandwich was created in 1967 by M. J. "Jim" Delligatti, an early McDonald's owner and operator, at his Uniontown, Fayette County, McDonald's. He developed his brainchild because sales were down and he thought that the way to get things back up were to expand the menu. McDonald's agreed to let him test a large sandwich that featured two patties, which he called the Big Mac. It was a hit, so he introduced them at three of his other McDonald's in Pittsburgh. From there, well, you know what happened.

Food and Drink

Boysenberry

**Knott's Berry Farm
8039 Beach Boulevard
Buena Park, California
714-220-5200**

Today it's a popular theme park, but Knott's Berry Farm really does have its roots planted in berries, as the name says. In fact, this is where the Boysenberry was born. In 1923, a man named Rudolph Boysen crossed a loganberry with a raspberry near this site, and he called the resulting hybrid the "boysenberry."

Ten years later, in 1933, a Buena Park farmer named Walter Knott started planting boysenberries right here on what he called "Knott's Berry Farm." The depression took hold, and his wife fixed up a roadside stand and began hawking freshly baked pies, plus fresh preserves, and delicious home-cooked chicken dinners.

So many people came around to visit the stand (and buy her wares) that Walter thought it would be a good idea to create an old west ghost town so waiting customers would have something to do—and so Knott's Berry Farm was born. Today, Knott's Berry Farm features 165 shows, attractions, and rides.

Food and Drink

Cheeseburger I

2776 Speer Boulevard
Denver, Colorado

Smile and say "cheeseburger!" In 1935, Louis Ballas, owner of the Humpty-Dumpty Drive-In in northwest Denver, put a slice of cheese on a hot burger, and the rest is history. The world's first "cheeseburger"—a term patented by Ballas—is honored with a small memorial at 2776 Speer Boulevard, now the parking lot of Key Bank.

The Cheeseburger II

Kaelin's Restaurant
1801 Newburg Road
Louisville, Kentucky
502-451-1801

Carl and Margaret Kaelin *may* have beaten Ballas by one year. Shortly after opening their new restaurant in 1934, Kaelin was cooking a hamburger when he decided to add a slice of American cheese (seems he liked the extra "tang" from the cheese). He christened his new creation the "cheeseburger." A proclamation from the mayor of the city of Louisville designates every October 12th (the date the cheeseburger was invented) as "Kaelin's Cheeseburger Day" here in Louisville.

Cheeseburger III

The Rite Spot
1500 West Colorado Boulevard
Pasadena, California

Then there are those who believe that Lionel Sternberger first came up with the "cheese hamburger" back in 1926 while working the grill at a place called The Rite Spot (which is no longer there). Sternberger had purchased a roadside burger stand here—the former Hinky Dick—which was located on historic Route 66 just before the entrance to the neighboring town of Eagle Rock.

Food and Drink

Coca-Cola

107 Marietta Street
Atlanta, Georgia

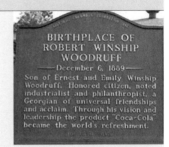

Woodruff, Robert Winship

1414 Second Avenue
Columbus, Georgia

On May 8, 1886, druggist Dr. John Stith Pemberton (a former Confederate officer) invented "Coca-Cola" syrup. It was mixed in a 30-gallon brass kettle hung over a backyard fire. After he made a jug of the syrup he took it down to "Jacobs Pharmacy" and talked Willis E. Venabele into mixing it with water and selling it for five-cents a glass. It was marketed as a "brain and nerve tonic" in drugstores and sales averaged nine drinks per day.

Pemberton's bookkeeper, Frank M. Robinson, was the person who suggested the name "Coca-Cola," which was chosen because both words actually named two ingredients found in the syrup. He also suggested that the name be written in the Spencerian script, a popular penmanship of that time. It was from his pen that the "Coca-Cola" signature originated. Pemberton liked the easy to remember name, so history was born.

On November 15, 1886, John G. Wilkes (who was drunk) walked into a drugstore complaining of a headache and requested a bottle of "Coca-Cola" syrup. To get instant relief, he asked the "soda jerk" to mix up a glass on the spot. Rather than walk to the other end of the counter in order to mix it with cold tap water, the clerk suggested using soda water. The man remarked that it really tasted great. Soon after, "Coca-Cola" was in fizzy, carbonated form.

The building at 107 Marietta Street where the drink was invented is no longer there. Jacob's Pharmacy, where Coca-Cola formula was dispensed for the first time, was located at the southwest corner of Peachtree and Marietta streets (the site of what is now the Wachovia tower).

Robert Winship Woodruff was born in Columbus, Georgia on December 6, 1889. He was the man who shepherded Coca-Cola into the huge international brand that it is today. At just 33 years old, he took command of The Coca-Cola Company in 1923 and shaped the young soft drink enterprise and its bottler franchise system into a corporate giant with the world's most widely known trademark. A man of enormous stature and personal magnetism, Mr. Woodruff's influence over the affairs of The Coca-Cola Company was absolute until his death in 1985. His birthplace is honored with a historical marker.

Food and Drink

Coca-Cola Bottle

Root Glass Company
Corner of Third Street and Voorhees Streets
Terre Haute, Indiana

Biedenharn Candy Company Museum

1107 Washington Street
Vicksburg, Mississippi

Terre Haute is the birthplace of the Coca-Cola bottle. The Chapman Root Glass Company invented the "Hobbleskirt," or "contour," bottle specifically for Coca-Cola. They modeled the bottle after a cocoa bean. The bottle was first patented on November 16, 1915, and then renewed on December 25, 1923. The actual shape of the bottle was patented in 1960. A historic marker has been placed at the site of the bottling company. The bottling company is long gone, and a gas station and restaurant now sit at the site. At the Vigo County Historical Society Museum located at 1411 South 6th Street in Terre Haute, visitors can see a huge collection of original Coca-Cola artifacts as well as exclusive products in their gift shop and a rare mold of the original bottle.

The Biedenharn Candy Company Museum is in the restored 19th-century candy store and soda fountain where Joseph Biedenharn first bottled Coca-Cola in 1894. Coca-Cola memorabilia, a bottle collection and antique bottling equipment are displayed.

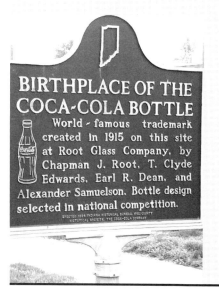

Food and Drink

Corn Dog

Cozy Dog
2935 South Sixth Street
Springfield, Illinois
217-525-1992

The corn dog, named first the "Crusty Cur" and then the "Cozy Dog," was invented by Ed Waldmire Jr., and made popular here at his restaurant. Here's how he once told the story: "In Muskogee, Oklahoma, I saw an unusual sandwich called 'corn-dog.' This sandwich was a wiener baked in cornbread. The corn-dog was very good, but took too long to prepare. The problem was how to cover a hotdog with batter and cook it in a short time. In the fall of 1941, I told this story to a fellow student at Knox College whose father was in the bakery business, and then gave it no further thought.

"Five years later while in the Air Force stationed at Amarillo Airfield, I received a letter from my fellow student, Don Strand. To my surprise he had developed a mix that would stick on a wiener while being french-fried. He wondered if he could send some down that I could try in Amarillo. Having plenty of spare time, I said 'yes.'

Using cocktail forks for sticks, the U.S.O kitchen in which to experiment, we made a very tasty hotdog on a stick, that we called a "crusty cur." They became very popular both at the U.S.O. in town, and at the P.X. on the airfield. My friend continued to send mix and we continued to sell thousands of crusty curs until I was discharged—honorably—in the spring of 1946. We decided to sell them that spring. My wife did not like the name

'crusty curs.' Through trial and error and discarding dozens of names, we finally decided on the name 'Cozy Dogs.'"

Cozy Dogs were officially launched on June 16, 1946 and today at the Cozy Dog Drive-In, you'll still find the delicious, innovative hot-dog-on-a-stick at this classic American restaurant.

Food and Drink

Dr. Pepper Museum

300 South 5th Street
Waco, Texas
254-757-1025

Dr Pepper Company is the oldest major manufacturer of soft drink concentrates and syrups in the United States. It was created, manufactured and sold beginning in 1885 here in the Central Texas town of Waco. Dr Pepper is a "native Texan," originating at Morrison's Old Corner Drug Store (originally located in Waco at the corner of 4th and Austin, it can now be seen here at this museum).

The origin of Dr Pepper is this: Charles Alderton, a young pharmacist working at Morrison's store, is believed to be the inventor of the now-famous drink. Alderton spent most of his time mixing up medicine for the people of Waco, but in his spare time he liked to serve carbonated drinks at the soda fountain. He liked the way the drug store smelled with all of the fruit syrup flavor odors mixing together in the air. He decided to create a drink that tasted like that scent. He kept a journal, and after numerous experiments he finally hit upon a mixture of fruit syrups that he liked.

As to the name, Morrison is credited with naming the drink "Dr. Pepper" (the period was dropped in the 1950s). Unfortunately, the exact origin is unclear, though the museum has collected over a dozen different stories on how the drink became known as "Dr Pepper." The exceptional museum tour includes some interesting smells and flavors in the Old Corner Drug Store, a tour of the bottling room, the chance to crown a soft-drink bottle and shoot a "Waco" in the soda fountain, plus a sample-size fountain treat.

Food and Drink

French Dip Sandwich

Philippe the Original
1001 North Alameda Street
Los Angeles, California
213-628-3781

Philippe the Original is one of the oldest and best-
known restaurants in Southern California, if not the
world. It was established in 1908 by Philippe
Mathieu, the man thought to have created the "French Dip Sandwich." Here's the story:
One day in 1918, while making a sandwich, Mathieu inadvertently dropped the sliced
French roll into a roasting pan filled with juice still hot from the oven. The patron, a
policeman, said he would take the sandwich anyway and returned the next day with some
friends asking for more dipped sandwiches. And so the "French Dip Sandwich" was born—
so-called because of either Mathieu's French heritage, the French roll the sandwich is
made on, or because the officer's name was French. Whatever the reason, people love
this place for all the *right* reasons—great food, great prices and great history.

Ice Cream Sundae Birthplace #1

1404 15th Street
Two Rivers, Wisconsin

On July 8th, 1881, some claim that the first ice cream sundae was served by accident
here at this address in Two Rivers. Druggist Edward Berner, owner of Ed Berner's Ice
Cream Parlor, was asked by a man named George Hallauer for some ice cream topped
with syrup soda. Realizing how good it tasted, Berner decided to add the dish to his regular menu and charged a nickel, the same price as a serving without syrup. However,
the nickel price created too small a profit margin, and so it was decided that the treat
would only be served on Sundays to maintain costs.

Sometime later, on a day other than Sunday, a ten-year-old girl insisted on being served
a dish of ice cream "with that stuff on top," saying they could "pretend it was Sunday."
Not only did she persuade Berner to serve her the special dessert, but, after that, the
confection was sold every day in many flavors. It eventually lost its Sunday-only association and came to be called an "Ice Cream Sundae" when a glassware salesman
placed an order with his company for the long canoe-shaped dishes in which it was
served, and referred to the bowls as "Sundae dishes."

Nearby at the Washington House Hotel Museum in Two Rivers, you'll find a replica of Ed
Berner's ice cream parlor. Additionally, the Wisconsin State Historical Society recog-
nizes Two Rivers as the birthplace of the sundae and in 1973 a historical marker was
placed in Two Rivers Central Memorial Park to commemorate the event.

Food and Drink

Ice Cream Sundae Birthplace #2

216 East State Street
Ithaca, New York

The story here goes that one hot Sunday afternoon in 1891, John M. Scott, the pastor of the Unitarian Church, and one of his faithful parishioners, Chester Platt, retired to the latter's drug store for something cool. Here, Mr. Platt supposedly got two dishes of ice cream from Miss DeForest Christiance, who was tending the soda fountain. He plopped a candied cherry on top of each dish of ice cream and covered the whole thing with cherry syrup, resulting in what many Ithaca folks think was the real first ice cream sundae.

JELL-O Museum

23 East Main Street
LeRoy, New York
585-768-7433

JELL-O, perhaps America's most famous dessert, was born here in LeRoy, located in upstate New York. In 1845, a man named Peter Cooper patented a product that was "set" with gelatin. But it never caught on with the public. However, in 1897, Pearle Wait, a carpenter here in LeRoy, was concocting a cough remedy and laxative tea in his home. He experimented with gelatin and came up with a fruit-flavored dessert that his wife, May, named Jell-O. He tried to market his product but he lacked the capital and the experience.

In 1899, he sold his formula to a fellow townsman, Frank Woodward, for just $450. Woodward already had some success in manufacturing and selling and was one of the best-known manufacturers of proprietary medicines. At first, sales were so slow that Woodward gave his plant superintendent the chance to buy the JELL-O rights for $35. But before they could complete their deal, sales took off. By 1906, sales reached $1 million.

The marketing was brilliant—they'd send out well-attired salesmen to demonstrate JELL-O and distribute 15 million copies of a JELL-O recipe book containing celebrity favorites and more. In 1923, Woodward's Genesee Pure Food Company was renamed JELL-O Company and later merged with Postum Cereal to become the General Foods Corporation. In 1997, the JELL-O Museum opened its doors in LeRoy. The museum features JELL-O artwork by famous artists such as Max Parrish and Norman Rockwell, and showcases memorabilia from the more than 100 years in the brand's history.

Food and Drink

Kellogg Company

235 Porter Street
Battle Creek, Michigan

A plaque here reads: "At the age of fourteen, Will Keith Kellogg (1860–1951) began working as a salesman for his father's broom business. Later he worked with his brother Dr. John Harvey Kellogg, at the Battle Creek Sanitarium. In 1894, John, assisted by Will, developed a successful cereal flake. It was first served to patients at the sanitarium and later sold by the Sanitas Food Company.

"In 1906, W. K. Kellogg launched his own food company to sell Toasted Corn Flakes cereal. The company grew to be the largest manufacturer of ready-to-eat cereals in the world. Kellogg's early personal philanthropies included assistance to rural teachers, to British children orphaned by war, to the blind and to a number of hospitals and medical programs. In 1930 the W. K. Kellogg Foundation was established to promote the health and well being of children. Today, it is among the world's largest philanthropic organizations.

"Will manufactured the first boxes of cereal in a three-story building on Bartlett Street at the rate of thirty-three cases per day. In 1907 the original factory building was destroyed by fire, and part of the present structure was erected on this site. Kellogg Company sold more than one million cases of cereal in 1909, and by 1911 the company's advertising budget had reached $1 million. In 1917, production capacity reached nine million boxes per day. In 1980, United States production of Kellogg's ready-to-eat cereals required more than 110,000 bushels of corn, 225,000 pounds of bran, 9,000 bushels of wheat and 12,000 pounds of wheat germ each day. By its seventy-fifth anniversary in 1981, Kellogg Company had forty-seven plants operating in twenty-one countries."

The site is not open to the public.

Kool-Aid

508 West First Street
Hastings, Nebraska

The town of Hastings, Nebraska is known as the "Birthplace of Kool-Aid" because Nebraska native Edwin Perkins invented the powdered soft drink here in 1927. To honor Kool-Aid on its milestone birthday, the Hastings Museum permanently dedicated a 3,300 square-foot exhibit to portray the Kool-Aid story.

The museum is located at 1330 North Burlington Avenue in Hastings. There, you'll find artifacts including rare early packets, a Kool-Aid cartoon suit worn by its jug mascot and a large interactive exhibit that tells the story of Kool-Aid and inventor Edwin Perkins. You'll also find a commemorative sign at the site where it was invented.

Food and Drink

Lobster Newburgh

Delmonico's
56 Beaver Street
New York City, New York
212-509-1144

In 1836, the Delmonico brothers (Giovanni and Pietro) opened this now-famous restaurant in lower Manhattan. Since then, it's not only served some of the city's best meals—it's actually been the birthplace of some of the world's most famous dishes. For instance, in the mid-1800s, shipping magnate Ben Wenberg asked chef Charles Ranhofer to prepare a meal he had discovered in South America—chunks of lobster sautéed in butter and served in a sauce of cream and egg flavored with paprika and sherry. The meal was such a success that it was added to the Delmonico's menu as Lobster Wenberg.

However, some time later, Wenberg consumed too much wine from Delmonico's renowned cellars and got into a fight. He was banned from Delmonico's forever and his name was taken off the menu. But they did not want to lose the dish, so "Wenberg" became "Newburgh"—and that's how Lobster Newburgh began.

In 1876, the Baked Alaska also originated at Delmonico's. It was created in honor of the newly acquired territory of Alaska. George Sala, an Englishman who visited Delmonico's in the 1880s, said: "The 'Alaska' is a baked ice.... The nucleus or core of the entremets

is an ice cream. This is surrounded by an envelope of carefully whipped cream, which, just before the dainty dish is served, is popped into the oven, or is brought under the scorching influence of a red hot salamander."

It was later popularized worldwide by Jean Giroix, chef in 1895 at the Hotel de Paris in Monte Carlo. And Eggs Benedict was also created at Delmonico's, back in the 1860s, in response to a complaint that their menu never changed. A couple named Mr. and Mrs. LeGrand Benedict, regulars at the upscale restaurant, asked for something new. To oblige, the chef served up eggs on ham served on a muffin and covered in Hollandaise sauce. They loved it, and so Eggs Benedict was born.

Food and Drink

Oreos

Chelsea Market
88 10th Avenue
New York City, New York
212-247-1423

Today in this funky, cobblestone-floored old building you'll find unbelievably appetizing places such as Manhattan Fruit Exchange, The Lobster Place, the bakery for Sarabeth's Bakery, Fat Witch Brownies and more (including some of the offices for Major League Baseball). But way back, this was once the head-quarters of Nabisco and the actual birthplace of the Oreo cook-ie. From 1898-1958, Nabisco occupied this building and Oreos were born here in 1912. In fact, some of the original red brick ovens are still visible in the MLB.com offices.

Pepperidge Farm

Sturges Highway at Ridge Common
Fairfield, Connecticut

Margaret Rudkin was a Connecticut housewife and mother of three young children. In the early 1930s, she discovered that one of her sons had an allergy to commercial breads that contained preservatives and artificial ingredients. So, in 1937, she started baking her own preservative-free bread for her ailing son. Eventually she hit upon a mouth watering whole-wheat loaf that contained only natural ingredients.

Encouraged by her family, Margaret Rudkin began selling her delicious, freshly-baked bread at a local grocery store here in Fairfield (it's called Mercurio's, located at 508 Post Road). The bread caught on with locals and as her business grew, she felt compelled to give her bread business a name. So, she dubbed it in honor of the farm she lived on— Pepperidge Farm (named for the Pepperidge tree located in the front yard). Today, you can still get a glimpse of the original Pepperidge Farm, exactly as it appears on the product packages. A good deal of the property has been sold and subdivided. However, the iconic, vine-covered, stone farmhouse is there, along with the inspirational Pepperidge tree.

Food and Drink

Pepsi

256 Middle Street
New Bern, North Carolina
252-636-5898

This spot was once a pharmacy where pharmacist Caleb Bradham invented "Brad's Drink" in 1898, which he later patented as Pepsi-Cola in 1903. Bradham, like many pharmacists of the day, operated a soda fountain in his drugstore, where he served his customers homemade beverages, the most popular of which was the aforementioned "Brad's Drink." The concoction's recipe included carbonated water, sugar, vanilla, rare oils, pepsin and cola nuts. (It was later renamed Pepsi after the pepsin and cola nuts used in the recipe.)

Pepsi-Cola went bankrupt in 1923, after Bradham lost his money in the stock market. Then it was bought in 1931 by the Loft Candy Company. Today at the actual place where the drink was invented, there is a recreated soda fountain. Visitors can purchase a wide variety of Pepsi memorabilia inside the store. The birthplace of Pepsi is owned and operated by Pepsi-Cola Bottling Company of New Bern, Inc. It first opened its doors on the 100th Anniversary of Pepsi-Cola.

Reuben Sandwich

Blackstone Hotel
302 South 36th Street
Omaha, Nebraska

This is the birthplace of the famous Reuben sandwich: the delicious combination of rye bread, corned beef, Swiss cheese, and sauerkraut. It was dreamed up at this historic hotel back in 1925 to feed participants in a late-night poker game. Created by a local grocer named Reuben Kulakofsky (hence the sandwich name), hotel owner Charles Schimmel loved the sandwich so much that he put it on the hotel restaurant menu. Bigger exposure would come later when Fern Snider, a one-time waitress at the Blackstone, entered the Reuben in a national sandwich competition in 1956. The entry won the top prize, and thus vaulted the sandwich into history.

Food and Drink

Russell Stover

Highway 24
10½ miles south of Alton, Kansas

In 1921 in Omaha, Nebraska, Russell and Clara Stover introduced an ice-cream creation called the Eskimo Pie. It was a chocolate-covered ice cream square in a small bag and sales exploded the first year they introduced it. At first, it looked as if they'd hit the mother lode, but the patent was too expensive to protect and so they sold their business and moved to Denver where they decided to go into the candy-making business.

From their bungalow home, they started "Mrs. Stover's Bungalow Candies." Clara made the candy and Russell was the salesman. In 1931, they moved their by-now thriving business to Kansas City. Here the couple weathered the Depression and the sugar-short World War II years that followed. But they eventually emerged as a multi-million dollar a year enterprise with world-wide sales. Sixty-six-year-old Russell Stover died May 11, 1954. Clara Stover survived him by 20 years. She carried on the candy business until selling out in 1960. She died on January 9, 1975 at the age of 93. But her candy lives on under the same familiar name. Today, the Russell Stover Birthsite Marker stands next to the field that was the site of the home where Stover was born in 1888.

The Tomato

1792 Graham Road
Reynoldsburg, Ohio

Alexander W. Livingston (1821-1898) was a plant and seed merchant. He became internationally known through his development of the tomato for commercial use. In 1870, after working and experimenting with seeds and plants for several years, he introduced the Paragon Tomato, the first commercial variety grown in these fields. A plaque saluting Reynoldsburg as the birthplace of the tomato and Alexander W. Livingston, the noted horticulturist who developed the domestic strain of the Paragon tomato, can be found in front of the Reynoldsburg Police Station.

Food and Drink

Tomato Juice

French Lick Springs Resort and Spa
8670 West State Road 56
French Lick, Indiana
800-457-4042

In 1917, the world famous chef Louis Perrin at the French Lick Resort ran out of oranges to serve for breakfast, so he created tomato juice. The renowned hotel has hosted dignitaries like Franklin D. Roosevelt, Lana Turner, Bing Crosby and Bob Hope.

The Ford Automobile

220 Bagley Avenue
Detroit, Michigan

It was here in 1892 where Henry Ford began experimenting with the motorized vehicle in his workshop, a small one-story brick structure, once located on this site. His invention was quite simple compared to today's automobiles. It consisted of a two-cylinder machine mounted in a light frame geared to bicycle wheels. That unpretentious auto was the start of the Ford Motor Company, which played a major part in the automobile industry that changed the face of Michigan and the world. A plaque marks the spot.

Ford, Henry

Greenfield, Michigan

A plaque in this condominium parking lot reads: "At this intersection stood the home in which Henry Ford was born on July 30, 1863. The farmhouse was owned by Ford's parents, William and Mary Ford, and in 1944 it was moved to Greenfield Village. In a space of less than ten years at the beginning of this century, the founder of Ford Motor Company developed three separate and distinct concepts, any of which would have assured him an honored niche in history. He designed and built the Model T Ford car, 'the car that put the world on wheels.' He inaugurated the moving automotive assembly line and developed the process of mass production on which modern industry is based. By instituting the five-dollar wage for an eight-hour day, he promulgated a new economic concept that opened the door to mass distribution. Henry Ford was also a pioneer in the field of aviation and in the development of the farm tractor."

Garland, Judy

2727 Highway 169 South
Grand Rapids, Minnesota
800-664-5839

This is the birthplace of Frances Ethel "Baby" Gumm, known to the world as Judy Garland. She spent her first four and a half years living in the two-story, white-framed house that was built in 1892. Today at the house, a one-acre memorial garden includes a field of poppies and the famous "Judy Garland" roses. Oral histories and photographs allow visitors to see the house as it was, down to the exact details (like the ukulele perched on top of the small grand piano). Nearby, The Children's Discovery Museum located at 2727 US Highway 169 South houses classic *Wizard of Oz* memorabilia and artifacts such as the original carriage used in the 1939 movie classic and a complete *Wizard of Oz* memorabilia exhibit (218-326-1900).

Gas Automobile

1915 South Webster Street
Kokomo, Indiana
765-456-7500

Elwood Haynes built the world's first gas automobile here in his garage on Main Street in 1893–94. In addition to creating the "first horseless carriage," Haynes is also known

for inventing stainless steel and an alloy used in the space program, today called "stellite." At this museum located in his old house you can take a look at his life and contributions to science and industry. In 1910 Haynes donated his Pioneer auto to the Smithsonian Institution in Washington, DC, where it is on permanent display. Haynes died on April 13, 1925.

Hilton Hotel

300 Block of Conrad Hilton Avenue
Cisco, Texas

Conrad Hilton was born on December 25, 1887, in the tiny town of San Antonio, New Mexico. He grew up working in the family hotel, and after a few years in New Mexico, he enlisted in the Army as America entered World War I. Upon returning to New Mexico, he held hopes of opening a bank. He had no luck in New Mexico so he headed to Cisco, Texas. He was on the verge of buying a bank here, but, when the bank owner raised the promised sale price, Hilton gave up the effort. Frustrated, he went looking for a place to sleep for the night and found that there were no rooms available. He saw that the owner of the Mobley Hotel, Henry L. Mobley, was renting all available beds for eight-hour shifts. So, Hilton gave up the banking idea and instead bought the Mobley in 1919.

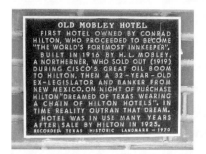

As Conrad's experience and successes grew, he decided to expand his hotel concept to other Texas cities. He purchased other hotels in Texas, forming the Hilton Hotels Corporation in 1946. In the 1950s the company began to diversify into other travel-related services, including car rentals and credit cards.

In 1924 he sold the Mobley to his mother, Mary Hilton, where it stayed in the family until 1931. Over the years, this first Hilton has had many functions. It has been a boarding house, nursing home, and a private residence. It then remained vacant for many years and was becoming rundown when the Hilton Foundation put up $1.2 million dollars for its restoration. Today, the hotel is used for the Cisco Chamber of Commerce, museum, park, and community center. The Mobley has also earned its place in the National Register of Historic Buildings.

Holiday Inn

4941 Summer Avenue
Memphis, Tennessee

The world's first Holiday Inn opened here in August of 1952. It was the brainchild of Memphis entrepreneur Kemmons Wilson, who thought the world needed a better place to stay. At one time this place featured 120 rooms with innovations like a bathroom, phone and air conditioning in each room. It would later become a Royal Oaks Motel. Then, in 1995, it was torn down to make way for the funeral home that's there now.

Ice Hockey

Long Pond
Windsor, Nova Scotia

It is believed that this is the birthplace of Canadian hockey. According to scholars, in the early 1800s, King's College School Boys began adapting the Irish field game of Hurley to the ice here on Long Pond. The Long Pond can still be seen on Howard Dill's property just off the campus of what is now King's-Edgehill School.

Keaton, Buster

Off Highway 54 and Xylan Road
Piqua, Kansas

A plaque in a field where there was once a house reads: "Joseph F. 'Buster' Keaton was born in Piqua, Kansas on October 4, 1895. Buster's parents, Joseph and Myra Keaton, were appearing in a traveling medicine show with stock company on a bill, which included the later famous magician Harry Houdini.

"According to the story Joseph later told interviewers, a cyclone struck Piqua and blew away the circus performance tent. When he returned to his boarding house after chasing around the countryside looking for a tent, he found his wife had given birth to their first child. Buster Keaton made his first stage appearance when he was just 24 hours old in the Catholic Hall, which was serving as a substitute theater for the evening's performance. When he was five years old, his family began touring vaudeville as 'The Three Keatons'. . . ." Next to the field is a small but excellent museum dedicated to the comic genius's life. Piqua is located in the southeast corner of Kansas, about 100 miles southwest of Topeka.

Kermit the Frog

Leland Chamber of Commerce
Located on the bank of Deer Creek, one and ½ miles west of the intersection
of Highway 82 and Highway 61.
Leland, Mississippi
888-307-6364

The small town of Leland (12 miles west of Greenville) is where Muppet-creator Jim Henson spent much of his childhood. It is here where Henson met his boyhood friend Kermit Scott, who is believed to have later inspired him to create Kermit the Frog. Today, Leland pays tribute to Hensen (and Kermit) through an exhibit located within their Chamber of Commerce. The exhibit was given by The Jim Henson Company as "a gift to the people of Leland." It features a tableau honoring Kermit the Frog's birth on Deer Creek, photographs from the Henson family album, a video center with many of Jim Henson's early works and a gift shop. A separate room is filled with Muppet memorabilia.

Kindergarten

919 Charles Street
Watertown, Wisconsin

Margarethe Meyer Schurz started the first kindergarten in the U. S. here in Watertown in 1856. Margarethe, who was born in Germany, had studied to be a teacher. She married Carl Schurz, and together they moved to the United Kingdom. While there, Margarethe taught school with her sister.

When she and Carl came to the U. S., they lived here in Watertown and Margarethe taught her daughter and other children of relatives and neighbors. The children learned through

arts and crafts, music and play. Historically, this was the first time that young children got together and learned rules by having fun, which constituted the first modern kindergarten. This system was adopted quickly throughout the U. S. and remains a staple of American education today. The original school-house is open for tours.

The Marx Brothers

179 East 93rd Street
New York City, New York

The Marx Brothers, of course, were sibling come-
dians of vaudeville, stage plays, and film. The
brothers were Groucho (Julius Henry Marx,
1890-1977), Chico (Leonard Marx, 1887-1961),
Harpo (Adolph Arthur Marx, 1888-1964), Zeppo
(Herbert Marx, 1901-1979) and Gummo (Milton
Marx, 1892-1977). This apartment in upper
Manhattan was where the brothers were born
and spent the early years of their life before
becoming international stars. Their film careers
included such classic comedies as *Duck Soup,
Horse Feathers* and *A Night at the Opera.* After
the movie work stopped in the 1940s, Groucho
enjoyed a solo career as a film actor, television
game show emcee, and superb raconteur both in
concerts and on talk shows.

Motel

2223 Monterey Street
San Luis Obispo, California

The plaque on the building reads, "Motel Inn. This is the site of the
world's original and first motel. Construction started in 1925 at a
cost of $80,000. The word "motel" was first thought of here by
architect Arthur Heinemen. Dedicated October 22, 1988 by Native
Sons of Golden West, Frank Company, Grand President and San
Luis Obispo Parlor No. 290." Though a large part of the original
structure was recently razed, part of the building still remains.

In 1925, Los Angeles architect Arthur Heineman built the first
motel in San Luis Obispo (which is abut halfway between San
Francisco and L.os Angeles). Heinemen came up with the term
"motel" by combining the words "motor" and "hotel." When he
opened, $1.25 a night got guests a cute, two-room bungalow with
a kitchen and a private adjoining garage. All the units faced a central courtyard, which housed the swimming pool and included picnic tables for social gatherings.

Naval Aviation

Ocean View Boulevard
Norfolk, Virginia

A plaque here reads: "On Nov. 14, 1910, man proved that planes could fly from ships when a Curtiss bi-plane piloted by E. B. Ely took off from the deck of the cruiser U.S.S. Birmingham at anchor off Old Point Comfort, flew two miles to Willoughby Spit and landed on the beach near here."

Plutonium

Gilman Hall
University of California at Berkeley
Berkeley, California

On the night of February 23, 1941, G.T. Seaborg, A.C. Wahl and J. W. Kennedy discovered plutonium in the third floor lab here (room 307) at Gilman Hall. Plutonium was used in several of the first atomic bombs, and is still used in bomb making. It has also been used as a compact energy source on space missions such as the Apollo lunar missions. Today, a plaque in the hall commemorates the discovery.

Room 307, Gilman Hall, was declared a National Historic Landmark in 1966 on the 25th anniversary of the discovery of plutonium. All of Gilman Hall was designated a National Historic Chemical Landmark in 1997, followed by its listing in the National Register of Historic Places in 2003. Gilman Hall has been used continuously by the College of Chemistry for 80 years. It is now occupied by the Department of Chemical Engineering.

Public School

Tremont and School Streets
Boston, Massachusetts

The first public school in America was established by Puritan settlers in 1635 in the home of Schoolmaster Philemon Pormont and was later moved to School Street. Here along the Freedom Trail, a portrait statue of Benjamin Franklin overlooks the site of the oldest public school in America which Franklin, Samuel Adams, and John Hancock once attended. It later became Boston Latin School, which is still in operation in the Fenway section of Boston. A tile design inlaid in the sidewalk marks the exact location of the school.

Religion

Christian Scientists

Located in front of the former Christian Science home on the south side of Pleasant Street (Route 9) west of downtown Concord, New Hampshire.
Concord, New Hampshire

While living at her "Pleasant View" home (1892 to 1908) once located on this site, Mary Baker Eddy founded the First Church of Christian Scientist in Boston, the headquarters of the Christian Science movement. From "Pleasant View" she guided its worldwide activities and gained fame as a religious leader and writer.

The buildings erected on this site in 1927 served as a home for retired Christian Science practitioners and nurses until 1975. The former Christian Science home, known as Pleasant View Home, was listed on the National Register in 1984. Mary Baker Eddy is buried at Mt. Auburn Cemetery in Cambridge, Massachusetts.

Religion

Gideon Bible

Boscobel Hotel
1005 Wisconsin Avenue
Boscobel, Wisconsin
608-375-4714

The Boscobel Hotel is best known today for being the site of a meeting that resulted in the founding of the Gideons International Society. In September, 1898, John H. Nicholson, a traveling sales- man from Janesville, Wiscon- sin, attempted to check into the Central House, but as no single rooms were available, the hotel manager asked him to share a room with another salesman, Samuel E. Hill of Beloit, Wisconsin. During their stay at the hotel, the two men discussed the need for an organization of commercial travelers that would provide "mutual help and recognition for Christian travelers."

In 1899, the two men met again and were joined by another salesman, W.J. Knights of Janesville, Wisconsin. In July of that year the organization known as the Christian Commercial Travelor's Association was formed. Its object was the fellowship of "Christian traveling men of the world."

Although the first organizational meeting took place in Janesville, the Gideons have always identified the Boscobel Hotel as the location of its founding. From its modest beginnings in Boscobel and Janesville, the Gideons have grown into an international organization whose name is familiar even to those who are unfamiliar with the organi- zation itself. The Gideon Bible, distributed by the organization, is now familiar to every American traveler.

A plaque in room 19 commemorates where the history took place, but that's not all room 19 may be famous for. During the winter of 1960, Senators Hubert Humphrey and John F. Kennedy were battling for the Democratic presidential nomination. Wisconsin was an early primary state; thus, J.F.K and his wife Jackie stayed here on March 25th, and leg- end persists that it may have been that exact night that J.F.K. Jr. was conceived, in the very room where the Gideon Bible was conceived. (John-John was born November 25th of that year.)

Religion

The Methodist Church

Barratt's Chapel
6362 Bay Road
Frederica, Delaware
302-335-5544

This chapel is where the Methodist Church of America was organized in 1784, when American preachers met here in rural Delaware to organize it. They elected Francis Asbury as their first bishop and began to develop their own life, a life free of the Church of England.

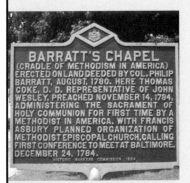

The chapel now serves as a museum that focuses on Methodism on the Delmarva Peninsula. It has books, records, letters, and memorabilia on display. There is an 11-acre cemetery with graves dating from 1785 to the present, including Barratt family graves. The chapel exterior is much as it was in 1784, except for a gable window added on the west end and the conversion of two large first floor windows into doors. On the inside there have been several changes. A metal star on the floor marks the historic meeting of Thomas Coke and Francis Asbury on November 14, 1784.

Seventh Day Adventist Church

Washington, New Hampshire
Directions: On the east side of NH 31, just south of Old Stoddard Road. Take second left, opposite the Common, 2.3 miles on Millen Pond Road to the site of this building.

In April 1842, a group of citizens in this town banded together to form "the first Christian Society." In the Adventist movement of 1842-43, they espoused the Advent hope. In January 1842, these Washington Sabbath-keepers, after meeting for many years as a loosely knit group, organized the first Seventh Day Adventist Church on this site.

The Republican Party

The Little White Schoolhouse
303 Blackburn Street
Ripon, Wisconsin
920-748-6764

The Republican Party was born in the early 1850s by anti-slavery activists and individuals who believed that government should grant western lands to settlers free of charge. The first informal meeting of the party took place here in Ripon, a small town northwest of Milwaukee. The first mass meeting in the country that definitely and positively cut loose from old parties and advocated a new party under the name "Republican" was held in this schoolhouse, March 20, 1854. Alvan Earle Bovay, a local lawyer, led 54 of the area's 100 eligible voters in forming this new political organization to "protect the voters against the Nebraska swindle" which threatened to extend slavery. (Ripon is also known as "Cookietown U.S.A.," the home of the world's largest baked cookie.)

Restaurants

A&W

13 Pine Street
Lodi, California

A&W Restaurants, which claims to be the first U.S. franchise restaurant chain, was founded here in the northern California town of Lodi. On a sweltering day in June of 1919, an entrepreneur named Roy Allen was passing through town on the day a homecoming parade was taking place to honor World War I veterans. Seizing the opportunity, he mixed up a batch of ice-cold creamy root beer and sold it from a beverage cart to the thirsty locals. Soon, on this spot, he opened his very first root beer stand and the rest is history. After the huge success of this first root beer stand, Roy Allen opened a second stand in the nearby city of Sacramento. In 1922, Allen partnered up with Frank Wright, a worker from the first stand in Lodi. Combining the "A" and "W" initials, the men officially formed what we know today as A&W Restaurants.

Restaurants

Bob's Big Boy

4211 West Riverside Drive
Burbank, California
818-843-9334

The oldest surviving Bob's Big Boy is located in Southern California. It was designed by Wayne McAllister and built in 1949 (the original Bob's was in Glendale). Today, this structure has been declared a national landmark.

Burger King

3090 Northwest 36th Street
Miami, Florida

In 1954, David Edgerton opened the first Burger King hamburger stand here. Burgers and shakes were 18 cents each. The Whopper, which appears in 1957, sold for 37 cents.

Dunkin' Donuts

534 Southern Artery
Quincy, Massachusetts
617-472-9502

Dunkin' Donuts started in 1946 when a man named William Rosenberg founded Industrial Luncheon Services, a company that delivered meals and coffee break snacks to customers on the outskirts of Boston, Massachusetts. The success of Industrial Luncheon Services led Rosenberg to open his first coffee and donut shop, the "Open Kettle." In 1950, the Open Kettle became the first Dunkin' Donuts. Today, with over 6,000 Dunkin' Donut Shops worldwide, the company is the largest chain of coffee, donut, and bagel shops. You'll still find a Dunkin' Donuts on this site.

IHOP

4301 Riverside Drive
Toluca Lake, California

The first International House of Pancakes restaurant opened at this site in 1958 by a man named Al Lapin. The restaurant, whose menu was originally based on pancakes, quickly grew in popularity. By 1962, there were 50 IHOP locations. Lapin was the one who actually chose the familiar blue roof and A-frame architectural style. Over the years, a number of items have been added to the menu, and today IHOP has a full lunch and dinner menu. (The structure here, though no longer an IHOP, is the original building, so you'll be able to notice the famous, iconic A-frame structure.)

Restaurants

Jack in the Box

6720 El Cajon Boulevard
San Diego, California

In 1951, a businessman named Robert O. Peterson opened the first Jack in the Box restaurant in San Diego on the main east-west thoroughfare leading into city. Equipped with an intercom system and drive-thru window, the tiny restaurant served up hamburgers to passing motorists for just 18 cents, while a large jack-in-the-box clown kept watch from the roof.

Kentucky Fried Chicken

3900 South State Street
Salt Lake City, Utah

This was the site of the world's first Kentucky Fried Chicken restaurant. Known as the original Harman's Kentucky Fried Chicken, it was here in 1952 where Colonel Harland Sanders made the business deal with local Pete Harman that launched the famous fast food. Sanders was visiting from his home in Louisville, Kentucky, fried chicken recipe in hand. Harman ran a hamburger place called the Do Drop Inn. He decided to take a chance on the 65-year-old, down-on-his-luck Sanders. So, on August 4, 1952, the first bucket of chicken was served. (Chicken dinners then cost $3.50 and included 14 pieces of chicken, mashed potatoes, rolls and gravy. The same meal would cost about $25 today.) Today, KFC, as it is popularly known, is a fast food phenomenon with 12,000 restaurants in 80 countries. As of this writing, a KFC museum is being built on this site.

McDonald's

400 North Lee Street
Des Plaines, Illinois
847-297-5022

The McDonald's #1 Store Museum is a re-creation of the first McDonald's restaurant opened on this site, April 15, 1955, by McDonald's Corporation founder Ray Kroc. The original red-and-white-tiled restaurant building featuring the Golden Arches underwent several remodels through the years and was finally torn down in 1984. The present facility was built according to the original blueprints with some modifications to accommodate Museum visitors and staff. The "Speedee" road sign is original and the customer service and food preparation areas contain original equipment. There are also displays featuring historical photos, early advertising, memorabilia, and a short video presentation. (While this is the first Kroc-opened McDonald's, the very first McDonald's was in San Bernardino, as outlined in *James Dean Died Here*.)

Restaurants

Pizza Hut

1845 North Fairmount, Wichita State University
Wichita, Kansas

When the pizza craze started sweeping the nation in the late 1950s, two young college students attending the University of Wichita wanted to capitalize on the trend. Brothers Frank and Don Carney opened the first Pizza Hut restaurant on June 15, 1958. The pair had had been approached by the owner of this small building (then located at the corner of Kellogg and Bluff Streets). She wanted a respectable neighborhood business there and she had read a November 1957 Saturday Evening Post article about the pizza craze. The brothers jumped into action.

Interestingly, the building's structure influenced the name of what would become the famous worldwide pizza chain. The building had a sign that would only accommodate nine characters. The brothers wanted to use "Pizza" in the name, which left room for just three extra letters. A family member of theirs suggested that the building looked like a hut–and so Pizza Hut was born. In the 1980s, the first Pizza Hut building was moved to the Wichita State University campus. It is still used as a meeting place (not to mention a reminder of how far a good idea can go).

Restaurants

Subway

Jewett Street
Bridgeport, Connecticut

Subway Restaurants was founded in the summer of 1965 in Bridgeport, Connecticut. It was the brainchild of 17-year-old Fred DeLuca and his family friend Dr. Peter Buck, with its purpose being to earn money for Fred's college tuition. With a one thousand dollar loan from Dr. Buck, Fred opened up the sub shop, then called "Pete's Super Submarines."

In the early days, Fred would personally purchase and deliver all of the produce used by the restaurants from the famous Hunts Point Market in the Bronx. He would remove the passenger and rear seat of his 1965 VW Beetle (his first brand new car) and load it up with crates of fresh vegetables and drive back to Connecticut. When the business started to expand with more locations, he traded in the Beetle for a VW van.

Today, there are more than 20,000 locations in 71 countries, making it the second largest fast food franchise in the world. (Note—in 1968 the fifth sandwich shop was opened, and marked the first time the name Subway was used. The oldest continuously operating location is at 1 River Street in Milford, Connecticut.)

Taco Bell

7112 Firestone Boulevard
Downey, California

In 1962, Glen Bell opened the first Taco Bell restaurant here in Downey, California (in 1964 the first Taco Bell franchise was sold). Interestingly, the "Bell" in the name "Taco Bell" is the last name of the founder. Glen Bell would go on to expand Taco Bell worldwide, then sell it for $130 million.The actual building still stands, but it's now occupied by a local taco stand, Seafood & Tacos Raul.

Restaurants

Wendy's

257 East Broad Street
Columbus, Ohio
614-464-4656

On November 15, 1969, the late, great Dave Thomas opened the very first Wendy's restaurant (named for his daughter) and it still stands today. The building was at one time a car dealership. Today, in addition to being a restaurant, it also serves as a living history museum for the popular chain. Its interior features comforting touches like carpeted floors, Tiffany-style lamps and plenty of foliage. The signature square burgers are made-to-order, and chicken sandwiches are available grilled or fried. Thick fries, meaty chili and stuffed baked potatoes round out a menu that includes a cool, ultra-thick chocolate Frosty.

Wienerschnitzel

900 West Pacific Coast Highway
Wilmington, California
310-513-8744

In 1961, fast food entrepreneur John Galardi was thinking about how to stand out in the fast food business, which was still in its infancy. Then, the 23-year old had a brainstorm: Hot dogs! Soon after, the first Der Wienerschnitzel opened here in Wilmington, California. In 1962, a second restaurant was built that featured Der Wienerschnitzel's signature red A-frame roof. The breakthrough design pioneered the drive-thru concept in Southern

California. Since then, the company has changed its name to simply "Wienerschnitzel" (it also has over 300 stores in 10 states and Guam). A plaque on the restaurant at this location details its history. Today, Wienerschnitzel is the world's largest hot dog chain, selling more than 75 million hot dogs per year.

Retail

J.C. Penney

722 J.C. Penney Drive
Kemmerer, Wyoming

J.C. Penney (1875–1970) got started in retail when he bought a butcher shop in Longmont, Colorado. In 1898, he went to work for Thomas M. Callahan and William Guy Johnson of Fort Collins, Colorado, who ran a small chain of stores known as "Golden Rule Stores." Penney was assigned to the company's store in Evanston. He was such a huge success that the owners offered him a shot to become a partner in a new Golden Rule store to be opened in Kemmerer. In the early part of 1902, 27-year-old Penney arrived by train here to start the new business. The spread-out mining town had approximately

1,000 residents, a company store that operated on credit and 21 saloons where a good deal of spare cash was spent. The store opened on April 14, 1902, and the first day's receipts totaled an impressive $466.59. The store was open seven days a week, opening on Sundays at 9:00 A.M.

Two breakthrough retail ideas—cash only and do unto others as you would have them do unto you—were the basis for James Cash Penney's new business venture. He named the store the Golden Rule and by 1912, there were 34 Golden Rule stores with sales exceeding $2 million. In 1913, the chain incorporated under the laws of the state of Utah as the J.C. Penney Company, Inc., and the Golden Rule Store name was phased out. By 1928, the J.C. Penney Company had 1,023 stores across the country.

J.C. Penney Museum

312 North Davis Street
Hamilton, Missouri
816-583-2168

The J.C. Penney birthplace and museum contains items belonging to J.C. Penney and explains his contributions to American retailing. The home was moved to its original farm site and renovated to its 1875–1900 appearance. It's open year round; admission is free to the public.

Retail

Target

1515 West County Road B
Roseville, Minnesota
651-631-0330

On May 1, 1962, the first Target store opened (as part of The Dayton Company) in Roseville, Minnesota, a suburb of St. Paul. They were the first retail store to offer well-known national brands at discounted prices. Today, more than 1,107 Target stores operate in 47 states, including Target Greatland stores, and Super Target stores.

Wal-Mart

105 North Main Street
Bentonville, Arkansas
501-273-1329

This free museum is on the site of Sam Walton's original 5 & 10 cent store in Bentonville, Arkansas (Bentonville is now Wal-Mart world headquarters). The Wal-Mart visitors center traces the origin and growth of Wal-Mart. The center was created as an educational and informative facility for those interested in this American retailing success story.

Ruth, Babe

216 Emory Street
Baltimore, Maryland
410-727-1539

George Herman "Babe" Ruth, Jr., was here born February 6, 1895. From humble waterfront beginnings he would become the most famous athlete of all time, baseball's greatest star. His power and charisma would forever change the game. The birthplace features hundreds of artifacts and treasures from Ruth's days at St. Mary's Industrial School for Boys, including his hymnal and bat, the scorebook from his first professional game and items from his father's saloons. Rare photos show George as a toddler with his parents and young George with his St. Mary's team.

Spark Plugs

541 Tremont Street
Boston, Massachusetts

Albert Champion invented the spark plug here in his auto supply store in Boston's South End in 1907. Champion, who was born in France, came to America in 1889 to compete in a series of races. He brought with him bicycles, tricycles, motorcycles and other wheeled contraptions to work on as he developed his interest in mechanics. In 1907, his tinkering paid off as he came up with the sparkplug—the device inserted in the head of an internal-combustion engine cylinder that ignites the fuel mixture by means of an electric spark.

Albert Champion then turned his hobby into the Champion Ignition Company. However, the investors in the Champion Ignition Company eventually left Albert high and dry and took the Champion name with them. But that didn't stop Albert from making spark plugs. He united with the Buick Motor Co. to continue manufacturing spark plugs. To this very day, his mark is on every spark plug manufactured by AC Delco's spark plug division. After all, AC stands for "Albert Champion." There is now an art gallery on the site.

Strauss, Levi

1866-1416 Battery Street
San Francisco, California

Twenty-four-year-old Levi Strauss came to San Francisco from New York in 1853 to open a west coast branch of his brothers' dry goods business. Levi, a German immigrant, had spent several years in New York learning the dry goods trade. In San Francisco, one of Levi's customers was Jacob Davis, a Reno-based tailor who often purchased bolts of cloth from the wholesale house of Levi Strauss & Co. Jacob had a customer who regularly ripped the pockets of the pants that Jacob made for him. He tried to think of a way to strengthen the difficult customer's pants, but to no avail.

One day, he had an idea: put metal rivets at the points of strain, such as on the pocket corners and at the base of the button fly, to strengthen the pants. The unique "riveted pants" were at once a smash not just with that one man, but many other customers as well. Jacob, fearful that the idea could get stolen if not protected, wanted to apply for a patent on the process. However, he lacked the $68 that was required to file the papers. In need of a business partner, he pitched the idea to Levi Strauss. Strauss loved the idea and thought it viable.

So, on May 20, 1873, the two men received patent #139,121 from the U.S. Patent and Trademark Office. That day is considered the official "birthday" of blue jeans. This address is the site of the original Levi Strauss store where the pants were first sold. Levi Strauss & Company, after seven years of declining sales, closed their last U.S. sewing plant on January 8, 2004.

Striking Clock

Benjamin Banneker Historical Park
300 Oella Avenue
Catonsville, Maryland
410-887-1081

This is the homestead of Benjamin Banneker, the first renowned African-American man of mathematics and science. Banneker first achieved national acclaim for his scientific work in the 1791 survey of the Federal Territory (now Washington, D.C.). At age 22, in the mid-1750s, Banneker created the first all-American-made wood clock of this colonial

region right on this site. Banneker is also well known for his six almanacs published between 1792 and 1797. He has also been noted for his exchange of letters with Thomas Jefferson on the equality of men and the "injustice of the State of Slavery."

At this park and museum you'll see archaeological artifacts of Bannekers' era (including pieces of lens, lead pencils, and instruments most likely used by Benjamin Banneker himself); artifacts formerly held by the Ellicott family—best friends of Banneker (including his work table, candle molds, candlesticks); and books and other publications donated to the Museum (especially on African-American history).

Superman

10622 Kimberly Avenue
Cleveland, Ohio

In 1934, Glenville High School students Jerry Siegel and Joe Shuster created the famous "Superman" character here at Siegel's house. The building is now listed on the National Register of Historic Places. After they came up with the idea for Superman, they tried to sell their inspiration to the newspaper syndicates but were repeatedly rejected for four long years. They finally had it developed before they graduated.

In the meantime, they had begun producing work for the fledgling Detective Comics, Inc., predecessor to today's DC Comics, with their most prominent creation being Slam Bradley. Finally, in early 1938, Siegel and Shuster sold the rights to Superman to DC for a reported $130, as well as a contract to supply the publisher with material. The first story, cobbled together by re-pasting the newspaper strip samples, appeared in Action Comics #1.

Supermarkets

Piggly Wiggly
79 Jefferson Street
Memphis, Tennessee

The very first self-service market opened September 6, 1916, operating under the name Piggly Wiggly. It was an unusual but instantly popular concept: shopping baskets, open shelves, no clerks to shop for the customer—these were all unheard of at the time. While Piggly Wiggly was the first self-service market, the first supermarket was the King Kullen Grocery Company in New York. It opened in 1930 in a garage at 171-06 Jamaica Avenue in Jamaica, Queens.

While working as a general sales manager for Mutual Grocery and Kroger Stores in Illinois, Michael J. Cullen pitched the idea of a supermarket to the company's president in writing. He included his innovative ideas such as separate departments, merchandise on shelves and discount pricing. But, they ignored him. He moved east and opened America's first supermarket on August 4, 1930. (His young son misspelled the family name in a cute fashion and the store name was born.) Within six years, King Kullen was a chain with 17 stores throughout Queens and Nassau County, with $6 million in annual sales. Today, King Kullen has approximately 50 stores throughout Long Island and Staten Island—and it is still a family-run business.

Television

Farnsworth's Green Street Lab
202 Green Street
San Francisco, California

A plaque here reads: "Farnsworth's Green Street Lab—In a simple laboratory on this site, 202 Green Street, Philo Taylor Farnsworth, U.S. pioneer in electronics, invented and

patented the first operational all-electronic 'television system' on September 7, 1927.

The 21-year-old inventor and several dedicated assistants successfully transmitted the first all-electronic television image, the major breakthrough that brought the practical form of this invention to mankind. Further patents formulated here covered the basic concepts essential to modern television. The Genius of Green Street, as he was known, died in 1971."

The Typewriter

North 4th and West State Streets
Milwaukee, Wisconsin

A plaque here reads: "At 318 State Street, approximately 300 feet northeast of here, C. Latham Sholes perfected the first practical typewriter in September, 1869. Here he worked during the summer with Carlos Glidden, Samuel W. Soule, and Matthias Schwalbach in the machine shop of C.F. Kleinsteuber. During the next six years, money for further development of the typewriter was advanced by James Densmore, who later gained the controlling interest and sold it to E. Remington and Sons of Ilion, N.Y."

Volleyball

Corner of High and Appleton Streets
Holyoke, Massachusetts

Volleyball was invented here in Holyoke, Massachusetts in 1895 by William G. Morgan, an instructor at the Young Men's Christian Association (YMCA). Morgan had carried out his undergraduate studies at the Springfield College of the YMCA which is where he met James Naismith, who, in 1891, had invented basketball. After graduating, Morgan spent his first year at the Auburn (Maine) YMCA. Subsequently, during the summer of 1896, he moved to the YMCA at Holyoke (Massachusetts), where he became Director of Physical Education.

Morgan decided to blend elements of basketball, baseball, tennis, and handball to create a game for his classes of businessmen, a game which would demand less physical contact than basketball. In doing so, he created the game of Volleyball (at that time called

"Mintonette"). As for the net, Morgan borrowed that idea from tennis, and raised it 6 feet 6 inches above the floor, just above the average man's head. The original YMCA where the game was created burned down in the 1940s. Today, a marker commemorates the game's creation (a Dollar Store sits on the actual site). As well, the interesting Volleyball Hall of Fame is located in Holyoke at 444 Dwight Street, 413-536-0926.

Wayne, John

216 South Second Street
Winterset, Iowa
515-462-1044

Marion Robert Morrison, a.k.a John Wayne, was born here on May 26, 1907. The son of a pharmacist, he grew up to become one of Hollywood's most popular movie stars.

Visitors to his restored birthplace will see an impressive collection of John Wayne memorabilia such as the eye patch worn in the movie *True Grit*, a hat worn in *Rio Lobo,* and a prop suitcase used in the film *Stagecoach.*

Hundreds of rare photographs of the Duke are on display as well as letters from Lucille Ball, Gene Autry, Maureen O'Hara, Jimmy Stewart, Kirk Douglas, Bob Hope, Ronald Reagan and George Burns. Many celebrities and dignitaries have visited the childhood home of John Wayne since its opening. On November 3, 1984, President Ronald Reagan commented that the birthplace of John Wayne is an inspiring tribute to a good friend and a great American.

Webster, Daniel

Franklin, New Hampshire
603-934-5057
Directions: From Tilton, take exit 20 of Interstate 93, follow Route 3 south (west) through Franklin to Route 127. Take 127 south and follow the signs to the Daniel Webster Birthplace.

The Daniel Webster Birthplace is associated with the birth and early childhood years of Daniel Webster, one of our country's most respect-

ed orators and statesmen. While the site affords a view of the early years of Daniel Webster, it also provides a glimpse of 1700's farm life in the infant years of the U.S. Webster served as a U.S. Congressman from New Hampshire and Massachusetts; and Secretary of State under Presidents Harrison, Tyler and Fillmore. In all, Webster spent 40 years in public service, helping to mold the loose collection of states into a single unified nation. One theme in particular stands out from his many impassioned speeches: "The Union, one and inseparable, now and forever."

Whitman, Walt

246 Old Walt Whitman Road
Huntington Station, New York
516-427-5240

Built in approximately 1819 by Walt Whitman Sr., this weathered farmhouse and the surrounding West Hills served as inspiration for Walt Whitman, one of America's greatest
poets. Though he left the birthplace at an early age, Whitman returned here often. There
are maps available for auto-hiking tours of Whitman-related sites in historic and beautiful West Hills (including the highest point on Long Island—Jayne's Hills). Tours of the
home are also available.

X-treme Sports

Fort Adams State Park
Newport, Rhode Island

Staged by ESPN, the 1995 X-Games, held at Fort Adams State Park in Newport, Rhode
Island was created to be the largest gathering of extreme athletes ever and the biggest
production event in the history of ESPN. One hundred and fifteen cameras were used
including helmet cams, dirt-jump cams, point-of-view cameras mounted on top of the
climbing wall and halfpipe. There were even cameras mounted on the wheels of skate-
boards and street-luge sleds. This is thought to be the most pivotal moment in the
launching of X-treme Sports as a national phenomenon.

History and Tragedy

Air Mail

Bellefonte Air Mail Field
830 East Bishop Street
Bellefonte, Pennsylvania
Take PA 550 to Bellefonte Area High School.

A marker here details the fact that the initial stop on the first scheduled westbound air mail flight was made here by Pilot Leon D. Smith on December 18, 1918. The site for the field was chosen by pioneer aviator Max Miller and was in regular use for airmail until 1925. Although carrier pigeons had long been used to send messages (an activity known as pigeon mail), the first mail to be carried by an air vehicle was on January 7, 1785 on a balloon flight from Dover, England to France near Calais. Balloons also carried mail out of Paris and Metz during the Franco-Prussian War (1870), drifting over the heads of the Germans besieging those cities.

Aviation

College Park Aviation Museum
1985 Corporal Frank Scott Drive
College Park, Maryland
301-864-6029

Founded in 1909 for the Wright Brothers' instruction of the first military aviators, College Park Airport is home to many other "firsts" in aviation, and is particularly significant for the well-known aviators and aviation inventors who played a part in this field's long history. In 1909, Wilbur Wright taught Lieutenants Frederic Humphreys, Frank Lahm, and Benjamin Foulois to fly here. Humphreys became the first military pilot to fly solo in a government airplane. Some other "firsts" that took place here:

• 1909: First woman passenger to fly in the U. S.
On October 27, Mrs. Ralph Van Deman (her first name is lost to history), wife of Captain Ralph Van Deman, became the first woman in the United States to go aloft in an airplane when she flew at College Park as the passenger of Wilbur Wright. Mrs. Van Deman was a close friend of Katherine Wright (sister to Wilbur and Orville).

• 1909: First officer to fly a military airplane
Lt. Frederic Humphreys was the first military pilot to fly solo in a military airplane. He received his flight instruction from Wilbur Wright at College Park, alongside Lieutenant Frank Lahm and Lieutenant Benjamin Foulo.

• 1909: First U.S. Naval officer to fly in a heavier-than-air machine
During a nine-minute flight on November 3, Lieutenant George C. Sweet, USN, flew as a passenger of Lieutenant Frank Lahm, U.S.A.

• 1911: First testing of a bomb-aiming device from an aero
Inert bombs were dropped into the goldfish ponds at the end of the airfield using a bombsight developed by Riley E. Scott.

• 1912: First testing of a machine gun from an airplane
On June 7th, a Lewis Machine Gun was fired by Captain Chandler from a Wright B, with Lieutenant Milling as pilot.

• 1918-21: First U.S. Postal Air Mail Service
The regular U.S. Postal Air Mail flights were inaugurated on August 12, 1918, from College Park to Philadelphia to New York.

• 1924: First controlled helicopter flight
Emile and Henry Berliner based their flight experiments at College Park from 1920 to 1924. After their success at College Park, they moved to the Naval Air Station in Anacostia, where they worked with the Navy on continued experiments.

In 1998, a museum opened on this site and visitors can enjoy and experience all of the history that's taken place here. Hellmuth, Obata and Kassabaum, the firm that designed the Smithsonian's National Air and Space Museum, also designed this 27,000 square foot museum. Visitors enter a soaring hall with the Prop Shop gift shop on the left. In the curved entry hall are photomurals and text panels detailing the events leading up to the founding of the College Park Airfield in 1909. Through a scaled-down replica of the 1909 hangar and past an animatronic Wilbur Wright is the main gallery, which features aircrafts and exhibits detailing the history of the College Park Airport.

Byck, Samuel Joseph

Baltimore/Washington International Airport
BWI exit off of I-195
Baltimore, Maryland

Samuel Joseph Byck was an unemployed tire salesman who attempted to hijack a plane from the Baltimore/Washington International Airport on February 22, 1974. His goal was to crash into the White House and kill United States President Richard M. Nixon. Before takeoff, Byck shot and killed one of the pilots on the DC-9 Delta Airlines Flight 523, wounded another, and grabbed a female passenger and ordered her to "fly the plane." He was shot and wounded through the cabin door by police during the attempt and committed suicide; a gasoline bomb was found under his body.

It was later discovered that Byck had sent a tape recording detailing his plan to news columnist Jack Anderson. It was also revealed that Byck had been arrested the previous December for protesting in front of the White House, dressed in a Santa suit. Byck had come to the notice of the Secret Service in 1972, when he had first threatened Nixon, whom he had resented ever since the Small Business Administration had turned him down for a loan. Byck had also sent bizarre tape recordings to various other public figures including Jonas Salk, Abraham Ribicoff, and Leonard Bernstein.

Canada

Charlottetown, Prince Edward Island

More than one hundred years ago, a small group of elected officials gathered here in Charlottetown, Prince Edward Island. They were meeting to discuss the possibility of uniting three Maritime jurisdictions, but representatives also appeared at the conference to raise a broader issue, and sow the seed of a concept to establish a larger union and create a country. This historic event of 1864 led to the founding of Canada. Visiting today, you can relive and learn about the history of the island and the history of Canada, as this is her official birthplace.

Carver, George Washington

Diamond Grove, Missouri
Directions from Westbound Interstate 44: Take exit 18, go south on Alternate U.S. Highway 71 to the town of Diamond. Go west 2 miles on County Road V, then south about 1 mile on County Road 16Q.
Directions from Eastbound Interstate 44: Take exit 8A, go south on Alternate U.S. Highway 71, turn left and go east on County Road V, then south about 1 mile on County Road 16Q.

George Washington Carver (1864–1943) became a famous American agricultural chemist. However, he was born a slave on this farm in Missouri. In 1896, he joined the staff of Tuskegee Institute as director of The Department of Agricultural Research, retaining that post the rest of his life. His efforts to improve the economy of the South (particularly for African-Americans) included the teaching of soil improvement and of diversification of crops. He discovered hundreds of uses for the peanut, the sweet potato, and the soybean and thus stimulated the culture of these crops. He devised many products from cotton waste and extracted blue, purple, and red pigments from local clay.

In 1953, his birthplace here was made a national monument. The park consists of 210 acres of the original 240-acre Moses Carver homestead. The visitor center includes a museum with exhibits that trace George W. Carver's life from his birth through his youth at the Carver farm to his role as an artist, educator and humanitarian, as well as his world

renowned work as a scientist. The ¾-mile walking trail winds its way through the woodland and tall grass prairie. Included at the monument are the Carver bust, birthplace site, boyhood statue, William's Pond, 1881 Moses Carver dwelling and Carver family cemetery.

Douglas, Frederick

Congress Street (at the end of St. Antoine Street)
Detroit, Michigan

On March 12, 1859, two famous Americans met several of Detroit's African-American residents here in the home of William Webb. They were John Brown, the famed antislavery leader, and Frederick Douglas, an ex-slave and internationally recognized antislavery orator and writer. The purpose of the important meeting was to discuss methods of abolishing American Negro slavery.

The men sought a solution through political means and orderly democratic processes. Although they differed on tactics to be used, they were united in the immortal cause of American Negro freedom. Among the prominent members of Detroit's Negro community reported to have been present were: William Lambert, George DeBaptiste, Dr. Joseph Ferguson, Reverend C. Monroe, Willis Wilson, John Jackson, and William Webb.

Edison, Thomas

James Dean Died Here documented the famous Menlo Park lab and spot where Edison first invented the light bulb. Here are some other historic sites related to the great inventor:

Birthplace
9 Edison Drive
Milan, Ohio
419-499-2135

Thomas Alva Edison, inventor of the phonograph, the incandescent light bulb, and many other devices, was born in Milan, Ohio, in 1847. Here at the Edison Birthplace Museum, you'll find a collection of rare treasures including examples of many of Edison's early inventions, documents, and family mementos. After Edison's death, the opening of his birthplace to the public as a memorial and museum became the private project of his wife, Mina Miller Edison, and their daughter, Mrs. John Eyre Sloane. It opened on the centennial of the inventor's birth in 1947. Today, the Edison Birthplace Association, Inc. maintains this National Historic Site.

Edison, Thomas

Central Park

Fourth Street and Park Avenue
Louisville, Kentucky

During the Southern Exposition held here 1883–1887, the public saw an electric light for the very first time, thanks to Thomas Edison, who introduced his incandescent light bulb to huge crowds. The city built an enormous exposition building, thought to be the largest wooden structure in the world at the time: 13 acres under one roof. The building and grounds (Central Park was the midway) were illuminated by over 4,800 incandescent electric lights, the largest concentration anywhere at that time, even more than in New York City. (With Edison's influence, Louisville was one of the earliest electrically lit neighborhoods in the nation.)

Edison House

729-31 East Washington Street
Louisville, Kentucky
502-585-5247

At age 19, in 1866, Thomas Edison came here to Louisville to work as a telegraph key operator. With his adroit skill at receiving telegraph messages, Thomas Edison easily found a job with the Western Union located on Second and West Main Street— about eight blocks from the Edison House. There are many artifacts available for viewing at this home, including both cylinder and disc phonographs, and Edison Business Phonographs. An Edison Kinetoscope, the first home motion picture projector, is also on display in the museum.

Three-Wire Electric Lighting System

2350 McGregor Boulevard
Fort Myers, Florida
239-334-7419

The first successful use of a three-wire electric lighting system was made here on July 4, 1883, in the City Hotel building in Sunbury. Thomas A. Edison directed the work. (The Edison Electric Illuminating Co. plant was nearby at 4th and Vine Streets.) A plaque marks the spot where the hotel used to be.

BIRDS-EYE VIEW OF LOUISVILLE FROM THE RIVER FRONT AND SOUTHERN EXPOSITION 1883

Edison, Thomas

Winter Home

2350 McGregor Boulevard
Fort Myers, Florida
239-334-7419

This was the winter home of Thomas A. Edison, beautifully situated along the Caloosahatchee River. Thomas Edison first visited Florida in 1885, which is when he purchased this property and built his vacation home. Finished in 1886 and dubbed "Seminole Lodge" by the Edisons, the home was a winter retreat and workplace for the prolific inventor until he died in 1931. (Edison's good friend Henry Ford purchased the neighboring property in 1915.)

The furnishings at Seminole Lodge are those of the Edisons, including brass "electroliers," electric chandeliers manufactured in Edison's own workshop. The house is surrounded by a mature tropical garden that was originally planted as an experimental garden but grew to include thousands of varieties of plants from all over the world. The site also includes Edison's Laboratory, the Edison Museum and the first swimming pool built in Florida. On weekdays, visitors are offered narrated river cruises aboard a replica of Edison's 1903 electric motor launch, The Reliance.

Flag Day

Ozaukee Highway I (½ mile east of Waubeka)
Fredonia, Wisconsin

Over three quarters of a century ago, a 19-year-old, $40-a-month schoolteacher, stirred by a deep love of the American Flag, held the first Flag Day exercises in a little country schoolhouse located near Fredonia. Bernard J. Cigrand, who later became a professor of dentistry and a college dean, began a lifelong crusade on June 14, 1885, to honor the adoption of the Stars and Stripes by the Continental Congress on June 14, 1777.

Thirty-one years later, in 1916, his devotion to the Flag was rewarded when June 14th was declared National Flag Day by President Woodrow Wilson, who said, "the Flag has vindicated its right to be honored by all nations of the world and feared by none who do righteousness." In 1949, long after Dr. Cigrand's death, Congress and the President of the United States proclaimed the American Flag would be displayed on all government buildings on June 14th and asked the American people to join in the observance of the Flag's anniversary.

Franklin, Benjamin

Birthplace

17 Milk Street
Boston, Massachusetts

George Washington called Benjamin Franklin the "Father of our country." Thomas Jefferson described him as "a harmonious human multitude." The philosopher Immanuel Kant dubbed him "A

modern Prometheus," after the ancient Titan in the Greek myth who steals fire from the heavens and gives it to mankind. Ben Franklin was born here and lived here until he was 17 years old, when he left his family to find fame and fortune in Philadelphia. A bust of Franklin stands at the site, which is now occupied by an office building.

Christ Church

2nd Street, above Market Street
Philadelphia, Pennsylvania
215-922-1695

In June 1752, Ben Franklin was here to conduct one of his most important experiments involving lightning. While waiting for the steeple on top of this church to be completed (it was to act as the "lightning rod"), he grew impatient and decided that a kite would be able to get close to the storm clouds just as well. Ben needed to figure out what he would use to attract an electrical charge; he decided on a metal key, and attached it to the kite. Then he tied the kite string to an insulating silk ribbon to protect the knuckles of his hand. At the first sign of the key receiving an electrical charge from the air, Franklin knew that lightning was a form of electricity. (Franklin's 21-year-old son William was the only witness to the event.)

Christ Church holds a lot of other American history as well. Founded in 1695, it was the first parish of the Church of England (Anglican) in Pennsylvania. It is also the church where the American Episcopal Church was born. Those who worshiped regularly at Christ Church include George Washington, Benjamin Franklin, Betsy Ross, Robert Morris, Absalom Jones, Benjamin Rush, John Penn (William Penn's grandson), Francis Hopkinson and many others.

Visitors are welcome to tour the church. Tours of the burial ground are also offered; there, you'll find the resting places of Benjamin Franklin and Dr. Benjamin Rush, signer of the Declaration of Independence and "Father of American Psychiatry."

Franklin, Benjamin

Final Residence

Chestnut Street between 3rd and 4th Streets
Philadelphia, Pennsylvania

A plaque here reads: "Printer, author, inventor, diplomat, philanthropist, statesman, and scientist. The eighteenth century's most illustrious Pennsylvanian built a house in Franklin Court starting in 1763, and here he lived the last five years of his life."

Franklin died on April 17, 1790 at the age of 84. Twenty-thousand mourners attended his funeral at Philadelphia's Christ Church Burial Ground.

Old South Meeting House

308 Washington Street
Boston, Massachusetts

Best remembered as the site of the tax protests that led to the Boston Tea Party in 1773, the Old South Meeting House has been the site of religious, political and social debate for over 300 years. This brick meeting house was built in 1729 to replace the Cedar Meeting House, which its dissident Puritan congregation had outgrown.

African-American poet Phillis Wheatley worshipped here, and Benjamin Franklin was baptized here. In 1876, the venerable structure was nearly demolished, but Bostonians rallied to rescue the Old South Meeting House. It was the first instance of successful historic preservation in New England. From the meeting of more than 5,000 colonists on December 16, 1773 (which started the Boston Tea Party) to today, the Old South Meeting House has been the site of historic debates effecting the fate of the community, the state of Massachusetts, and of course, the nation.

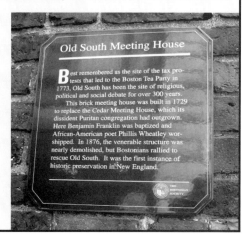

Gonzalez, Elian

2319 Northwest 2nd Street
Miami, Florida

Elian Gonzalez was the little boy who was rescued by a fisherman on Thanksgiving Day, 1999, after his mother tried to cross the Florida Straights with him in an inner tube (she drowned). He was brought to Miami where he was taken in by his Cuban relatives. His father came over from Cuba to reclaim him.

After a lengthy legal battle, there was a controversial raid on this house in the neighborhood called "Little Havana." During the raid, Elian was taken at gunpoint from his family. He eventually returned to Cuba with his father.

Grant, Ulysses S.

3 East 66th Street
New York City, New York

It is generally thought that among Presidential memoirs, which are typically banal and self-serving, there is one that actually has earned a place among other great historical books—the "Personal Memoirs of Ulysses S. Grant." After recently losing his personal fortune to a Wall Street scam artist, Grant wrote this book out of desperation and out of his passionate desire to tell his story of the great Civil War. Sadly, he was suffering the ill effects of what would soon be diagnosed as throat cancer. Plain and simple, he needed money for his family.

In this challenging situation he wrote what has been described as one of the most gripping accounts of the Civil War ever told. Gore Vidal, who wrote a critically acclaimed novel about Abraham Lincoln, said of Grant's memoir, "It is simply not possible to read Grant's *Memoirs* without realizing that the author is a man of first-rate intelligence."

Mark Twain, who became a close friend of President Grant, described it as comparable to

Caesar's *Commentaries*. "I was able to say in all sincerity that the same high merits distinguished both books," Twain said, "clarity of statement, directness, simplicity, manifest truthfulness, fairness and justice toward friend and foe alike and avoidance of flowery speech. General Grant was just a man, just a human being, just an author . . . The fact remains and cannot be dislodged that General Grant's book is a great, unique and unapproachable literary masterpiece."

The book earned Grant's estate close to $450,000 in royalties. It was written during the period Grant lived in this house (1881 to 1885—the year he died). The house has since been torn down and an apartment building now sits on the site.

Hale, Nathan

1131 Third Avenue
New York City, New York

A plaque on the side of this Banana Republic store commemorates the spot where revolutionary war-hero Nathan Hale was hanged by the British. (It is believed that Hale was hanged from a tree near what is now the intersection of Third Avenue and East 66th Street in Manhattan—defined in colonial times as the five-mile stone on the Post Road, where there was a tavern called The Dove.)

Before his hanging, Hale was allowed to give a speech from the gallows, part of which, according to tradition, included the words "I only regret that I have but one life to lose for my country." No official records of any sort having been kept of Hale's speech, it is impossible to verify that he actually delivered this memorable line; however, rumor of it subsequently spread throughout the colonies, making a martyr of Hale and boosting morale for the revolutionaries.

Just after Hale's death, rumors about his demise must have circulated through the American camp, but no American letters or other documents written about Hale in New York at the time survive. The only contemporary accounts are very terse and were written by British soldiers.

Hanging (Last Public in America)

One Executive Boulevard
Owensboro, Kentucky

The last public hanging in America was held here in 1936, when a 22-year-old black man named Rainey Bethea was hanged for the murder of a 70-year-old white woman. Bethea was charged with raping and murdering Lischia Edwards in her upstairs apartment at 322 East Fifth Street on June 7, 1936. He was arrested three days later on the riverbank at First and Davies Streets. The public outrage that followed the hanging resulted in the complete abolition of public executions in the United States. Today, the International Rooms of the Executive Inn Rivermont are located on the exact site where the gallows stood.

Heart Mountain Relocation Center

U.S. Highway 14
Cody, Wyoming
307-754-2689

On February 19, 1942, President Roosevelt signed Executive Order No. 9066, granting the Secretary of War the authority to establish military areas from which any or all persons might be excluded. This order translated into the evacuation of more than one hundred thousand Japanese and Japanese Americans from the West Coast of the United

States. Japanese-Americans who were unable to leave the Pacific Coast on their own were ordered to relocation camps administered by the War Relocation Authority.

One of these 10 camps, Heart Mountain Relocation Center, was located between Powell and Cody, Wyoming. At its peak, Heart Mountain interned more than ten thousand Japanese-Americans and was the third largest community in Wyoming. Area residents initiated the Heart Mountain Memorial Park after World War II. The park includes plaques, a sidewalk and a graveled parking area. There is also a concrete slab (moved from Block 25) and three standing hospital buildings.

Henry, Patrick

St. John's Church
2401 East Broad Street
Richmond, Virginia
804-649-7938

This is one of the most historic sites in America, for it was right here that the Virginia Convention of 1775 met

to discuss the question of taking arms against the British. Delegates to the Convention included Thomas Jefferson and George Washington.

It was here that Patrick Henry delivered the famous words "Give me liberty or give me death!" as he took his stand on independence from the British. (Buried in the churchyard are Henry Clay, George Whythe, and Elizabeth Arnold Poe, mother of Edgar Allen Poe.)

Kennedy, Ted

Lawrence Cottage
Chappaquiddick, Massachusetts

Mary Jo Kopechne was the woman killed in the automobile that Senator Ted Kennedy drove off the Dyke Bridge in Chappaquiddick in 1969. That night, she had attended a party here at the Lawrence Cottage with several others including Susan Tannenbaum, Maryellen Lyons, Ann Lyons, Rosemary Keough, Esther Newburgh, Joe Gargan, Paul Markham, Charles Tretter, Raymond La Rosa, John Crimmins, and Ted Kennedy. Kopechne left the party with Kennedy around midnight. Moments later, their car plunged off the nearby Dyke Bridge, killing the young woman. Kennedy, who was never able to offer a clear, consistent version of the night's events, saw his political future forever compromised.

Kinko's

4133 South Danville Drive
Abilene, Texas
325-698-3300

This is the Kinko's from which the mysterious (and evidently forged) documents regarding President Bush's service in the National Guard were faxed to CBS in New York several weeks before the 2004 Presidential election. The network, anchor Dan Rather and producer Mary Mapes all came under extensive fire for the shoddy reporting. In January of 2005, an independent team found CBS guilty of gross negligence both in their reporting and the subsequent denials once their story was challenged. Four executives were fired as a result of the story, though anchorman Dan Rather managed to keep his job (he had already announced he was stepping down as the anchor, effective March 2005).

Kinte, Kunta

One Dock Street
City Dock
Annapolis, Maryland
410-263-7973

City Dock is the site of the historic Annapolis waterfront park. It includes many shops and restaurants in the area. At the head of the City Dock is a brass plaque, which memorializes the 1767 arrival of Kunta Kinte, the inspirational slave brought from Africa aboard a slave ship. When his descendant, Alex Haley, published the landmark book Roots, Kinte's name became a rallying symbol for African-Americans seeking to understand their pasts. Haley has now been honored with a life-size statue symbolizing the value of pride in one's heritage.

Labor

Avondale Mine Disaster Historical Marker

Plymouth Township (east side of U.S. Route 11)
Avondale, Pennsylvania

At 10:00 A.M., September 6, 1869, one of the worst disasters in the history of anthracite mining in the United States occurred at the Avondale Mine. A fire originating from a furnace at the bottom of a 237-foot-deep shaft roared up the shaft killing 110 miners, 80 percent of whom were Welsh. On September 9, 1869, the last body was removed from the mine. The disaster also killed two boys, ages 10 and 14, who began working just that day. A plaque marks the location of the mine.

Battle of the Overpass

Miller Road overpass (at the Ford River Rouge Plant)
Dearborn, Michigan

A marker here remembers the place where Ford "Servicemen" beat Walter Reuther and other union leaders on the overpass bridge in 1937. Photos of the incident destroyed the Ford Co.'s credibility, forcing it to recognize the union in 1941.

CIO Founding

Boardwalk
Atlantic City, New Jersey

At the President Hotel, UMWA President John L. Lewis punched Carpenters Union President Bill Hutcheson in the face, stormed out, and formed the Congress of Industrial Organizations in 1938. A marker in the boardwalk identifies the exact spot where the incident occurred.

Ford Hunger March

Ford Rouge Plant
10520 Fort Street
Dearborn, Michigan

Three thousand unemployed autoworkers braved the cold on March 7, 1932, to demand jobs and relief from Henry Ford. The marchers got too close to the gate and were gassed. After regrouping, they were sprayed with water and shot at. Four men died immediately.

Labor

Henry, John

Top of Big Bend Mountain
Talcott, West Virginia

A statue here commemorates the 1870 site where John Henry beat a machine in a steel-driving contest and became the most sung about hero in American folklore. It has been said that the contest cost him his life and his ghost lives in the Big Bend tunnel (located near the statue). As legend has it, John Henry died after competing with a steam-powered drill in an attempt to prove that he could work faster than a machine. Visitors may view the twin Chesapeake and Ohio railroad tunnels, 6,500 feet long, where Henry is said to have worked in 1873.

Italian Hall

Italian Hall Memorial Park
7th and Elm Streets
Calumet, Michigan

On December 24, 1913, area copper miners had been on strike for five months. The miners were fighting for better pay, shortened workdays, safer working conditions and union recognition. That day, during a yuletide party for the striking miners and their families, someone yelled, "Fire!" Although there was no fire, 73 people died while attempting to escape down a stairwell that had doors that opened inward. Over half of those who died were children between the ages of six and 10. The perpetrator of the tragedy was never identified. (The strike ended in April 1914.)

The Italian Hall was built in 1908 as headquarters for Calumet's benevolent society. The society, organized along ethnic lines, encouraged and financially aided immigrants and provided relief to victims of hardship. Following the 1913 Christmas Eve tragedy, the hall continued to be used for nearly five decades. The two-story, red brick building was razed in 1984. Through the efforts of the Friends of the Italian Hall and Local 324 of the AFL-CIO, the site of the building became a memorial park dedicated to the people who lost their lives in 1903.

Labor

Ludlow Massacre Monument

Junction of Del Aqua and Colorado and Southern Railroad tracks
Ludlow, Colorado

A monument here marks the site where striking miners and their families were killed in their tent colony on April 20, 1914. On that day, 20 innocent men, women and children were killed in the Ludlow Massacre. The coal miners in Colorado and other western states had been trying to join the UMWA for many years. They were bitterly opposed by the coal operators, led by the Colorado Fuel and Iron Company. Upon striking, the miners and their families had been evicted from their company-owned houses and had set up a tent colony on public property.

The massacre occurred in a carefully planned attack on the tent colony by Colorado militiamen, coal company guards, and thugs hired as private detectives and strikebreakers. Later investigations revealed that kerosene had intentionally been poured on the tents to set them ablaze. The miners had dug foxholes in the tents so that the women and children could avoid the bullets that were randomly shot through the tent colony by company thugs. The women and children were found huddled together at the bottoms of their tents.

"Rosie the Riveter" Memorial

Corner of Regatta and Marina Bay Parkway
Marina Bay Park
Richmond, California

A sculpture here marks the accomplishments and remembers the hardships of the "Rosies," the women who worked in the Kaiser Shipyards during WWII. Shipyard No. 2 produced 747 warships. This is the first national memorial to honor and interpret American women's contributions to the WWII home front. (The memorial is in a public park and is open every day during daylight hours.) The park is in development and has a small visitor center in the City of Richmond's City Hall South where a Driving Tour Booklet can be obtained.

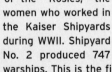

Lincoln, Abraham

Bellevue Place

333 South Jefferson Street
Batavia, Illinois

On May 19, 1875, the jury announced its verdict after 10 minutes of deliberation: "We, the undersigned jurors in the case of Mary Todd Lincoln, having heard the evidence in the case, are satisfied that said Mary Todd Lincoln is insane, and is a fit person to be sent to a state hospital for the insane. . . ." Ten years after Abraham Lincoln's assassination, a Chicago court declared his 56-year-old widow Mary insane and committed her to a mental institution.

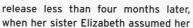

On May 20, 1875, she arrived here at Bellevue Place, a private, upscale sanitarium in the Fox River Valley. (Her focused efforts led to her release less than four months later, when her sister Elizabeth assumed her care in Springfield.) Bellevue Place still stands and has been converted to rental units and is not open to the public. Mary's quarters were on the second floor at the front; a reproduction of Mary's bedroom is in Batavia's Depot Museum, located at 155 Houston Street in Batavia, Illinois (Phone: 630-406-5274).

Lincoln Depot

10th and Monroe Streets
Springfield, Illinois
217-544-8695

This restored railroad depot, located a few blocks from Lincoln's home, was where he started his inaugural journey to Washington, D.C. Three months after his election, in November, 1860, Abraham Lincoln left Springfield for Washington, D.C. to become the 16th President of the United States. The special train that would take him there left the Great Western Depot on the rainy morning of Monday, February 11, 1861, the last day Lincoln spent in Springfield.

His son Robert stood at his side while he paid a special tribute to his friends and neighbors in a famous impromptu speech known as his "Farewell Address." Lincoln did not return to Springfield alive. Today, visitors can relive what it was like back then in the old brick depot that's just two blocks from the Lincoln home.

Lincoln, Abraham

Lincoln Family Pew

The First Presbyterian Church
321 South 7th Street
Springfield, Illinois
217-528-4311

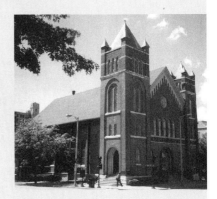

This church houses the original Lincoln family pew. The Lincolns purchased and used the pew for 10 years when the congregation worshipped in a previous building (no longer standing) at Third and Washington Streets. In that building, the pew was No. 20 on the left side, fifth row from the front. The Lincoln family began attending the church in 1850, after the death of three-year-old Edward Lincoln.

Lincoln Home

413 South 8th Street
Springfield, Illinois
217-492-4241

This is the only house that Abraham Lincoln ever owned. He and Mary Todd lived here for 17 years (they were married here in 1842). On February 11, 1861, Lincoln bid farewell to the citizens of Springfield, to his friends and neighbors of 24 years, and the special home where he had resided for 17 years: "My friends—No one, not in my situation, can appreciate my feeling of sadness at this parting. To this place, and the kindness of these people, I

owe everything." He was on his way to serve as President of a nation on the verge of Civil War. Today, the Lincoln home (which is the centerpiece of the Lincoln Home National Historic Site) is restored to its 1860's appearance, revealing Lincoln as husband, father, politician, and President-elect. There is a visitor center, and free Ranger guided tours of the home (tickets first come-first served).

London Museum

609 Main Street (Texas Highway 42)
New London, Texas
903-895-4602

On March 18, 1937, just 18 minutes before classes were to be dismissed for the day, a massive explosion destroyed the New London Junior-Senior High School, instantly killing over 300 students and teachers. (Because of this catastrophe, legislation was immediately created to put an odor in all gas to avoid another such tragedy.) The museum is located across the road from the rebuilt London School, exactly where the accident happened, on State Highway 42. As well, a 32-foot cenotaph that contains the names of the victims is located in the center of Highway 42.

Long, Huey

State Capitol Building
North 3rd Street on State Capitol Drive
Baton Rouge, Louisiana

Dr. Carl Austin Weiss shot and killed Governor Huey Long here in the State Capitol building on Sunday, September 8, 1935. He had come to the Capitol building for a special meeting of the state legislature. Long is thought to have been greeted by Dr. Weiss, a physician practicing in Baton Rouge, while walking down the main corridor.

Then, as reported by witnesses, Weiss shot Long at close range in the abdomen. Long cried out and then stumbled down the corridor. Weiss was immediately shot and killed by Long's bodyguards. The number of shots fired is not known. All told, 30 bullet wounds were found in front of Weiss's body: 29 in the back, and 2 in the head. But, it was impossible to tell how many bullet wounds were caused by the same bullet entering and exiting. Long died two days later from wounds sustained in the shooting. He is buried on the grounds, and his statue faces the Capitol.

As to why Weiss shot Long, the supposed story is as follows: Weiss had married Yvonne Pavy, the daughter of Judge Benjamin Pavy—one of the leading opponents of Huey P. Long. Unable to unseat Pavy in St. Landry Parish, Huey Long decided to gain revenge by having two of the judge's daughters dismissed from their teaching jobs. Long also warned Pavy that if he continued to oppose him he would say that his family had "coffee blood" (this was based on the story that Pavy's father-in-law had a black mistress). On September 8, 1935, Weiss was told that rumors were circulating that his wife was the daughter of a black man. Weiss was so furious over the news he supposedly decided to kill Long.

McCarthy, Joseph

Colonnade Room
McClure Hotel
1200 Market Street
Wheeling, West Virginia
304-232-0300

On February 9, 1950, the Republican senator from Wisconsin, Joseph R. McCarthy, addressed 275 members of the local Republican's women's club here at the McClure Hotel in Wheeling, West Virginia. That date was the famous night McCarthy declared he had a list of 57 people in the State Department who were known to be members of the American Communist Party.

"While I cannot take the time to name all the men in the State Department who have been named as members of the Communist Party and members of a spy ring, I have here in my hand a list of 205—a list of names that were known to the secretary of state and who, nevertheless, are still working and shaping policy of the State Department," McCarthy said in his speech, presenting a scrap of paper. In fact, the list of names was not a secret and had been previously published by the Secretary of State in 1946. These people had been identified during a preliminary screening of 3,000 federal employees.

For the next two years, Joseph McCarthy investigated various government departments and questioned many people about their political past. Some people lost their jobs after they admitted they had been members of the Communist Party. McCarthy made it clear to the witnesses that the only way of showing that they had abandoned their left-wing views was by naming other members of the party. This witch-hunt and anti-communist hysteria became known as McCarthyism. Today, the McClure still stands, but it has become the Ramada Plaza City Center Hotel.

Memorial Day

Waterloo, New York

HISTORIC NEW YORK

MEMORIAL DAY

On May 5, 1866, the residents of Waterloo held the first complete, community-wide observance of Memorial Day. They dedicated the entire day to honoring the Civil War dead in a solemn and patriotic manner. Throughout the village, flags, draped in mourning, flew at half mast. Ladies prepared wreaths and bouquets for each veteran's grave. Businesses closed, and veterans, civic organizations and townspeople marched to the strains of martial music to the village cemeteries. There, with reverent prayers and patriotic ceremonies, the tradition of Memorial Day was born.

Henry C. Welles, a prominent citizen, first proposed the idea for a day completely devoted to honoring the Civil War dead. General John B. Murray, the Seneca County Clerk, who had commanded the 148th New York Infantry Regiment in the war, quickly advanced the thought and marshalled community support. Since that year, Waterloo has annually observed Memorial Day. New York, in 1873, became the first state to proclaim Memorial Day, or Decoration Day, as it was originally called, a public holiday.

In May, 1966, a joint resolution by the United States Congress and a proclamation by President Lyndon B. Johnson officially recognized Waterloo as the birthplace of Memorial Day.

THE STATE EDUCATION DEPARTMENT

In the summer of 1865, a local druggist in Waterloo named Henry C. Welles had the idea to remember the patriotic dead by placing flowers on their graves. Nothing resulted from this suggestion until he advanced the idea again the following spring to General John B. Murray. Murray, a civil war hero, jumped on the idea and began recruiting the help of others in the community.

On May 5, 1866, Waterloo was decorated with flags at half-mast, draped with evergreens and mourning black. Veterans, civic societies and residents, led by General Murray, marched dramatically to the three village cemeteries. One year later, on May 5, 1867, the ceremonies were repeated. In 1868, Waterloo joined with other communities in holding their observance on May 30th, in accordance with General Logan's orders. It has been held annually ever since.

One hundred years later, Waterloo held the first formal, annual observance of a day dedicated to honoring the war dead. On March 7, 1966, the State of New York recognized Waterloo by a proclamation signed by Governor Nelson A. Rockefeller. This was followed by recognition from the Congress of the United States. The House of Representatives and the Senate unanimously passed House Concurrent Resolution 587 on May 17th and May 19th, 1966 respectively. This reads in part as follows: "Resolved that the Congress of the United States, in recognition of the patriotic tradition set in motion one hundred years ago in the Village of Waterloo, NY, does hereby officially recognize Waterloo, New York as the birthplace of Memorial Day. . . ."

Then, on May 26, 1966, President Lyndon B. Johnson signed a presidential proclamation recognizing Waterloo as the birthplace of Memorial Day. It should be noted that at least 24 communities around the country lay claim to being the birthplace of Memorial Day. Waterloo remains the "official" birthplace because that community's first observance one hundred years earlier in 1866 was considered so well planned and complete. Other communities that had the foresight and good moral sense to conduct similar remembrances are Boalsburg, Pennsylvania; Mobile, Alabama; Montgomery, Alabama; Camden, Arkansas; Atlanta, Georgia; Milledgeville, Georgia; New Orleans, Louisiana; Columbus, Mississippi; Jackson, Mississippi; Vicksburg, Mississippi; Raleigh, North Carolina; Cincinnati, Ohio; Charleston, South Carolina; Fredericksburg, Virginia; Portsmouth, Virginia; Warrenton, Virginia; and Washington, D.C.

Molasses Disaster

Commercial Street between Copps Hill and the playground of North End Park
Boston, Massachusetts

The Boston Molasses Disaster occurred in the North End neighborhood of Boston at the Purity Distilling Company facility on January 15, 1919. At the time, molasses was the U.S.'s primary sweetener, used to make all types of confectionery, and also rum. A 50-foot tall molasses tank containing as much as 2.5 million gallons of molasses exploded. The explosion was of sufficient force to cut the girders of the nearby, elevated railroad and lift a train off the rails. Some close buildings were also collapsed by the blast. The molasses flowed out in a wave between eight-and-15-feet high, moving at 35 miles per hour and exerting a force of 2 tons per foot.

Twenty-one people were killed and 150 were injured as the hot molasses crushed, asphyxiated, and cooked many of the victims to death. It took over six months to remove the molasses from the cobblestone streets, theaters, businesses, automobiles, and homes. The harbor ran brown until summer. Purity Distilling paid out one million dollars in damages (equivalent to around one hundred million dollars today) in one of the first class-action lawsuits held in Massachusetts. The cause of the accident has never been proven.

Money

Crane & Company Museum
Main Street
Dalton, Massachusetts
413-684-2600

The paper for all United States currency has been made in this factory since 1842. The patented method that Crane & Company uses still involves embedding silk threads into banknote paper, a method created to thwart counterfeiters. At this fine museum visitors will experience the entire process of making money and view things such as samples of paper used for currency and the invoice for paper sold to Paul Revere to print America's first money in 1775.

Mother Jones

Mother Jones Prison

Jones, Mary Harris "Mother"
Prison Site on West Virginia 61
Pratt, West Virginia

Mary Harris "Mother" Jones was held here as a prisoner during the West Virginia Mine Wars. A prominent labor leader and organizer, Mother Jones was arrested after arriving to speak to Governor William E. Glasscock on February 12, 1913. She was held under the charges of stealing a machine gun, trying to blow up a train, and conspiracy to commit murder. Mother Jones was sentenced to 20 years in jail, but was released after just 85 days, shortly after sending this message to John W. Kern through her underground railway:

"From out of the military prison wall of Pratt, West Virginia, where I have walked over my eighty-fourth milestone in history, I send you the groans and tears and heartaches of men, women, and children as I have heard them in this state. From out these prison walls, I plead with you for the honor of the nation, to push that investigation, and the children yet unborn will rise and call you blessed."

The Mother Jones Prison, the boarding house where Jones was held, was designated as a National Historic Landmark on April 27, 1992. The owners demolished the building between April 1 and May 10, 1996. The Landmark designation of the Mother Jones Prison was withdrawn on September 22, 1997, and it was removed from the National Register of Historic Places.

Burgess Farm

Powder Mill and Riggs Roads
Adelphi, Maryland

This marks the place of Mother Jones's death at the Burgess Farm on November 30, 1930. Jones spent the last two years of her life being cared for by Lillie May Burgess. (She had celebrated her 100th birthday at the farm on May 1, 1930.)

After her death, the farm was converted into the Mother Jones Rest Home and then became the property of the Hillandale Baptist church.

MOTHER JONES
"GRAND OLD
CHAMPION OF LABOR"
MARY HARRIS "MOTHER" JONES,
THE LEGENDARY LABOR ORGANIZER,
SPENT A LIFETIME FIGHTING FOR UNIONS
AND THE RIGHTS OF WORKERS.
SHE DIED AT THE BURGESS FARM NEAR
HERE ON NOVEMBER 30, 1930,
AGED 100 YEARS.
MARYLAND HISTORICAL TRUST
MARYLAND STATE HIGHWAY ADMINISTRATION

Mother Jones

Miners' Monument

Union Miners' Cemetery
North edge of Mt. Olive on North Lake Street (this cemetery is split by North Lake Street); the eastern side is adjacent to Cavalry Cemetery. The western side is adjacent to Immanuel Lutheran Cemetery.
Mount Olive, Illinois

A granite spire marks the grave of Mother Jones (1830–1930), the fiery champion of organized labor. She's buried next to her boys (four miners killed in a skirmish between striking workers and mine guards at the Virden Min in 1898) in the 1930's only union-owned cemetery.

Mother Jones is honored today by the political magazine that bears her name. She lived in an era when women couldn't allowed to vote. "You don't need a vote to raise hell," she commented about that. "You need convictions and a voice." She perhaps is most famous for her saying, "Pray for the dead, and fight like hell for the living."

Mothers Against Drunk Driving (MADD)

Mothers Against Drunk Driving (MADD)
Sunset Avenue at New York Avenue
Fair Oaks, California

On May 3, 1980, 13-year-old Cari Lightner was walking home with a friend when she was hit and killed by a repeat-offender drunk driver. (He had just been released on bail two days earlier from another drunk-driving accident.) This was the inspiration for the group Mothers Against Drunk Driving, or MADD, which has become one of America's most popular non-profit organizations. The group included the girl's mother, Candace Lightner. Since MADD's inception, more than 2,300 anti-drunk driving laws have been passed.

Patton, General George S.

Located off I-10, about 30 miles east of Indio at Chiriaco Summit.
Chiriaco Summit, California
760-227-3483

The George S. Patton Memorial Museum was established to honor the late General George S. Patton and the thousands of men who served with him both at the Desert Training Center and overseas. The museum was actually the entrance to Camp Young, command post for the Desert Training Center during World War II.

Major General George S. Patton, Jr., established the D.T.C. in response to a need to train American combat troops for battle in North Africa during World War II. The camp, which began operation in 1942, covered 18,000 square miles. It was the largest military training ground ever to exist. Over one million men were trained at the 11 sub-camps (seven in California). Today, exhibits display memorabilia from the life and career of General Patton. The exhibit halls include the many and varied aspects of military life with particular focus on the Desert Training Center and soldiers of World War II.

President's House in Philadelphia

Market Street (near Sixth Street)
Philadelphia, Pennsylvania

It no longer exists, but this was the site of the original "White House." It stood just north of the entrance to the new Liberty Bell Center, which partially covers the site of some of the house's back buildings and stands just in front of the site of the slave quarters Washington ordered to be built.

It served as the Executive Mansion of the United States from 1790 to 1800 during Philadelphia's tenure as the nation's capital. It was George Washington's "White House" for over six years, John Adams's "White House" for almost four years, and British Army headquarters from 1777-78. In addition, Benedict Arnold began his betrayal here.

The site of the President's House lies directly across Market Street from the entrance to the Independence Visitor Center. The foundation of the front wall of the main house lies underneath the sidewalk, about 20 feet south of the Market Street roadway. A public bathroom was built on the site and stood squarely atop the footprint of the main house until its removal on May 27, 2003.

As of this writing, work is being done here to construct a new site for the Liberty Bell.

Roosevelt, Theodore

28 East 20th Street
New York City, New York

Theodore Roosevelt, the 26th President of the United States, was born here in 1858 on the site where this Greek Revival house (a replica of the original) now stands. He lived here until 1872 when his family relocated to Europe. The original house was demolished in 1916, but was then rebuilt to its original specifications in 1923. The five-story brick building includes a parlor, library, nursery, dining room and master bedroom featuring satin with rosewood trim decor. Now a public museum, it is full of period furniture and Roosevelt memorabilia.

Roosevelt, Theodore

Inaugural Site
641 Delaware Avenue
Buffalo, New York
716-884-0095

While vacationing in the Adirondack Mountains of New York, Vice President Theodore Roosevelt learned the news that President William McKinley was not expected to survive bullet wounds incurred days earlier during an assassination attempt in Buffalo, New York. When Roosevelt completed the grueling 15-hour journey to Buffalo, President McKinley had indeed died. Deeply saddened over McKinley's tragic death, Roosevelt arrived at the home of his friend Ansley Wilcox. Here, in the library of this stately Greek Revival house, Roosevelt took the oath and became the 26th President of the United States.

Interestingly, in his haste to make it to Buffalo, Roosevelt had not packed any formal clothes. Consequently, he was forced to borrow a long frock coat, trousers, waistcoat, four-in-hand tie, and patent leather shoes. It was a tragic day, but a profound one as well:

Roosevelt's 1901 inauguration marked a turning point in the role of the presidency, launching a dramatic change in national policy and propelling the United States into the realm of world affairs. This turning point was the birth of the modern presidency. The house where the inauguration took place has been restored and is open to the public as the Theodore Roosevelt Inaugural National Historic Site.

San Diego Presidio

Presidio Park in Old Town (next to parking lot across Presidio Drive
from the Serra Museum)
San Diego, California

The first of the famous California missions was established here. A marker details: "Soldiers, sailors, Indians, and Franciscan missionaries from New Spain occupied the land at Presidio Hill on May 17, 1769 as a military outpost. Two months later Fr. Junipero Serra established the first San Diego Mission on Presidio Hill.

Officially proclaimed a Spanish presidio on January 1, 1774, the fortress was later occupied by a succession of Mexican forces. The presidio was abandoned in 1837 after San Diego became a pueblo." This spot is also the site of the first white settlement on the West Coast of the United States. The historic Serra Museum sits right next to the site, which is located in beautiful old town State Historic Park.

Silkwood, Karen

State Highway 74 (about seven miles south of Crescent, Oklahoma)

Karen Silkwood died on November 13, 1974 in a fatal one-car crash after what's been reported as falling asleep at the wheel. Since then, her story has achieved worldwide fame (even being made into the major motion film, 1983's *Silkwood*) and generated a ton of controversy. Silkwood was a chemical technician at the Kerr–McGee's plutonium fuels production plant in Crescent, Oklahoma (she was also a member of the Oil, Chemical, and Atomic Workers' Union and a staunch activist who was critical of plant safety).

The week before her death, Silkwood was supposedly gathering evidence for the Union to support her claim that Kerr–McGee was negligent in maintaining plant safety (along with being involved in a number of odd, unexplained exposures to plutonium). November 13, 1974, Karen Silkwood was driving her 1973 white Honda Civic south on Route 74 towards Oklahoma City. At about 8:05 P.M., the Oklahoma State Highway Patrol was notified of a single car accident seven miles south of Crescent. Dents in the back of her car raised suspicions, causing some to wonder whether she'd been run off the road or not (to date, nothing's been proven, and tests did show an elevated amount of sleep inducing-drugs in her system).

"Sit-In"

132 South Elm Street
Greensboro, South Carolina

On February 1, 1960, four black college students sat down at a "whites only" lunch counter here at what was then a Woolworth store on South Elm Street. They refused to leave when asked. Within a week, the "sit-in" (as it was called) spread across the south. Today, a historical marker commemorating the sit-in that occurred in the Woolworth Building can be found outside, along with bronzed footprints of the lunch counter protest leaders.

Soviet Transpolar Landing Site

Near the intersection of Cottonwood and Sanderson Streets, west of San Jacinto.
Riverside, California

Three miles west of this site, on July 14, 1937, three Soviet aviators completed a transpolar flight from Moscow in 62 hours and 17 minutes, establishing a new world nonstop distance record of 6,305 miles. The huge, single-engine aircraft, an Ant-25 Military Reconnaissance Monoplane, was shipped back to the Soviet Union and placed in a museum. Aircraft commander Mikhail Gromov, co-pilot Andrei Yumashev and navigator Sergei Danilin became generals in World War II.

BELIAKOFF
Navigator   CHEKALOFF
                   Pilot   BAIDUKOFF
                                  Co-Pilot

Taft, William Howard

Riverside Mission Inn
3649 Mission Inn Avenue
Riverside, California
909-784-0300

The Mission Inn, one of American's grand hotels, has been a gorgeous Riverside landmark since the completion of its first wing in 1903. Many artifacts are currently housed in the Mission Inn Museum including lacquered Asian temple guardians, life-size papal court figures, Spanish and Mexican terra cotta, and hundreds of bells. The Mission Inn

has hosted many presidents over the years, including President Theodore Roosevelt, President William Howard Taft, President Ronald Reagan, and others. Both Bette Davis and Richard Nixon got married here.

Of these famous visits, President William Howard Taft's stay at the Mission Inn on October 12, 1909, may be the most memorable. Following an early-morning tour of Southern California, the President participated in a local ceremony to honor Father Junipero Serra, founder of the California Missions. After the ceremony, Taft returned to the Mission Inn where he was escorted to the Presidential Suite (now the Presidential Lounge) to prepare for a banquet in his honor in the hotel's dining room.

State and local dignitaries were in attendance, along with nearly one hundred others. Having prepared carefully for the President's visit, the hotel owner commissioned his craftsmen to build a special chair to accommodate Taft's 300-pound frame. Following a whirlwind day of events, President Taft bid adieu to his guests and left Riverside on the 9:30 P.M. train. Following Taft's visit, the handcrafted chair was placed in the hotel lobby where it remains today for all to sit in. (The museum also offers tours.)

After the Presidency, Taft served as Professor of Law at Yale until President Harding made him Chief Justice of the United States, a position he held until just before his death in 1930.

Tammany Hall

100-102 East 17th Street
New York City, New York

This was the site of last headquarters of Tammany Hall, the corrupt political club that dominated New York City politics for decades. The club was named for an Indian chief whose anti-English policies appealed to the largely Irish-American New York politicians. The structure, designed to resemble New York's Federal Hall, was built in 1929. In 1943, the building was sold to the International Ladies Garment Workers Union. The main meeting hall, named Roosevelt Auditorium, became one of the most important centers for union activities in New York City. In 1984, the hall was renovated for use as an off-Broadway theater.

Tesla, Nikola

New Yorker Hotel
481 8th Avenue
New York City, New York
212-971-0101

Nikola Tesla, the brilliant, Serbian-American inventor, electrical engineer, and scientist died here. After his graduation from the University of Prague in 1880, Tesla worked as a telephone engineer in Budapest, Hungary. By 1882, he had devised an AC power system to replace the weak direct-current (DC) generators and motors then in use.

He came to the United States in 1884 and began working for Thomas Edison. However, Edison advocated use of the inferior DC power transmission system, which caused friction between he and Tesla. By 1886, Tesla was out on the street. In 1887, Tesla had enough money from backers to build a laboratory of his own in New York City, so he created one.

In 1888, his discovery that a magnetic field could be made to rotate if two coils at right angles are supplied with AC current (90 ohm) out of phase made possible the invention of the AC induction motor. Tesla would later invent a high-frequency transformer called the Tesla Coil, which made AC power transmission practical. From 1891-1893, Tesla lectured before huge audiences of scientists all over the world. George Westinghouse purchased the patents to Tesla's induction motor and made it the basis of the Westinghouse power system, which still underlies the modern electrical power industry today.

Tesla died alone of heart failure here in this hotel, in room 3327, some time between the evening of January 5th and the morning of January 8, 1943. Despite selling his AC electricity patents, he was essentially destitute and died with significant debts. At the time of his death, Tesla had been working on some form of teleforce weapon, or death ray, the secrets of which he had offered to the United States War Department on the morning of January 5th. The papers are still considered to be top secret.

Immediately after Tesla's death became known, the FBI instructed the Office of Alien Property to take possession of his papers and property, despite his U.S. citizenship. All of his personal effects were seized on the advice of presidential advisors. FBI head J. Edgar Hoover declared the case "most secret," because of the nature of Tesla's inventions and patents.

Titanic

Pier 59
South of Chelsea Piers, past 14th Street
New York City, New York

This rusting pier (the Cunard's pier) was where the Titanic was due to dock back in April 1912, before she sank in the icy Atlantic Ocean. Nearby at Pier 54 was the departure point for the Lusitania's first voyage and also where the Titanic's survivors returned onboard the Carpathia.

Tulsa Race Riot

419 North Elgin Avenue
Tulsa, Oklahoma

In terms of lives lost, the Tulsa Race Riot stands as the most devastating race riot in United States history. On May 31, 1921, Dick Rowland, a black shoe-shiner, was accused of assaulting Sarah Page, a white elevator operator in the Drexel Building (319 South Main Street). Following Rowland's arrest and the publication of a fabricated newspaper story asserting a sexual assault, mobs of blacks and whites gathered near the jail.

The whites intended to lynch Rowland, and the blacks were there to defend him. (An alleged eyewitness account claims that the violence started when a white man was killed while trying to wrest a gun from a black man.) Factor in that this happened in the racially and politically charged atmosphere of northeastern Oklahoma, a hotbed of Ku Klux Klan activity at that time, and you have a lethal situation.

By June 1st, white mobs had invaded the segregated black part of town and destroyed the Greenwood district, known nationally as the "Black Wall Street" (for its economic success). Dozens of businesses, 1,256 homes, many churches and a hospital were destroyed in an area covering 35 blocks. Estimates of the dead range up to 300. After the governor declared martial law, black people were rounded up by the National Guard and put into the baseball stadium. Several black families fled for more peaceful cities; only a percentage returned to rebuild. No one was ever arrested or charged for the mass murder and arson that happened that day. This site, the Mt. Zion Baptist Church, had been dedicated just a few weeks before the riot. This source of deep pride for many local black Tulsans was tragically destroyed during the catastrophe (along with more than half a dozen other black churches.) However, it has since been rebuilt on the exact site—a symbol of re-growth and perseverance that harkens back to a tragic event.

Tuskegee Institute National Historic Site

1212 West Montgomery Road
Tuskegee, Alabama
334-727-3200

In 1881, at the age of 26, Booker T. Washington became the first principle of a newly formed Normal School for Negroes in Tuskegee, Alabama. This began a lifelong quest for excellence that oversaw the growth of Tuskegee Institute. The Historic Campus District still retains the original buildings built by the students of the Institute, with bricks made by students in the Institute brickyard.

In 1896, George Washington Carver joined the faculty and revolutionized agricultural development in the South in the early twentieth century. The legacy of these two men,

and the history of this great institution of higher education has been preserved to tell the story of men and women, former slaves, who struggled to make their place in American society. The site, located on the campus of Tuskegee University, became a part of the National Park System in 1974.

Vikings

L'Anse aux Meadows
Located on the tip of the Great Northern Peninsula, 433 kilometers north of Deer Lake along the Viking Trail (Route 430).
Newfoundland, Canada
709-623-2608

If you are jogging near Mount Auburn Hospital on the Cambridge side of Memorial Drive in Cambridge, Massachusetts, you'll probably see a plaque at your feet: "On This Spot in the Year 1000 Leif Erikson Built His Home in Vinland." However, this marker has proved to be bogus; the Vikings never made it that far. But, they did make it here, to the tip of the Great Northern Peninsula of the island of Newfoundland.

The remains of an 11th-century Viking settlement are evidence of the first European presence in North America. The excavated remains of wood-framed, peat-turf buildings are similar to those found in Norse Greenland and Iceland. L'Anse aux Meadows is the only authenticated Viking site in North America. It was established one thousand years

ago by the explorer Leif Eriksson during his adventures in eastern North America—500 years before Columbus's exploits in the "New World." Helge Ingstad and his wife Anne Stine rediscovered the site in 1960. L'Anse aux Meadows is now a National Historic Park and a UNESCO World Heritage Site, the first cultural site in the world to receive this designation.

Washington, George

Ferry Farm

268 Kings Highway (Route 3, east of Fredericksburg at Ferry Farm Road)
Fredericksburg, Virginia
540-370-0732

Ferry Farm is a place of legend and of rich and diverse history. A boy named George Washington grew to manhood here from 1738-1752 (ages six-19). This was also the setting of the stories of the Cherry tree and the silver dollar (really a stone) thrown across the Rappahannock River. In addition to being George Washington's boyhood home, this site was also an important part of the Union lines during the Battle of Fredericksburg. Ongoing archaeological digs have already revealed evidence of early Native American habitation. The work continues in search of the original farm buildings and houses of Washington's youth.

The visitor's center here, built in the 1960s, was once used as a boy's school. Today, it houses a gallery featuring the Ages and Stages of Washington's boyhood, displays of artifacts found on the site, the archaeology lab, and administrative offices.

Ingersoll's Inn

Tremont Street at Court Street
Boston, Massachusetts

A plaque here denotes: "In 1789, President George Washington stayed at Joseph Ingersoll's inn at this site while visiting Boston. Massachusetts Governor John Hancock's visit to meet Washington here is regarded as an early acceptance of federal sovereignty over that of individual states. Daniel Webster would later have law offices here, and Boston grocer S.S. Pierce started a thriving and long-lived provisions business in 1831."

Washington, George

McComb Mansion

39 Broadway
New York City, New York

On April 23, 1789, President-elect George Washington and Mrs. George Washington moved into the very first Presidential mansion at 3 Cherry Street at the corner of Franklin—just east of the present City Hall in Manhattan. (Today the site is occupied by one of the granite supports of the Brooklyn Bridge.) After finding that house too small, Washington moved here to the McComb Mansion in February, 1790.

The second Presidential mansion was considered one of the finest private buildings in New York. Here, the first lady supervised a household that included 21 servants (seven of the 21 were slaves). In October, 1790, after the national capital was moved to Philadelphia, the President left New York City for the last time. Today, a plaque marks this former site of the McComb Mansion.

It is one of the lesser known but still important Presidential landmarks in the United States, and an important place in the lives of George and Martha Washington.

Washington, George

Fraunces Tavern

54 Pearl Street
New York City, New York
212-425-1778

On December 4, 1783, nine days after the last British soldiers left American soil and thus ended the Revolution, General George Washington invited the officers of the Continental Army to join him in the Long Room here at Fraunces Tavern so he could bid farewell. At 12 o'clock noon the officers arrived

at the tavern and made their way to the Long Room (on the second floor). They met the General there, who first filled his glass with wine and then, turning to the officers, said, "With a heart full of love and gratitude I now take leave of you. I most devoutly wish that your latter days may be as prosperous and happy as your former ones have been glorious and honorable."

They toasted, and then Washington said, "I cannot come to each of you but shall feel obliged if each of you will come and take me by the hand," which each man did. Then, the officers escorted Washington from the tavern to the Whitehall wharf, where he boarded a barge that took him to Paulus Hook, (now Jersey City) New Jersey. Washington continued to Annapolis, where the Continental Congress was meeting, and resigned his commission. Today, Fraunces Tavern remains much as it did back then. There is a fine restaurant on the first floor, and you can also tour the rest of the building (including the Long Room and an excellent museum on the upper floors of the building).

World War I Attack

Nauset Heights Road
Orleans, Massachusetts

On July 21, 1918, this small town became the only American site shelled by an enemy during World War I. After it attacked a tugboat called the *Perth-Amboy* (along with three other barges), the German sub *U-156* fired upon the beach at Orleans. Locals watched as the shells landed harmlessly. Soon, an American seaplane chased the sub back out to sea. Today, a plaque marks the shelling site.

Zapruder, Abraham

Qualex Inc., Kodalux Processing Service
3131 Manor Way
Dallas, Texas

This is where Abraham Zapruder had his film developed of the assassination of John F. Kennedy. Immediately after shooting the historic footage, Zapruder headed to his office and locked the camera in a small safe. A *Dallas Morning News* reporter named Harry McCormack notified Forrest Sorrels, agent-in-charge of the Dallas Secret Service field office, saying that Zapruder might have in fact filmed the assassination. Later, the pair met Zapruder at his office. Zapruder then went with McCormack to the *Dallas Morning News* building where they planned to have the film developed.

However, the paper didn't have the technology needed. So, the film was taken to the paper's television branch, WFAA. There, they were told that the station's lab was set up only for black and white 16mm news film, not color. (WFAA did however take the opportunity to interview Zapruder himself, live, barely 90-minutes after the assassination.) On Zapruder's behalf, WFAA contacted the Eastman Kodak Company here on Manor Way, who offered to process his film right away.

Crime

An American Tragedy

Big Moose Lake–South Bay Area
The Adirondack Mountains
New York

In July 1906, Chester Gillette murdered his ex-girlfriend, Grace Brown, here at Big Moose Lake. The murder trial drew international attention as Brown's love letters to Gillette were read in court. On the morning of March 30, 1908, Gillette was executed by electrocution.

Theodore Dreiser saved newspaper clippings about the case for some 15 years before writing his famous novel, *An American Tragedy.* The 1951 film *A Place in the Sun,* starring Montgomery Clift, Elizabeth Taylor, Shelley Winters, Anne Revere, Keefe Brasselle and Raymond Burr, was based on the novel.

Anastasia, Albert

Park Central Hotel
870 Seventh Avenue
New York City, New York
212-247-8000

Albert Anastasia, also known as the "Mad Hatter" and "Lord High Executioner," was a Mafia boss remembered for running the contract killing syndicate known as Murder, Inc. On the morning of October 25, 1957, Anastasia entered the barbershop of this hotel. Anastasia's bodyguard parked the car in an underground garage and then took a little stroll. Anastasia relaxed in the barber chair, closing his eyes.

Suddenly, two men with scarves covering their faces marched in, shoved the barber out of the way, and shot Anastasia. After their first volley, Anastasia jumped to his feet and lunged at his killers; he was killed after several shots. Like many gang killings, the Anastasia murder remains unsolved.

Black Liberation Army

174 Avenue B (corner)
New York City, New York

On January 27, 1972, the Black Liberation Army assassinated police officers Gregory Foster and Rocco Laurie on this corner. After the vicious killings, a note sent to authorities portrayed the murders as a retaliation for the 1971 Attica prison massacre. Tragically, to date no arrests have been made.

Bonanno, Joe

36 East 37th Street
New York City, New York

In October 1964, mobster Joe Bonanno was kidnapped from in front of this address, then his lawyer's apartment. The event occurred shortly before Bonanno was scheduled to testify before a grand jury—and while Bonanno was apparently contemplating murdering crime boss Carlo Gambino. He re-emerged in a federal courthouse in 1966, saying he had been at his cousin's in upstate New York. Shortly after that, he retired to Arizona.

Capone, Al

Headquarters

4823 Cermak Road
Cicero, Illinois

Early in 1924, legendary gangster Al Capone made his headquarters here in a hotel called the Hawthorne Inn. At this site on the afternoon of September 20, 1926, 11 automobiles filled with Hymie Weiss gangsters, drove slowly past the Inn and poured more than one thousand bullets into the building, from machine-guns, pistols and shotguns. Capone was having lunch in a restaurant next-door, and thus escaped injury.

Later, the Inn was renamed the Towne Hotel, and remained a meeting place of the Chicago Syndicate through the 1960s. On February 17, 1970, a fire which started in the kitchen destroyed the hotel. Other Capone headquarters included the Four Deuces at 2222 South Wabash, the Metropole Hotel at 2300 South Michigan Avenue, and the Lexington Hotel at 2135 South Michigan Avenue, all located in Chicago.

Hideout

12101 West County Road CC
Couderay, Wisconsin
715-945-2746

This lakefront retreat was gangster Al Capone's hideout. Built in the 1920s by Capone for $250,000, the house was vacant until 1959 when it was made into a restaurant and museum. The home has bulletproof walls (18-inch thick fieldstone), a secret bunkhouse for the gang, a blockhouse with jail cells and a guard tower that was manned by armed guards with machine guns.

The 90-acre lake was supposedly used by airplanes to smuggle in liquor during Prohibition, and a dock on the lake let the gang roll barrels of booze into trucks. Today it's called The Hideout, and it's a fun, historical restaurant, bar, and museum that lets you experience a real gangster hideout firsthand.

Pony Inn

5613 West Roosevelt Road
Cicero, Illinois

On April 27, 1926, state attorneys William McSwiggen, Thomas Duffy, Myles O'Donnell and Jim Doherty pulled up in front of the Pony Inn, once located at this site. At the same time, gangster Al Capone's Cadillac approached as McSwiggen and his friends stepped out of their car. Slowly driving by, Capone opened fire with a machine gun, killing Duffy, Doherty and McSwiggen.

Cassidy, Butch

First Bank Robbery

San Miguel National Bank
129-131 West Colorado Avenue
Telluride, Colorado

On June 24, 1889, Butch Cassidy kicked off his notorious life of crime by robbing the San Miguel National Bank, then located here on a portion of Main Street. (The old bank burned and was replaced by the Maher Building in 1892; the Maher still stands today.) Cassidy had been riding with the McCarty gang, known as the Wild Bunch.

After a few days of drinking and playing cards, they robbed the San Miguel National Bank of about $24,000. Cassidy was almost apprehended at what is now Society Drive, but he managed to escape. It was a valiant attempt, but Butch wrenched the man's prized pearl-handled gun from his hand and bolted out of town with the money, never to be seen in town again.

Hole-in-the-Wall

Kaycee, Wyoming
Directions: To access the area, take Interstate 25 south from Kaycee to the TTT Road exit. At TTT Road exit, drive south about 14 miles to Willow Creek Road (County Road 111). Take this road west for about 18 miles to a primitive two-track road that bears north. This is County Road 105. As you travel along County Road 105 there are a number of livestock gates that must be opened and closed.

The Hole-in-the-Wall is approximately 40 miles southwest of Kaycee, Wyoming. It's a colorful and scenic red sandstone escarpment that is rich in legend of outlaw activity in the late 1800s, most notably Butch Cassidy and the Wild Bunch Gang. The "hole" is a gap in the Red Wall that, legend has it, was used secretly by outlaws to move horses and cattle from the area. The area is primitive in nature, with no services.

Cassidy, Butch

Robbers' Roost

Outlaw Trail
San Rafael Swell, Utah
Directions: Travel 3.2 miles north on State Route 158 (Deer Creek Road) from State Route 157 (Kyle Canyon Road). On the right is a parking area and the trailhead is on the left.

This was a popular outlaw hideout for over 30 years. Robbers' Roost is located along the Outlaw Trail, the infamous route in southeastern Utah where many notorious bandits hid out while on the run from the law. Fresh horses were reserved here and there was a large weapons cache. Butch Cassidy considered it an ideal hideout due to the many lookout points on all sides of the canyons.

Butch Cassidy's original corral remains in Robbers' Roost, in addition to a stone chimney, caves, and several carvings. Due to the difficult terrain, a maze of canyons, and extreme heat the Roost was never successfully penetrated by authorities (but it is a popular hiking spot).

The Cheerleader Killing Plot

Grandy's Restaurant
8 Uvadle Avenue
Channelview, Texas

It was one of the most shocking and selfish criminal plots imaginable, a tabloid-ready spectacle that became the talk of the nation. In January, 1991, Wanda Holloway, a house-wife in Channelview, Texas was furious that her daughter, Shanna, failed to make her junior high cheerleading squad for two years in a row. She got it in her head that Shanna's chances were thwarted by another girl, Amber Heath, and so she hatched a plot to have Amber's mother killed (which, in her twisted mind, would mean Amber, who would be in mourning, would be unable to compete for her spot on the squad).

Holloway actually made a payment to a hit man for the contract killing of Verna Heath in the parking lot of this restaurant. Thankfully, the contract was never carried out, and Wanda Holloway was convicted of soliciting capital murder. She was sentenced to 15 years in prison. Today, she is out on probation. Not one but two TV movies were made out of the case—*The Positively True Adventures of the Alleged Texas Cheerleader-Murdering Mom* and *The Cheerleader Murdering Mom.*

Coll, Vincent "Mad Dog"

314 West 23rd Street
New York City, New York

Back in the 1930s, this was the site of a drugstore where on February 8, 1932, Dutch Schultz's gang rubbed out mobster Vincent "Mad Dog" Coll. Supposedly, Coll had accidentally killed a child during a shoot-out, bringing unwanted attention to the Mob.

Dillinger, John

Boarding House Arrest

320 West First Street
Dayton, Ohio

John Dillinger was arrested here at the boarding house that once stood on this site on September 22, 1933. Acting on a tip, local detectives burst into the room and surprised Dillinger, who was visiting with his girlfriend.

Dillinger, John

Crown Point Jail House

One block south of the old Courthouse Square on Main Street
Crown Point, Indiana

President Reagan got married here—so did Rudolph Valentino, who drove three times around the ornate high-towered courthouse, waving to assembled throngs. (Today, "Valentino's," an ice cream parlor in the basement of the courthouse, is named after him.) Others married here include football player Red Grange, Muhammad Ali and Michael Jackson's parents.

However, while Crown Point was was a well-known marriage-mill in the 1920s, its greatest international fame came from the escape of desperado John Dillinger. On January 30, 1934, Dillinger was captured in Tucson, Arizona. Due to a bank robbery in Chicago, which resulted in a murdered police officer, Lake County gained priority to prosecute Dillinger, and he was shipped here to Crown Point.

While incarcerated here, Dillinger carved a gun from a wooden washboard or a bar of soap (local legend varies), and stained the fake gun with black shoe polish. This is the tool he used to stage his escape. The breakout occurred during the early hours of March 3, 1934, and the prop was soon replaced by an automatic gun that Dillinger took from a guard.

The jail is not open for tours at this point, though it is visible from the street.

Dillinger, John

Hotel Congress

311 East Congress Street
Tucson, Arizona
520-622-8848

On January 22, 1934, an early morning fire tore through this historic hotel. Hotel patrons, including the notorious John Dillinger and six of his gang members, were all forced to flee from the hotel. Unbeknownst to anyone, Dillinger and company had holed up in the hotel as a means of laying low after a series of bank robberies. The gang had been staying on the third floor when the desk clerk called them with the notice to evacuate.

Two firemen helped the gangsters move their heavy luggage (later revealed to have contained a small arsenal and $23,816 in cash). Later, once the fireman recognized the gang from photos published in *True Detective* magazine, they knew who was in their midst. A stakeout ensued and they were finally captured at a house located at 927 North Second Avenue.

In just five hours, without firing a single shot, the small town police force of Tucson had nabbed some of the country's most feared criminals—something that the combined forces of several states and the FBI had failed to do. When captured, Dillinger simply muttered, "Well, I'll be damned." The gangsters were arraigned in town (people could even pay a buck to see Dillinger sitting in his jail cell) and then were transported to the Crown Point jail in Indiana—from which he eventually escaped.

Little Bohemia

142 Highway 51 South
Manitowish Waters, Wisconsin
715-543-8433

After John Dillinger, Public Enemy #1, comitted a crime, he'd often flee here to the Little Bohemia restaurant to hide out until the heat cooled off.

In April 1934, the FBI almost captured Dillinger and his gang at Little Bohemia. But, after a shootout, they escaped in a rowboat. The original bullet holes can still be seen in the windows and walls of the back dining room, and news articles are on display in the entry way.

Dillinger, John

Merchant's National Bank

229 South Michigan Street
South Bend, Indiana

At 11:30 A.M., on Saturday, June 30, 1934, this one-time South Bend bank entered crime history as the last bank to be robbed by the notorious John Dillinger. Some say Baby Face Nelson (who was present with Dillinger) was the shooter while others say it was a man named Homer VanMeter. Three men (including Dillinger) went into the bank and surprised the 25 customers inside. Dillinger fired his machine gun into the ceiling.

South Bend police officer Howard Wagner, 29, was directing traffic at Wayne and Michigan when he noticed a group of people in front of the bank. When the shots rang out, he went to investigate, and was gunned down by the lookouts before he was able to draw his own weapon. Dillinger was shot to death less than a month later as he left the Biograph Theater in Chicago on July 22, 1934. While the original Merchant's National Bank building still stands, today it is a restaurant.

Durst, Robert

2213 Avenue K
Galveston, Texas

It was here in this four-plex apartment house where bizarre multimillionaire Robert Durst rented a room across the hall from Morris Black—whom he would eventually kill in September 2001. Durst was arrested the next month in Pennsylvania and charged with the crime of killing Morris Black, dismembering Black's body, and placing the remains in bags before dumping them in Galveston Bay.

In court, Durst claimed the killing was an act of self-defense. Stunningly, on November 12, 2003, a Galveston jury found Durst not guilty. Durst originally had come to Galveston to escape media attention surrounding a new investigation into the 1982 disappearance of his first wife, Kathleen. His family runs The Durst Organization, a privately held billion-dollar New York real estate company.

Genovese, Kitty

80-20 Austin Street
Kew Gardens
Queens, New York

On March 13, 1964, Catherine "Kitty" Genovese arrived here at her home at around 3:15 A.M. She parked about one hundred feet from her apartment's door, and was approached by a man named Winston Moseley. Genovese may have changed direction towards a nearby police call box, but Moseley overtook her and stabbed her.

Genovese screamed out; her cries were heard by several neighbors, one of whom shouted at the attacker. Moseley ran away, and Genovese made her way towards her own apartment, seriously injured. Witnesses saw Moseley enter his car and drive away, only to return five minutes later.

He systematically searched the apartment complex, following the trail of blood to Genovese, who was laying, barely conscious, in a hallway. He proceeded to rape and rob her, finally delivering a fatal stab wound. The entire attack sequence took approximately half an hour.

A few minutes after the final portion of the attack, a witness, Karl Ross, called police. Police and medical personnel arrived within minutes and Genovese was taken away by ambulance and died en route to the hospital. Later investigations revealed that at least 38 individuals nearby had heard or observed portions of the attack. Many were entirely unaware that an assault or homicide was in progress; some thought that what they saw or heard was a lovers' quarrel.

Media attention of the Genovese murder led to reform of the NYPD's telephone reporting system; the system in place at the murder was often inefficient and directed individuals to the incorrect department. The dramatic press coverage also led to serious investigation of what is called the "bystander effect" by psychologists. In addition, some communities organized neighborhood watch programs and the equivalent for apartment buildings to aid people in distress.

Gonzales, Julio

The Happy Land Social Club
1959 Southern Boulevard
The Bronx, New York

On March 25, 1990, a tragic fire took place at The Happy Land Social Club, an un-licensed disco frequented primarily by Hondurans. A man named Julio Gonzales was tossed from the club for arguing with his girlfriend (who also worked there). He bought $1 worth of gasoline, poured it in the club's doorway and lit it, setting of a catastrophic fire that killed 87 people (but not Gonzalez's girlfriend—she is one of the five who survived). Gonzalez is now serving 25-year to life prison sentence. Today, in front of 1959 Southern Boulevard, a monument stands in memory to the dead. It's an eight-foot-tall concrete obelisk, surrounded by a high metal fence. The names of the victims are engraved on the sides of the structure, a final reminder of 87 lost lives.

Greenglass, David

209 High Street, Number 4
Albuquerque, New Mexico

David Greenglass, brother of convicted spy Ethel Rosenberg and the other half of the alleged spy ring, supposedly exchanged atomic bomb secrets here at his apartment with Soviet agents in 1945. Eventually, Greenglass decided to be a prosecution witness against his sister and his brother-in-law in exchange for immunity for his wife Ruth, so that she might remain with their two children. Greenglass received a 15-year sentence for his role in the passing of information concerning the atomic bomb. He and Ruth remained together after he was released from prison. On June 19, 1953, Ethel and Julius Rosenberg were put to death in the electric chair.

James, Jesse

First Daylight Robbery
103 North Water Street
Liberty, Missouri
816-781-4458

The first bank robbery in the U.S. in daylight hours took place in Liberty, Missouri, on February 13, 1866 at the Clay County Saving Association Bank. The Jesse James-Youngers gang got away with $62,000–$42,000 in bonds; $518 in United States Government Revenue Stamps and the rest in gold, silver coins and greenbacks. The Liberty Bank today is open to the public as the Jesse James Bank Museum.

James, Jesse

Junction of Highways CC & 49
Gads Hill, Missouri

On January 31, 1874, five men robbed the Little Rock Express on its way from
St. Louis to Little Rock at a small southeast Missouri town called Gads Hill.
A bold and daring crime that resulted in no casualties, the Gads Hill robbery
did much to add to the legend of the James-Younger gang.

Jordan, James

State Route 74 (near Interstate 95)
Lumberton, North Carolina

On July 23rd, 1993, basketball great Michael Jordan's father James was murdered here
in North Carolina by two locals: Daniel Green, age 21, and Larry Martin Demery, age 20.
Jordan was shot in the chest as he slept in his car outside a country store after a drive
from Wilmington to Charlotte, North Carolina, where he had attended the funeral of a
friend. For three days after they ditched the body in a swamp near Bennettsville, South
Carolina, Green and Demery went joyriding in Jordan's $40,000, 1993, red, Lexus
coupe—picking up dates and calling family and friends from the cellular phone.

A jury went on to find the two men guilty of first-degree murder, first-degree armed robbery and conspiracy to commit armed robbery. Today, they are both serving life terms
in jail.

Junta, Thomas

51 Symonds Way
Reading, Massachusetts
781-942-2271

This was the scene of the infamous "Hockey dad killing" that took place on July 5, 2000
when Junta, a 6-foot 1-inch tall, 270-pound truck driver — fought twice with Michael
Costin, 6-foot, 156 pounds. The second fight proved fatal for Costin. The two men had
argued over what Junta described as rough play during hockey drills in which both men's
sons were participating.

This incident is considered the worst example of the national problem of "sideline rage"—
parental violence in youth sports. A crowd of children, including sons of both Costin and
Junta, witnessed the beating, and several youngsters shouted for the men to stop.
Thomas Junta was sentenced to six to 10 years in state prison for the fatal beating.

McVeigh, Timothy

520 East Flint Hills
Junction City, Kansas

Terrorist Timothy McVeigh, the Oklahoma City bomber, stayed here at the Dreamland Motel the day before the bombing in 1995. He rented the infamous Ryder truck locally at Elliot's Body Shop, also in Junction City.

Miranda Law
Miranda, Ernesto

17 South Second Avenue
Phoenix, Arizona

For nearly 40 years police have been reading suspects their rights because of a landmark 1966 United States Supreme Court case, *Miranda vs. Arizona*. That case had its origins here in an interrogation room of the Phoenix Police Department. In 1963, Ernesto Miranda was arrested in Phoenix, Arizona for armed robbery of a bank worker. He already had a record for armed robbery, and a juvenile record including attempted rape, assault, and burglary. While in police custody he signed a written confession to the robbery, and to kidnapping and raping an 18-year-old woman 11 days before the robbery. After the conviction, his lawyers appealed on the grounds that Miranda did not know he was protected from self-incrimination.

The case made it all the way to the Supreme Court, where the conviction was overthrown. In a landmark ruling issued in 1966, the court established that the accused have the right to remain silent and that prosecutors may not use statements made by defendants while in police custody unless the police have advised them of their rights, commonly called the Miranda Rights. The case was later retried; Miranda was convicted on the basis of other evidence, and served 11 years.

He was paroled in 1972, and died in 1976 at the age of 34, after being stabbed in a bar fight. A suspect was arrested but chose to exercise his right to remain silent, and was released. The building where the famous interrogation took place still stands today; it's used for various city functions (but it's no longer the police station).

Mitnick, Kevin

4550 Tournament Drive, Apartment 202
Raleigh, North Carolina

It was here at the Players Club apartments that infamous computer hacker Kevin Mitnick was arrested. Though Mitnick was supposedly the model for the David Lightman character in the 1984 movie *Wargames*, in fact, the screenwriters had never heard of him when they created the movie.

Morgan Bank

23 Wall Street
New York City, New York

Just before lunchtime on Wednesday, September 16, 1920, a horse-drawn wagon rode up to the Morgan Bank in lower Manhattan. Without warning, it blew up—the wagon had held dynamite and shrapnel that blasted into the crowd. The explosion killed over 30 people and injured hundreds of others. All that remained of the horses were four hooves found near a neighborhood church.

The fatal explosion also caused $2 million worth of damage and shattered windows as far as half a mile away. Some officials suspected that members of the working class and/or political radicals were responsible for the bombing. The officials speculated that it might have been an act of revenge. (The government had recently arrested and violently suppressed many anarchists, socialists, labor organizers, and communists.)

Investigators went to 5,000 horse stables to try to trace the bombers, but no evidence was found. Today, the limestone exterior of the Morgan building still has pockmarks from the explosion that happened more than 75 years ago.

Nesler, Ellie

423 North Washington Street
Sonora, California

On April 2, 1993, Ellie Nesler walked into a "Gold Country" courtroom and shot twice-convicted child molester Daniel Driver 35 times in the head as he faced seven molestation charges, including one related to her young son. This set off a national debate as to whether what she did was right. Some criticized her for taking the law into her own hands, but many praised her for seeking her own justice.

Nesler served three years of a 10-year manslaughter sentence when a court overturned the conviction due to juror misconduct. Today, she is back in a California prison on charges related to manufacturing methamphetamine.

O'Hair, Madalyn Murray

Cooksy Ranch, 100 miles west of San Antonio
Real County, Texas

In 1960, Madalyn Murray sued the Baltimore-Maryland School District, protesting the unconstitutionality of her son William participating in Bible readings in the Baltimore public schools. This suit reached the United States Supreme Court, which handed down a decision in 1963, voting 8-1 in her favor and effectively banning "coercive" public prayer and Bible-reading in public schools in the United States.

This ruling sparked such an outcry that in 1964 *Life* magazine referred to Madalyn Murray as "The most hated woman in America." O'Hair founded the group American

Atheists in 1963 and remained its leading spokesperson until 1995, when she and two of her adult children vanished after leaving a note saying they would be away temporarily. The trio appeared to have taken with them at least $500,000 in American Atheist funds; one private investigator concluded that they had fled to New Zealand.

Eventually, suspicion turned to David Roland Waters, an ex-convict who had worked at the American Atheist offices. Police concluded that he and accomplices had kidnapped the O'Hairs, forced them to withdraw the missing funds, and then murdered them. Waters eventually pled guilty to reduced charges. In January, 2001, he led police to three bodies buried on this remote Texas ranch, which proved to be O'Hair and her children.

Peterson, Scott

Berkeley Marina
Berkeley, California

Scott Peterson, a 32-year-old fertilizer salesman from Modesto, was convicted in 2004 of killing his wife Laci and their unborn son, Connor. Prosecutors say he killed her on the night of December 23, 2002, and dumped her body off his fishing boat in the San Francisco Bay the following day. In April, 2003, Laci Peterson's remains and the body of her child were discovered on the Richmond shoreline, less than two miles from the Berkeley Marina where Peterson admits he went fishing the day Laci went missing. The ensuing trial captivated the nation as the emotionless and seemingly unfazed killer barely reacted to the news of his guilty and death sentence convictions.

Purdy, Patrick Edward

Cleveland Elementary School
20 East Fulton Street
Stockton, California

On January 17, 1989, here at Cleveland Elementary School, 26-year-old Patrick Edward Purdy opened fire on an elementary schoolyard full of Asian-American children. He shot 106 rounds, killing five and wounding 30 before taking his own life. Purdy, who had expressed his dislike for Asian immigrants and Asian-Americans, had attended the school 15 years earlier.

Rothstein, Arnold

Park Central Hotel
870 Seventh Avenue
New York City, New York
800-346-1359

Arnold Rothstein was a New York gambler and mob boss, widely reputed to have been the brains behind the Black Sox scandal during the 1919 World Series. He never confessed, however, and no evidence could verify his connection to the affair. Rothstein was shot to death on November 6, 1928 at the employees' entrance to this hotel, following a spectacular three-day poker game in Manhattan, New York.

At the end of the game Rothstein owed $320,000 and refused to pay, claiming the game had been fixed. (Gambler George McManus was arrested for murder but was later acquitted for lack of evidence.) Interestingly, F. Scott Fitzgerald based his character Meyer Wolfsheim, Jay Gatsby's crooked associate in *The Great Gatsby*, on Rothstein. Rothstein also provided the model for gambler Nathan Detroit in the musical *Guys 'n Dolls.*

Schultz, Dutch

12 East Park Street
Newark, New Jersey

Dutch Schultz (born Arthur Flegenheimer) is one of the best-known New York mobsters of the Prohibition era (1920s–1930s). He dropped out of school in the fourth grade and turned to a life of crime. He started with pick-pocketing and petty theft, eventually moving up to bootlegging and smuggling—but his main mark would be left in bloody gang wars.

In 1933, he was acquitted of income tax evasion, but much of his power was lost to "Lucky" Luciano. Nevertheless, he was a board member in Luciano's national crime syndicate, and drew attention from special prosecutor Thomas E. Dewey. In 1935, he tried

to convince his associates to assassinate Dewey, but the infamous Murder Inc. opted instead to murder Schultz along with three associates.

The hit took place on the night of October 23, 1935, in the Palace Chop House. The restaurant is no longer there, but etched into the concrete wall of what used to be the eatery is a tribute to Schultz.

In the last few hours of his life, Schultz rambled continuously to the cops in his room at Newark City Hospital. The cops wanted details on the hit, but all Schultz did was wax on about dozens of other topics. In the years that have followed, Schultz's cryptic dying words have been literary inspiration for writers as various as E. L. Doctorow in *Billy Bathgate*, and perhaps most famously, William Burroughs in *The Last Words of Dutch Schultz*.

Sherrill, Patrick Henry

U.S. Post Office
200 North Broadway
Edmond, Oklahoma

On August 20, 1986, part-time letter carrier Patrick Henry Sherrill killed 14 co-workers in the post office here before taking his own life. Sherrill had a history of work problems and faced the possibility of being fired. The shooting spree began in the parking lot and ended in the mail-sorting room. This incident helped inspire the term "going postal."

Train Robbery

Bass, Sam

U.S. 138
Big Springs, Nebraska

A plaque here reads: "The first and greatest robbery of a Union Pacific Train took place near Big Springs on the night of September 18, 1877. The legendary Sam Bass and five companions—after capturing John Barnhardt, stationmaster, and destroying the telegraph—forced Union Pacific Express Train Number 4 to halt. A reported $60,000 in new $20 gold pieces and currency was taken from the Express car, while about $1,000 and a number of watches were taken from passengers. It is said that the accumulated loot from this, the Big Springs Robbery, was then divided by the outlaws beneath the Lone Tree growing on the north side of the River.

After making the division, the robbers then split into pairs and fled their pursuers. Joel Collins and Bill Heffridge were killed at Buffalo, Kansas. Jim Berry was killed near Mexico, Missouri, while Tom Nixon and Jack Davis were never located. After forming another band and robbing four trains in Texas, Sam Bass was killed by Texas Rangers at Round Rock, Texas, on July 21, 1878; it was his 27th birthday. His epitaph reads, 'A brave man reposes in death here, why was he not true?'"

The First Train Holdup

Seymour Chamber of Commerce
105 S. Chestnut Street
Seymour, Indiana

On October 6, 1866, thieves boarded an eastbound Ohio and Mississippi passenger train near Seymour, Indiana and entered an Adams Express Company car. Pointing guns at Adams Express employee Elem Miller, the masked bandits demanded keys to the safes. Miller held keys for the local safe only, so the robbers emptied that safe and tossed the other off the train intending to open it later.

Signaling the engineer to stop the train, the robbers, later identified as the infamous Reno brothers, made an easy getaway. Unaware of what had happened, the engineer sped off into the night while the thieves congratulated themselves on a job well done. Considered the first train holdup, the incident at Seymour was actually preceded by a similar train burglary: Exactly nine months before, bandits entered an Adams Express car en route to Boston from New York and stole over half a million dollars from safes on the unoccupied car. As in the Seymour case, detectives from the Pinkerton National Detective Agency quickly identified the criminals. Still, a wave of train robberies followed. Within weeks, two trains were derailed and their pay cars robbed.

Train Robbery

The Great Train Robbery

Truckee River Basin (Located at the railroad crossing near Verdi Inn)
Verdi, Nevada

The West's first train robbery occurred near this site on the night of November 4, 1870. Five men, led by a stage robber, Sunday School superintendent John Chapman, boarded the Central Pacific Overland Express at Verdi, Nevada. Two of the men took over the engine, one the express car, and two the rear platform.

One-half mile east, the engine and express car were halted and cut free. They proceeded for about five miles until they were stopped by a barricade. Here, the robbers forced the messenger to open up. Seizing $41,600 in gold coins, they rode off.

The uncoupled cars coasted downgrade and met the engine. The train proceeded to Reno. After a two-state chase, all were caught, tried and convicted. About 90 percent of the gold was recovered.

Marshfield Train Robbery

Marshfield Bridge
Marshfield, Indiana

One of earliest U.S. train robberies occurred May 22, 1868 at nearby Marshfield, a refueling and watering stop. The engine and express car were detached from Jeffersonville, Madison, and Indianapolis Railroad trains, and abandoned near Seymour. The notorious Reno Gang took U.S. treasury notes and government bonds from Adams Express Company safes in a car.

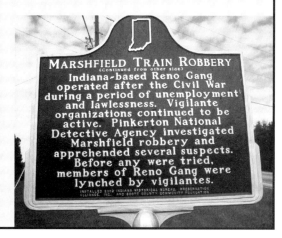

The Indiana-based Reno Gang operated after the Civil War during a period of unemployment and lawlessness. Vigilante organizations continued to be active. The Pinkerton National Detective Agency investigated the Marshfield robbery and apprehended several suspects. Before any were tried, members of Reno Gang were lynched by vigilantes.

Train Robbery

The Roundout Train Robbery

North side of Illinois Route 176 (just east of the toll road)
Lake Bluff, Illinois

On June 12, 1924, the largest train robbery in U.S. history occurred near here. Bandits who boarded the train in Chicago forced postal clerks to surrender sacks containing more than two million dollars in securities and cash. Local police apprehended the gunman within a few days.

The U.S. Postal Inspection Service investigated the case and identified the masterminds, one of whom was a trusted employee of the postal service. Some of the loot was never recovered. In all, eight men were convicted in federal court and sentenced within seven months of the robbery.

Weatherman

18 West 11th Street
New York City, New York

This odd-angled house (remodeled in Modernist style in 1978) was actually built in 1845, one of four houses on the block constructed by Henry Brevoort Jr., for his children; it was later the home of Charles Merrill (of Merrill Lynch), whose son, the poet James Merrill, was born here. But in 1970, it was a hideout for the radical Weatherman group (including Kathy Boudin), who used it as a bomb factory. On March 6, 1970, 60 sticks of dynamite accidentally exploded, killing three group members and destroying much of the house.

Most notable among the victims was Diana Oughton, a graduate student at the University of Michigan and former American Friends Service Committee Vista Volunteer in rural Guatemala. Her body was identified by a finger found 12 days after the explosion (the police estimated that she was standing within two feet of the blast).

White, Dan

San Francisco City Hall
Polk Street (between Grove and McAllister Streets)
San Francisco, California

On November 27, 1978, Dan White, a former San Francisco city supervisor who had recently resigned his position, climbed through a basement window at San Francisco's City Hall and then shot and killed both mayor George Moscone and supervisor Harvey Milk. Milk, a noted gay leader, became a martyr in death for the many causes he had taken up. In May of the next year, a judge gave White just seven years for the premeditated murders, prompting thousands to march on San Francisco's City Hall.

In what came to be known as the White Night Riots, the demonstration took a violent turn, resulting in significant property damage and the torching of twelve SFPD cruisers. White was released from prison in 1984. In 1985, he committed suicide with a garden hose hooked up to the exhaust pipe of his 1970 Buick Le Sabre.

During White's trial, defense attorneys stated that he was suffering from "diminished capacity," a defense that was permissible in California at that time. The lawyers argued that White suffered from depression and was therefore incapable of premeditation. Psychiatrist Martin Blinder testified that White was addicted to junk food and that too much sugar could have had an effect on the brain and worsened White's depression. This became derisively known as the "Twinkie Defense."

Wuornos, Aileen Carol

The Last Resort
5812 South Ridgewood Avenue
Port Orange, Florida

This biker bar was the end of the line for one of the worst serial killers in history, Aileen Carol Wuornos, on whom the 2003 movie *Monster* (starring Charlize Theron) was based. The background is this: a storeowner in Palm Harbor, Florida named Richard Mallory took a ride with Wuornos on November 30, 1989, and became her first victim. Six subsequent victims were found; one other has never been found.

She was eventually identified when she and a friend, Tyria Moore, drove off a road in a victim's car (this was several months before being apprehended). Wuornos plead self-defense for Mallory's murder, maintaining that he had attempted to rape her. She was convicted for this first murder in January, 1992, and put to death in 2002. Wuornos was arrested for the series of murders at this biker bar in 1991, after evidence had begun piling up against her.

Celebrity Deaths and Infamous Celebrity Events

Abdul, Paula

16358 Ventura Boulevard
Encino, California

At about at 1:30 P.M. on July 18, 1995, singer/host Paula Abdul arrived here at Delmonico's restaurant for lunch and became the victim of an afternoon car theft. She

briefly left her white 300SL Mercedes-Benz running unattended in front of the restaurant (she had gone to get a valet parking ticket). In an instant, two men jumped into her car and sped away. In recent years Abdul has become perhaps more famous than she ever was as a singer while performing as a judge on the TV show *American Idol.*

Adams, Nick

2126 El Roble Lane
Beverly Hills, California

This is where Nick Adams, who starred in TV's *The Rebel,* died of a drug overdose in 1968. The death remains a bit of a mystery today because no pill bottles or drug-related paraphernalia was found in the home.

Allen, Tim

Kalamazoo Airport
5236 Portage Road
Kalamazoo, Michigan

On October 2, 1978, comedian Tim Allen (*Home Improvement*) was arrested with 1.4 pounds of cocaine here at Kalamazoo Airport in Michigan. After testifying against his partner, Allen served two and a half years for felony drug possession. (Had he not testified, he might have received a life sentence.)

Begelman, David

Century Plaza Hotel
2025 Avenue of the Stars
Century City, California

This famous hotel is where former Columbia Pictures president David Begelman shot himself to death on August 7, 1995. Begelman, who pioneered the idea of "packaging" stars, writers and directors from one agency had also headed up Columbia Pictures. However, he gained infamy and fell from power in 1977 when he was accused of forging checks (Cliff Robertson's was the most notable) and misappropriation of funds; he was eventually convicted of grand theft. The scandal became the subject of David McClintick's 1982 bestseller *Indecent Exposure*.

Bennifer

The much-ballyhooed tabloid relationship between celebrities Ben Affleck and Jennifer Lopez in the early 2000s garnered much ridicule and produced one of the biggest bombs in Hollywood history—*Gigli.* Here are a few hotspots related to the on-again/off-again affair:

Brandi's Exotic Nightclub

595 Hornby Street
Vancouver, BC

On July 17, 2003 (the very night Bennifer's nauseatingly cozy Dateline interview aired), the Ben Affleck portion of Bennifer was seen here with professional party girl Tara Reid, as well as Christian Slater and his wife, Ryan Haddon. The night of booze, debauchery and lap dances led to a firestorm of publicity (Lopez was not present) that appeared to cause some conflict in the couple's relationship.

The Four Seasons Biltmore Hotel

1260 Channel Drive
Santa Barbara, California

In September 2003, it was widely speculated that the Bennifer marriage would take place here. However, it was called off and the couple issued the following statement: "Due to the excessive media attention surrounding our wedding, we have decided to postpone the date. When we found ourselves seriously contemplating hiring three separate 'decoy brides' at three different locations, we realized that something was awry. We began to feel that the spirit of what should have been the happiest day of our lives could be compromised, we felt what should have been a joyful and sacred day could be spoiled for us, our families and our friends." The couple broke up soon afterwards. Whatever!

Bennifer

Gigli

Mann National Theater
10925 Lindbrook Drive
Westwood, California

On July 27, 2003, this was the site of the world premiere for the infamous film, *Gigli*, starring Ben Affleck and Jennifer Lopez. The soon-to-be megaton flop revolved around two unbelievable gangsters who are assigned the task of kidnapping and watching over a prosecutor's mentally challenged brother while also keeping an open eye on each other to ensure the success of the operation. Ben played Gigli and Lopez played Ricky, a lesbian gangster. The film was so universally bad it seemed to derail both actor's careers and today ranks right up there with other classic failures such as *Heaven's Gate* and *Ishtar*.

Bolin, Tommy

16701 Collins Avenue
Miami, Florida

Legendary guitarist Tommy Bolin was found here in room 902 on December 4, 1976, dead from a heroin overdose at the age of 25. Bolin's band had opened the night before

for Jeff Beck, and following the well-received set he returned here to his room with several friends and hangers on. Bolin passed out in front of the group in the middle of the night while in mid-conversation and those present were unable to revive him. The innovative guitarist had already played in Deep Purple and The James Gang and, on the heels of his brilliant solo album, *Teaser*, was poised for his own stardom.

Bow, Clara

512 North Bedford Drive
Beverly Hills, California

Clara Bow was an American actress and sex symbol, best known for her film work in the 1920s and early 1930s. To some, Bow was the era's archetype of the flapper, but to many she was simply the "It Girl." That's because in 1927, Clara made *It*, a film that was essentially a vehicle for her sex appeal. Consequently, Bow was dubbed "The It Girl"–"It" being a euphemism for sex appeal, as defined by the British novelist Elinor Glyn.

This image was enhanced by many off-screen love affairs publicized by the tabloid press, most notably a rumor of an event that took place here at this house in which she enjoyed the intimate company of the entire U.S.C. football team. However, despite what other dalliances might have taken place here, many have debunked the U.S.C. myth.

During her heyday, Clara worked at an incredible pace, churning out 14 films in 1925 alone, and was successful in making the leap from silent to talking films. After being diagnosed as schizophrenic in 1949 and suffering a mental-health regimen that included shock treatments, Clara Bow died on September 26, 1965.

Boyer, Charles

6806 North Desert Fairways Drive
Scottsdale, Arizona

Legendary romantic leading man Charles Boyer starred in films throughout the 1930s and 1940s, always maintaining his famous French accent. In fact, after playing the suave jewel thief Pepe le Moko in 1938's *Algiers*, the cartoon skunk, Pepe le Pew, was introduced by Warner Bros. in honor of his character. Boyer lived for years in Arizona with his wife, Pat, who died in Phoenix from cancer in 1978. A mere two days after her death, Charles Boyer took a lethal overdose of Seconal while staying here at a friend's home. He was rushed to St. Joseph's Hospital in Phoenix where he died. (Sadly, the couple's only child, Michael Boyer (1944-1965) also committed suicide.)

Brando, Marlon

43 Fifth Avenue at East 11th Street
New York City, New York

As a young actor, Marlon Brando lived in a tiny apartment in this 11-story building in 1946. He shared it with an eccentric Russian violinist named Igor. According to biographer Charles Higham, Marlon Brando greatly enjoyed the Slav's company initially, but when he grew tired of him and wanted him to leave, he cut open the Russian's violin and filled it with horse manure, thus forcing Igor to leave. The great, reclusive actor died in California on July 1, 2004.

Bronstein, Phil

Los Angeles Zoo
5333 Zoo Drive
Los Angeles, California
323-644-4200

It was in the reptile house here in June 2001, that *San Francisco Chronicle* editor Phil Bronstein, the husband of actress Sharon Stone, was bitten on the foot by a Komodo Dragon in the Indonesian lizard's cage during the couple's private tour of the Los Angeles Zoo. The lizard got hold of Bronstein's foot after a zookeeper asked him to take off his white tennis shoes—it seems the five-foot-long reptile sometimes mistakes them for edible white rats. Bronstein managed to pry open the reptile's mouth and escape through a small feeding door in the cage.

The insider's tour was arranged by Stone as a Father's Day surprise for Bronstein, who had always wanted to see a Komodo dragon up close. The incident became fodder for several late night TV monologues.

Bruce, Lenny

Intersection of Rue Notre Dame and Normandy Drive
Miami Beach, Florida

On April 27, 1963, comedian and satirist Lenny Bruce was arrested at this intersection after police stopped him for a brake light violation and found hypodermic needles and a wide variety of pills in his car. (He was released on a $50 bond and ended up paying a fine.) The socially relevant performer had several other high-profile brushes with the law and eventually died in his Los Angeles home, purportedly from a drug overdose, on August 3, 1966.

Buckley, Jeff

Near Mud Island
Memphis, Tennessee

It was here where singer/songwriter Jeff Buckley, the 30-year-old son of singer Tim Buckley, drowned in May, 1997. Jeff Buckley, who was born in California's Orange County in 1966, had emerged in New York City's avant-garde club scene in the 1990s as one of the most acclaimed musicians of his generation, equally adored by fans and critics alike. His first commercial recording, the four-song EP *Live At Sin-é*, was released in December 1993, on Columbia Records. It featured Buckley, accompanying himself on electric guitar, in a small East Village coffeehouse.

His career was in full swing when on the evening of May 29, Buckley, hanging out with a friend at the Mud Island Harbor marina (half a mile inland off the Mississippi River in Memphis, Tennessee) decided to enter the water. He disappeared shortly after. After a 10-minute search, a friend called local police. The Memphis police department began dragging the waters that night but heavy rains hampered the search. Jeff Buckley was found three days later by passengers on a steamboat, who saw a body in a t-shirt tangled up in some branches on the riverside near Harbor Island.

Buckley, Tim

Santa Monica Hospital
2021 Arizona Avenue
Santa Monica, California

It was in the emergency room here where 28 year-old singer/songwriter Tim Buckley died at 9:42 P.M. on June 29, 1975. At first, authorities suspected that Buckley had suffered a heart attack, but then the county coroner's ruled his death was due to a heroin/morphine overdose (combined with alcohol). Ten days later, Richard Keeling, a research assistant in the music department at UCLA, was arraigned on charges of second-degree murder. According to reports, Keeling allegedly furnished Buckley with the lethal does of drugs. Under California law, this constitutes grounds for a murder indictment.

Capriati, Jennifer

Gables Inn
730 South Dixie Highway
Coral Gables, Florida

On May 16, 1994, a bloated and bleary-eyed Jennifer Capriati was arrested at this Coral Gables motel, in room 208, on a misdemeanor charge of marijuana possession (with two motel companions facing felony drug charges). The young tennis star had taken a break after some disappointing losses in 1993, but had already run into personal and legal troubles (she was nabbed for shoplifting in December 1993). As for the drug charges against her, she settled the misdemeanor charge by agreeing to attend drug counseling.

Capriati returned to the tennis tour in November of that year, but played in only one match, which she lost, and again went on sabbatical, this time for 15 months. Returning to the tour in 1996, she finally won a singles title in Luxembourg on September 25, 2000. In 2001, she began an earnest comeback, winning both the Australian Open and the French Open, and she successfully defended her Australian Open title the following year.

Crews, Tim

Little Lake Nellie
Clermont, Florida

On March 22, 1993, Cleveland Indians pitcher Tim Crews was killed in a tragic spring training boating accident that also took the life of Indians' closer Steve Olin and injured Southpaw Bob Ojeda. (They were pro baseball's first fatalities since 1979, when the Yankees' Thurman Munson crashed his Cessna Citation in Akron.) On March 22, Olin, Crews, and Ojeda, went out after dark in Crews's 18-foot bass boat. Traveling at about 60 miles per hour, they smashed into a wooden pier. Olin was killed instantly, Crews, 31, died of injuries the next morning at Orlando Regional Medical Center, Ojeda suffered lacerations on the head and eventually recovered.

Danson, Ted

Friar's Club
57 East 57th Street
New York City, New York

On October 8, 1993, actor Ted Danson created a firestorm of controversy by appearing in blackface at a Friars Club roast of Whoopi Goldberg. His seemingly offensive comments amused then-girlfriend Goldberg (who wrote the bit for him) but the incident became a huge embarrassment. They broke up soon afterward.

Dean, Howard

Hotel Fort Des Moines
1000 Walnut Street
Des Moines, Iowa
800-532-1466

It's been called the "I Have a Scream" speech (among other things). And most everyone agrees that democrat Howard Dean's January 2004 scream during his speech after a third place finish in the Iowa Caucus all but relegated him to the back of the pack. Late night (and pretty much all other) hosts had a field day with the now infamous audio that concluded, "Not only are we going to New Hampshire," Dean said. "We're going to South Carolina and Oklahoma and Arizona and North Dakota and New Mexico, and we're going to California and Texas and New York. And we're going to South Dakota and Oregon and Washington and Michigan. And then we're going to Washington, D.C., to take back the White House. Yeah!!!!!"

Depp, Johnny

I-10 near South Kino Parkway
Tucson, Arizona

On Tuesday, October 22, 1991, actor Johnny was here in Tucson for the filming of the movie *Arrowtooth Waltz* (eventually re-titled *Arizona Dream*). While here, he decided to take his 1991 black Porsche for a ride and at around 10:30 P.M.; police radar clocked him going 93 miles per hour in the westbound lanes of Interstate 10 (the posted speed limit was 55 miles per hour). Before actually pulling him over, Depp was clocked at 100 miles per hour. The 28-year-old actor had no ID on him and so he was driven to the Pretrial Services office of Superior Court. He was then released after posting a $305 bond.

Douglas, Michael

Sierra Tucson Centre
39580 Lago del Oro Parkway
Tucson, Arizona

Actor/producer Michael Douglas checked in here in 1992 at the bequest of his first wife. Tired of his alleged womanizing, she wanted him to seek help for what became infamously trumpeted in the tabloids as "Sexual Addiction." However, she still filed for divorce three years later. Douglas would go on to marry Catherine Zeta Jones, who, coincidentally, shares his same birthday. The only difference is, she's 25 years younger.

Fonda, Jane

Hopkins International Airport
5300 Riverside Drive
Cleveland, Ohio

On November 3, 1970, actress/activist Jane Fonda was arrested on her way to a speaking engagement at Bowling Green State College. After a skirmish that involved kicking a cop and customs official while trying to get to the ladies room, it was discovered that she had 102 plastic vials filled with various vitamins and other pills. She was arrested on charges of drug smuggling, and then released on a personal bond of $5000. Eventually, the Cleveland Municipal Court found in favor of Ms. Fonda and all charges were subsequently dropped.

Furlong, Edward

Meijer Grocery Store
4990 Houston Road
Florence, Kentucky

Edward Furlong was arrested in September 2004 for public intoxication following a bizarre incident at this Kentucky grocery store. According to the Florence Police Department, the 27-year-old *Terminator 2* star (in town to shoot a movie) and some buddies were getting rowdy and yanking lobsters out of the chain store's tank. When police arrived, Furlong, who smelled of booze, began to "turn around in circles" when an officer tried to frisk him.

The actor spent a few hours in custody before making bail on the misdemeanor count. While Furlong is known to be active in the People for Ethical Treatment of Animals, it is not clear whether he was trying to liberate the lobsters as part of his PETA platform. The actor is a vegetarian and has refused to wear leather in photo shoots in the past.

Gold Club

2416 Piedmont Road
Atlanta, Georgia

This now-closed strip club was the focal point of a huge scandal involving a group of professional athletes. The Gold Club was one of the most successful and high profile strip clubs on the East Coast. However, when it came under scrutiny by the FBI, testimony about sexual favors for celebrity athletes thrust the trial into one of the biggest sex scandals in professional sports history.

Fourteen weeks into the much-publicized racketeering trial, after NBA star Patrick Ewing and Atlanta Braves outfielder Andruw Jones testified about having received sexual favors from dancers, club owner Steve Kaplan made a plea deal. He agreed to pay a $5 million fine and serve three to five years in prison. The club has since closed.

Jackson, Janet

Reliant Stadium
Houston, Texas

Reliant Stadium, the first NFL stadium with a retractable roof, hosted the 2004 Super Bowl XXXVIII between the New England Patriots and Carolina Panthers. (The Patriots won 32-29 on Adam Vinatieri's 41-yard field goal with four seconds remaining.) The event also featured history's most controversial halftime show, the now infamous "wardrobe malfuntion" that featured Janet Jackson exposing her breast during a song and dance routine with Justin Timberlake.

The CBS network was heavily fined for the incident and though all parties involved claim the incident was unintentional, broad skepticism remained, many feeling that it was a calculated stunt designed to produce a shock effect (which it did).

An estimated 140 million people were watching the show when at the end, pop star Justin Timberlake popped off part of Jackson's corset, exposing her breast. Jackson spokesman Stephen Huvane said the incident "was a malfunction of the wardrobe; it was not intentional. . . . He was supposed to pull away the bustier and leave the red-lace bra."

Jackson, Michael

312 East Cook Street
Building E
Santa Maria, California

Singer Michael Jackson was arraigned here in Santa Maria on January 16, 2004, at the court of Santa Maria. He was admonished by the judge for turning up 20 minutes late and entered a plea of "Not Guilty." Hundreds of fans and an international media circus surrounded the event, which became notable for Jackson's bizarre, post-plea circus whereby he jumped on a van in front of the courthouse and began dancing for the throngs of people who showed up (as well as for the ever-present videographer Jackson had hired for the day).

Joel, Billy

Route 114
Sag Harbor, New York

In January 2003, singer/songwriter Billy Joel, then 53, was driving his blue 2002 Mercedes Benz south on Route 114 near Walker Avenue in Sag Harbor at about 10:30 P.M. when he apparently lost control of his vehicle, veered off the road and struck a tree. Paramedics rushed him by ambulance to East Hampton Airport, where he was airlifted to Stony Brook University Hospital. He was not given a Breathalyzer test and faced no charges in the incident.

Johnson, Don

Clark's Market
Aspen, Colorado

In the summer of 2004, a judge ordered actor Don Johnson to pay up the nearly $6,000 dollar tab owed to this Aspen grocery store. (He was also ordered to pay interest on the bill and court costs.) Don Johnson has starred in both the *Miami Vice* and *Nash Bridges* television series, as well as in the movie *Tin Cup.*

Keith, Brian

23449 Malibu Colony Road
Malibu, California

This is the home of actor Brian Keith (TV's Uncle Bill in *Family Affair,* and star of *Hardcastle and McCormick*), where he shot himself on June 24, 1997, following a long bout with emphysema and lung cancer.

Kevorkian, Jack

14555 Dixie Highway
Groveland Oaks Park
Holly, Michigan

On June 4, 1990, Janet Adkins, a 54-year-old Portland, Oregon woman with Alzheimer's disease, pushed the button on a "suicide machine" developed by Dr. Jack Kevorkian, causing her death. Dr. Kevorkian created the machine at his kitchen table using $30 worth of scrap parts from garage sales and hardware stores. The assisted suicide took place in the back of Dr. Kevorkian's 1968 Volkswagen van, here in this park. Dr. Kevorkian was present during this act, and it marks the beginning of more than one hundred assisted suicides over the next eight years by Kevorkian, utilizing his death machines.

In 1995, he even opened a "suicide clinic" in an office in Springfield Township, Michigan, but was booted out by the building's owner a few days after his first client died. On March 26, 1999, a jury in Michigan found Dr. Kevorkian guilty of second-degree murder for administering a lethal injection to a terminally ill man (the incident was videotaped and aired on the September 17, 1998 edition of *60 Minutes*). He was given a 10-25 year prison sentence.

Lamarr, Hedy

Former May Company Department Store
Wilshire Boulevard and Fairfax Avenue
Los Angeles, California

Before Winona Ryder made shoplifting headlines, there was Hedy Lamarr. In 1966, the actress was arrested for shoplifting here at the May Company. A jury found her not guilty and she sued the department store for $5 million. The bad publicity from this incident coupled with her controversial autobiography *Ecstasy and Me* (purportedly ghost written and not approved by Ms. Lamarr) brought an end to her movie career.

The Austrian-born film actress of the 1930s and 1940s gained fame by appearing nude in the 1932 Czech film Ecstasy. Once considered the most beautiful woman in the world, her other credits include *Lady of the Tropics* (1939) and Dishonored Lady (1942). Today, the May Company building still stands but it is part of the Los Angeles County Museum of Art.

 On a side note, Lamarr was also an inventor. In the 1940s, she and composer George Antheil received patent number 2,292,387 for their "Secret Communications System." This early version of frequency hopping used a piano roll to change between 88 frequencies and was intended to make radio-guided torpedoes harder for enemies to detect or to jam. The patent was little known for years because Lamarr applied for it under her then-married name of Hedy Kiesler Markey. Neither Lamarr nor Antheil made any money from the patent.

Love, Courtney

Plaid
76 East 13th Street
New York City, New York

Singer Courtney Love, while in the midst of a series of arrests (and bizarre public behavior) gave a surprise performance at Plaid, a lower Manhattan nightclub, for about 400 patrons on March 17, 2004. While on stage with her band, Love hurled a microphone stand into the audience and struck a 24-year-old man in the head. The man was taken to Cabrini Hospital (he fully recovered) while Love was booked at the 9th Precinct in the East Village and charged with reckless endangerment. Love had gone to the club after a controversial appearance earlier in the evening on *The David Letterman Show.*

Lowe, Rob

Atlanta Hilton and Towers
255 Courtland Street
Atlanta, Georgia

It was here in this hotel during the 1988 Democratic Convention that actor Rob Lowe videotaped himself with two women, one of whom was underage, thus setting off one of the biggest celebrity scandals of the decade. The Sunday night before the convention started, Lowe had flown in from Paris, attended a party thrown by Ted Turner, then went to hang out at Atlanta's Club Rio, where he met the two women (one of whom was 16). They went back to his hotel, and videotaped themselves. After Lowe passed out, the woman grabbed the tape and ran. Portions of the tape eventually made it to tabloid TV and were even sold commercially.

Lugosi, Bela

5620 Harold Way
Los Angeles, California

In the movie *Ed Wood* starring Johnny Depp, we see the real life relationship form between the filmmaker Wood and his hero, the over-the-hill horror legend, Bela Lugosi. This was the home depicted in the movie, the small, unpretentious house in a quiet part of Los Angeles where Lugosi lived until he died on August 16, 1956.

Martin, Billy

Potter's Field Road
Fenton, New York

Former Yankee ballplayer and manager Billy Martin was killed here on Christmas Day, 1989, in a one-vehicle accident that occurred near his home. The 61-year-old Martin was a passenger in his pickup truck when the vehicle skidded off an icy road and continued 300 feet down an embankment, stopping at the foot of Martin's driveway. William Reedy, Martin's longtime friend, survived the accident, but was charged with driving while intoxicated. Neither was wearing a seatbelt.

Miles, Sarah

Golden Star Motel
1046 East Pima Street
Gila Bend, Arizona

When actress Sarah Miles was filming the 1973 movie *The Man Who Loved Cat Dancing* here near Gila Bend, she became stuck in a tragic tabloid story when her younger boyfriend was found dead in the motel room they shared (it was then a TraveLodge Motel). On February 11, 1973, the 26-year-old aspiring screenwriter's body was found facedown near a pool of blood in the room of British actress Miles. Miles, then 31, was married, so this was extremely scandalous. (She later admitted to having an affair with the screenwriter.) The tabloids hinted at a violent altercation between Miles and her "friend" who had just returned to her room following a pre-38th birthday party for her costar in *The Man Who Loved Cat Dancing,* Burt Reynolds. In the end, the coroner found that the screenwriter died as a result of a drug overdose.

Minnelli, Liza

One West 29th Street
New York City, New York

The Marble Collegiate Church was built in 1854 for a congregation that dates back to 1628. A Dutch Reformed church, it is notable for being the pulpit of Norman Vincent Peale, who combined Christianity with motivational speaking in such books as *The Power of Positive Thinking.* Richard Nixon attended this church and was said to be greatly influenced by Peale. As well, Nixon's daughter Julie married Dwight Eisenhower II here in 1968. Other famous marriages here include the famous opera star Enrico Caruso to Dorothy Benjamin in 1918 and Donald Trump to Ivana Zelnicek in 1977 (he also met Marla Maples here). But perhaps the biggest marital spectacle took place here in 1992 when Liza Minnelli married the flamboyant David Guest. The pair was to star in a reality TV show together, but their match made in heaven soon disintegrated under charges of spousal battery.

Namath, Joe

Giants Stadium
50 State Highway 120
East Rutherford, New Jersey

It was while getting interviewed here on the sidelines of the Patriots vs. Jets game on December 20, 2003 that a clearly drunk Joe Namath told ESPN interviewer/sideline analyst Suzy Kolber that he wanted to kiss her (he said it twice). He also said he didn't care about what she was asking him about, because all he wanted to do was kiss her. He has since apologized to her and the audience for the embarrassing incident. Later, he publicly admitted to an alcohol problem, and underwent outpatient alcoholism treatment.

Newton, Helmut

Chateau Marmont Hotel
8221 Sunset Boulevard
Hollywood, California

Acclaimed fashion photographer Helmut Newton died here on January 23, 1993 after his Cadillac sped out of control from the driveway of the famous Chateau Marmont hotel and crashed into a wall directly across the street from the hotel's entrance. The 83-year old Newton saw his work appear in magazines such as *Playboy, Elle* and *Vogue*. He was perhaps best known for his stark, dramatic, black-and-white nude photos of women. Newton was taken by ambulance to nearby Cedars-Sinai Medical Center, where he died a short time later. (This hotel is also where actor John Belushi died.)

Norton, Emperor

537 California Street
San Francisco, California

One of the most mythical figures in California history was Joshua Abraham "Emperor" Norton, a highly eccentric 1800's citizen of San Francisco. His many celebrated activities included famously anointing himself as "Emperor of the United States" in 1859, becoming Emperor Norton I. Other notable activities included his ordering the dissolution of the United States Congress (which Congress ignored), and his numerous (and prophetic) decrees that a bridge be built across San Francisco Bay.

The King in Mark Twain's Huckleberry Finn is reportedly modeled after him. On January 8, 1880, Emperor Norton I dropped dead here on California Street, on his way to a lecture at the Academy of Natural Sciences. On January 10th, he was buried in the Masonic Cemetery. The funeral cortege was two miles long, and over one thousand people attended the ceremony.

On January 7, 1980 San Francisco marked the 100th anniversary of the death of its only monarch, Emperor Norton, with lunch-hour ceremonies at Market and Montgomery Streets.

Novarro, Ramon

3110 Laurel Canyon Drive
Los Angeles, California

This is where famed silent screen actor Ramon Novarro (star of Ben-Hur) was discovered murdered on Halloween night, 1968. Supposedly, two young crooks broke in looking for hidden money (which wasn't there) and then tortured the 69-year-old actor here in his home (eventually beating him to death). Many false rumors still circulate regarding the salacious details of the murder. Novarro was gay, which was still considered taboo in his day, thus prompting many illicit tales regarding his death.

Pacino, Al

Park Avenue
Woonsocket, Rhode Island

On January 7, 1961, two policemen sat in their parked squad car on Park Avenue, well into the graveyard shift. After noticing that the same car had passed them several times,

they pulled it over and then realized that all three occupants were wearing black masks and gloves. The driver was Vincent J. Calcagni, of Rhode Island; his two passengers were 19-year-old Bruce Cohen and 20-year-old Alphonse Pacino, both from New York City.

The cops searched the car's trunk and turned up a loaded .38 caliber pistol. The three men were then taken to the police station and booked, but there is no record of whether Pacino or the others were ever prosecuted or convicted.

Pappalardi, Felix

30 Waterside Plaza
New York City, New York

This is where Felix Pappalardi, the famed producer of the rock super-group Cream in the 1960s and bass player in the group Mountain was shot dead by his wife and collaborator Gail Collins. Police charged his wife in the slaying after receiving a call from her. When police arrived at the apartment, they said they found the musician lying on the bed in his underwear, a single bullet in his neck. Pappalardi, 41, was pronounced dead at the scene. A .38-caliber two-shot Derringer was lying nearby, police said.

Perry, Matthew

2233 Chelon Drive
Hollywood Hills, California

On the afternoon of May 20, 2000, *Friends* star Matthew Perry lost control of his green Porsche 911 near his home here and wound up careening his car through the front porch of a neighbor's home. No charges were filed.

After graduating high school, Perry was offered a leading role on the television series *Boys Will Be Boys* and he seized the opportunity to begin his chosen career. His other TV-series credits include regular roles on *Home Free* and *Sydney* as well as a recurring part on *Growing Pains* before landing his role on *Friends*.

Plato, Dana

Lake Video
Lake East Drive
Las Vegas, Nevada

In the early 1990s, former *Diff'rent Strokes* star Dana Plato donned a hat, coat and sunglasses, and robbed the video store once located here while brandishing a pellet gun. She would soon be arrested and sentenced to probation. Shortly after that, Plato was arrested and charged for forging prescriptions at an area drug store. She was also sentenced to probation in that case. In May 1999, Plato committed suicide in an Oklahoma trailer park.

Priestley, Jason

Canyon Drive (just north of Franklin Avenue)
Hollywood, California

Just after midnight on December 3, 1999, actor Jason Priestly crashed his new Porsche into a light pole and a parked car (a passenger in the car wound up with a broken arm). Though he claimed to have been trying to miss a deer, he was booked for drunk driving and eventually pleaded no contest. He was sentenced to five days in a work-release jail program.

Reynolds, Burt

12050 Ventura Boulevard
Studio City, California

Burt Reynolds used to shoot his show *Evening Shade* at CBS Studio Center near this former bookstore (now a restaurant). One evening in March of 1994, the actor was leaving the store carrying a box of books when he was jumped by two muggers. The attackers knocked Reynolds (who was wearing a cast on his arm at the time) down, but he got up and decked one of them. They ended up fleeing, empty-handed.

Rose, Pete

Jonathan's Café
212 South Main Street
Franklin, Ohio

This site was a central place in the Pete Rose betting scandal; it's the restaurant owned by Ron Peters where the ballplayer would go to place bets and collect money. Ron Peters had been an assistant golf pro at Cincinnati's Beckett Ridge Country Club when he started to see the revenue potential in booking the members' bets. After being fired in 1981, he opened Jonathan's Café with the money he made from bookmaking.

After being confronted here by officials from Major League Baseball, Peters began to cooperate in building the case against Rose. Rose, who was banned from baseball for life because of misconduct related to gambling on August 24, 1989, had a record 4,256 hits during his major-league career and led the Big Red Machine teams of 1975 and 1976 to World Series titles. Today, Jonathan's is gone, replaced by a gas station. Rose recently wrote a book in which he finally admitted to betting on baseball, thus shocking his many supporters who had believed his claim of innocence. Though there was talk of lifting his lifetime ban from baseball, as of this writing Rose is still banned from the game.

Ross, Diana

North Sabino Canyon Road (near East Tanque Verde Road)
Tucson, Arizona

On December 30, 2002, Motown diva and former Supreme Diana Ross was spotted weaving in her car in the southbound lanes of North Sabino Canyon Road. Tucson police pulled her over and, after taking a breath test, it was discovered she was twice over the blood-alcohol legal limit. Police on the scene said Ross couldn't walk a straight line and fell and laughed while trying to stand on one leg and count to 10.

In May of 2002, Ross had entered the Promises drug and alcohol rehabilitation center in Malibu, California before starting her world summer tour. In 2004, Ross was convicted of driving under the influence and ordered to spend two days in jail. She had telephoned into the city court hearing from New York to plead no contest to DUI. Two related charges were dropped.

Roth, David Lee

Washington Square Park
Greenwich Village, New York

On April 18, 1993, former Van Halen singer David Lee Roth was arrested here for pur-chasing marijuana for $10. Roth kept his record clean for the next year and so charges were dropped. Since then Roth has toyed with a Van Halen reunion which never quite got off the ground, and recently he has been training to become an Emergency Medical Technician in New York City.

Saldana, Teresa

Los Angeles City College
855 North Vermont Avenue
Los Angeles, California

On March 15, 1982, actress Theresa Saldana was assaulted in a parking lot here by an obsessed stalker, getting stabbed in the chest and abdomen 26 times. After a long and traumatic recuperation period, she organized "Victims for Victims," a support group for other attack victims. Her story was dramatized in the 1984 TV-movie *Victims for Victims: The Theresa Saldana Story*, in which she played herself.

Simmons, Richard

Terminal Four
Sky Harbor International Airport
Phoenix, Arizona

On Wednesday, March 24, 2004, famed exercise guru Richard Simmons was getting ready to leave for Los Angeles from terminal four. Waiting for his flight at America West's Gate A-9, he was busy signing autographs when 23-year-old Chris Farney, a Harley-Davidson motorcycle salesman, sarcastically yelled out, "Look! Richard Simmons! Drop your bags, let's rock to the '50s!"

The 54-year-old, 5 foot 4 inch Simmons went over to the 6-foot-2-inch, 255-pound Farney, admonished him not to make fun, and then slapped Farney on the right side of his face. Though witnesses described the slap as being light and even playful, police were called. Farney told cops that although he wasn't hurt, he felt Simmons should be held responsible for what he did. A contrite Simmons then got a bit excited and emotional; eventually he was cited for misdemeanor assault by touching and allowed to board his flight.

Slater, Christian

10445 Wilshire Boulevard
West Los Angeles, California

This high-rise condo is where actor Christian Slater was arrested for assault and battery on August 11, 1997. The 27-year-old actor was supposedly tearing through the halls half-

naked after getting into a heated argument with his girlfriend while attending a party. When the party host tried to play peacemaker, Slater allegedly bit him in the stomach. He later told the police that he had been binging on heroin and cocaine and going without sleep. Slater ended up serving 59 days in jail.

Smith, Elliot

1800 block of Lemoyne Street
Silverlake, California

On October 21, 2003, musician Elliot Smith fatally stabbed himself here in his apartment after arguing with a girlfriend, Jennifer Chiba. She told police that she and Smith were arguing when she locked herself in the bathroom. Then, after hearing a scream, she opened the bathroom door and found Smith standing with his back to her. When he turned around, she observed a kitchen knife in his chest. She then pulled the knife out of his chest and saw "two cuts" before he walked away and collapsed.

Chiba called 911 at 12:18 P.M. and performed CPR and first aid with a dispatcher's help until the paramedics arrived shortly after. Elliot Smith died at County-USC Medical Center 78 minutes later. The singer had been battling depression, drugs and alcohol for years, and had attempted suicide once before in 1997. During his lifetime, Elliott released five full-length albums as a solo artist as well as a number of singles. Elliott was nominated for an Academy Award for "Miss Misery", his musical contribution to the Academy Award-winning movie, *Good Will Hunting.*

Souljah, Sister

Hyatt Regency Hotel
400 New Jersey Avenue NW
Washington, DC

On June 13, 1992, Governor Bill Clinton spoke at the Rainbow Coalition convention in Washington. During his speech, he criticized questionable statements made by rap singer Sister Souljah (Lisa Williamson) in reference to the Los Angeles riots. The Reverend Jesse Jackson, founder of the Rainbow Coalition, was present at the event. He was quoted as saying he thought Clinton's comments were intended to embarrass and provoke him.

Clinton had repeated a Washington Post story that quoted Souljah saying after the Los Angeles riots, "If black people kill black people everyday, why not have a week and kill white people?" Clinton responded to the quote, saying: "If you took the words 'white' and 'black' and you reversed them, you might think David Duke was giving that speech." The move by Clinton helped present him to the nation as more of a centrist who was tough on crime and not influenced by special interest groups, and thus helped poise him for the Presidential election that he'd win in the coming months.

Spears, Britney

Aquarium and Pet Center
826 Wilshire Boulevard (9th Street and Wilshire Bouelvard)
Santa Monica, California

In the spring of 2004, Britney Spears, her sister, Jamie Lynn, and her mom visited this pet store to purchase a pair of puppies. As always, the paparazzi swarmed. One photographer claims that Britney's mom hit him with her Toyota Scion while she was backing out of the parking lot.

Video shot at the event shows only the aftermath with the cameraman on the pavement. The footage also captured a very upset Britney Spears who implored to her mother, "Mama, get in the car, get in the damn car!" Cops called to the scene prevented the Spears family from fleeing. When an ambulance arrived, the photographer, identified as Colin Reavley, was taken to the hospital where he was given X-rays (revealing no broken bones).

Stevens, Inger

8000 Woodrow Wilson Drive
Hollywood, California

This is where Swedish actress Inger Stevens committed suicide at age 36 on April 30, 1970. Stevens, whose real name was Inger Stensland, had her greatest success with her leading role in the TV series *The Farmer's Daughter,* and also with roles in TV episodes of series including *The Twilight Zone, Bonanza* and *The Alfred Hitchcock Hour.*

Stewart, Martha

Alderson Federal Prison Camp
Alderson, West Virginia

Nicknamed "Camp Cupcake," this is where celebrity homemaker and businesswoman Martha Stewart was sentenced to stay for five months in 2004 after being convicted of lying to investigators about a stock sale. Built in 1927, Alderson was the first federal prison for women, the vision of Eleanor Roosevelt and Mabel Walker Willebrandt, the first woman appointed to run federal prisons. It is set on a hill in rural West Virginia and it's known for its open environment. There are no metal fences surrounding the camp, and other famous women who have been sentenced here include Billie Holiday; Lynette "Squeaky" Fromme, a member of the Manson family who tried to shoot President Ford; and Sara Jane Moore, who also tried to kill Ford.

Stone, Oliver

2200 block of Benedict Canyon Drive
Beverly Hills, California

It was here where, around midnight on July 16, 1999, Oscar-winning director Oliver Stone was arrested on charges of drunken driving and felony possession of hashish (which

police allegedly found in his black Ford Mustang). Stone posted $12,500 bail and was released the next morning. Later, he would go on to plead no contest to the possession and DUI charges. In return for entering a drug rehab program, he received a suspended sentence.

Swayze, Patrick

Buckshot Road off Arizona 89A (in the Mingus West subdivision)
Just outside Prescott Valley, Arizona

Actor Patrick Swayze, star 1987's *Dirty Dancing* and 1990's *Ghost*, crashed his private plane here on June 1, 2000. Swayze was piloting his twin engine Cessna 414A from Van Nuys, California, to Las Vegas, New Mexico, where he had a ranch. But just after 10 A.M., his plane dropped off the radar at the Albuquerque traffic control center. Several hours later, police found Swayze's plane here on Buckshot Road. The plane had struck a streetlight, losing the right wing section from the engine outward, bounced, crossed an intersection, then struck a stop sign, another streetlight, and an electrical utility box. Trouble was, Swayze could not be found.

Later, three construction workers said that they helped Swayze hide the remnants of a 30-pack of Miller Lite and an almost-empty bottle of wine from the wreckage before Swayze took off. Eventually, the actor surfaced and reported that he was cruising at 13,000 feet when he heard a loud sound. Suspecting a loss in cabin pressure, he hunted out a landing spot along this road. He said he then hitched a ride with a local resident and called authorities. Reports indicate that he called his lawyer, his publicist and his wife. Ultimately, the Safety Board investigators reported a missing clamp and a disconnected hose, which could have caused the loss in cabin pressure.

Tiny Tim

410 Oak Grove Street
Minneapolis, Minnesota

It was here at the Women's Club of Minneapolis that oddball singer Tiny Tim suffered a fatal heart attack in November of 1996. The quirky cult figure who became famous for singing "Tiptoe Through the Tulips" and for getting married on *The Tonight Show* had suffered a heart attack the month before but had resumed performing. During a benefit concert here, Tim (real name Herbert Khaury) told his wife Susan Khaury during the performance that he felt ill. She was trying to help him back to their table when he collapsed and he died later at the local hospital.

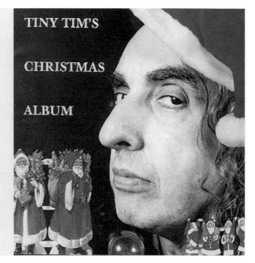

Valentino, Rudolph

Falcon Lair
1436 Bella Drive
Beverly Hills, California

Located a mere stone's throw from the Tate/Manson murder site, Falcon Lair, the Benedict Canyon home built in 1924 for actor Rudolph Valentino, is one of Hollywood's most legendary homes. The silent screen leading man (who died in 1926) lived here for just over a year, but his mark remains on the 4,700-square foot home, both for the rumors of his haunting it and for the salacious tales of the wild parties that took place here.

Valentino immigrated to the U. S. from Italy in 1913 and in 1921 found instant fame from the film *The Four Horsemen of the Apocalypse* (1921), largely due to a suggestive tango scene. Valentino was one of the first true sex symbols in America, and his exotic charm also made his next movies *The Sheik, Blood and Sand, Monsieur Beaucaire* and *The Son of the Sheik* major box office hits, particularly with women. By the time he died, Valentino's "Latin lover" persona had made him the idol of millions.

The words "Falcon Lair" still remain on the front gates from when Valentino christened it with the name. The house also boasts Napoleon Bonaparte's original war room, installed by the late tobacco heiress Doris Duke. Today the house is owned privately. Legend has it that Valentino's ghost can sometimes be seen looking out of his favorite window on the second floor, where city to ocean views can still be enjoyed (on those days when smog is light).

Valentino died while in New York to see his brother Alberto off to Italy. The star collapsed in his Ambassador Hotel room and was taken to the Polyclinic Hospital. After two emergency surgeries, and a brief recovery, Rudolph Valentino died Monday, August 23, 1926 at 12:10 P.M. of peritonitis.

Valentino, Rudolph

Hollywood Forever Cemetery
6000 Santa Monica Boulevard
Tomb 1205
Hollywood, California
323-469-1181

The Hollywood Forever cemetery is the final stop for many "old Hollywood" stars. Director John Huston, Jayne Mansfield, The Ritz Brothers and Carl Switzer (Alfalfa from *The Little Rascals*) are but a few of the famous graves here. But none is more talked about than the crypt of Rudolph Valentino.

Here's why: When Valentino died at the young age of 31 from peritonitis, many fans found this hard to accept. One such person was known as the legendary "Lady in Black," who, for the first 30 or so years Valentino was buried here, would mysteriously visit the grave dressed fully in black, always covering her face with a veil so no one could identify her. From the first day of Valentino's entombment, the Lady in Black would whisk in, place red roses in the flower holders, then rub her glove covered hand over his name and date of birth and death. Then, according to many reports, she would kneel before his tomb and pray.

Just who was the Lady in Black? Reportedly, she was a woman named Ditra Flame. As the story goes, as a child Ditra had become ill. Valentino, a friend of her mother, would visit her hospital bed, place a red rose and say, ". . . if I die before you do, you please come and stay by me because I don't want to be alone either. You come and talk to me." Ditra recovered and when Valentino died on August 23, 1926, she began her ritual. Although she died in the mid-1950s, many believe she still haunts the gravesite.

Vaughn, Vince

Firebelly Lounge
265 North Front Street
Wilmington, North Carolina

Actor Vince Vaughn was arrested here by North Carolina cops in April 2001, and charged with fighting in public for his part in a brawl outside the bar (he was in town filming a movie called *Domestic Disturbance*). During the fight, fellow actor Steve Buscemi was stabbed several times. Vaughn entered a no contest plea and the minor charge was dropped six months later. Timothy Fogerty, the man accused of stabbing actor Steve Buscemi, eventually pleaded guilty to a reduced charge in the incident and received a sentence of 180 days.

Velez, Lupe

732 N. Rodeo Drive
Beverly Hills, California

This is where actress Lupe Velez, dubbed "The Mexican Spitfire," committed suicide on December 13, 1944. She had made close to 50 movies in her lifetime, but none achieved the superstardom she'd hoped for. She had a number of highly publicized affairs before marrying famed swimmer Johnny Weissmuller in 1933.

The tense marriage lasted five years; they repeatedly split and finally divorced in 1938. She went on to have another emotionally draining affair, this time with Gary Cooper. In 1943, she returned to Mexico and starred in *Nana* (1944). Well-received, she returned to Hollywood. Lupe Vélez committed suicide with Seconal in Beverly Hills, California after

the end of her relationship with Harold Raymond, whose child she was carrying. The drug did not work, instead upsetting her stomach; she actually was found dead in her bathroom, having drowned in the toilet. Her suicide has gathered a cruel but grimly amusing story, made into a film by Andy Warhol in 1965 as *Lupe*.

Wallace, Mike

Luke's Bar & Grill
1396 Third Avenue
New York City, New York
212-249-7070

86-year-old CBS *60 Minutes* correspondent Mike Wallace was handcuffed and booked in August 2004, after arguing with New York parking-enforcement inspectors over where his driver had parked (or, presumably, double-parked) while Wallace was in this restaurant. According to the Taxi and Limousine Commission, Wallace became "overly assertive and disrespectful" and interfered with the inspectors, at one point lunged at one of them after being told to shut his mouth. Wallace was issued a summons for disorderly conduct and later released.

Williams, Ted

Alcor Life Extension Foundation
7895 East Acoma Drive, Suite 110
Scottsdale, Arizona

This is the cryonic facility where former Red Sox slugger Ted Williams is being kept on ice until the day when it might be possible to bring him back to life. After suffering a series of strokes and congestive heart failures, he died of cardiac arrest in Crystal River, Florida on July 5, 2002.

1941 — How Ted Hit .400

A public dispute over the disposition of Williams's body was waged after his death. Announcing there would be no funeral, John Henry Williams, Williams's son by his third wife, secretly had his body flown to the Alcor Life Extension Foundation and placed in cryonic suspension. Fearing John Henry was planning to sell their father's DNA for possible cloning, Barbara Joyce Ferrell, Williams's daughter by his first wife, sued, saying his will stated that he wanted to be cremated.

John Henry's lawyer then produced an informal family pact signed by Williams, John Henry, and his sister (Williams's daughter), Claudia, in which they agreed "to be put into biostasis after we die." The dispute was resolved on December 20, 2002 when Ferrell withdrew her objections after a judge agreed that a $645,000 trust would be distributed equally among the siblings.

Today, Williams's head—shaved and drilled with holes (it was also reportedly cracked as many as 10 times due to fluctuating temperatures)—resides at Alcor, resting in a nitrogen-filled steel can alongside his body, which is stored upright in a nitrogen-filled steel tank.

Let There Be Music

Aerosmith

**The Anchorage at Sunapee Harbor
17 Garnet Street
Sunapee, New Hampshire
603-763-3334**

Aerosmith was born right here, when New York drummer Steven Tyler met guitarist Joe Perry at this restaurant where Perry worked in 1970. According to legend, Tyler ate the best French fries he had ever had, and he wanted to meet the cook who made them. He walked into the kitchen and met the cook, who happened to be Joe Perry.

They ended up forming a power trio with Tom Hamilton on bass, and before long, they'd added drummer Joey Kramer and guitarist Brad Whitford. Today, 30 years later, Steven Tyler still eats at the Anchorage. Another Aerosmith landmark is Nipmuc Regional High School, located in nearby Upton, at 90 Pleasant Street. It was there on November 6, 1970, that Aerosmith appeared in their first-ever public performance.

Allman Brothers

The Big House
2321 Vineville Avenue
Macon, Georgia

Back in the 1960s and early 1970s, this big, rambling house was where the Allman Brothers lived communally. On the fateful night that guitarist Duane Allman was killed in a traffic accident, this was the last place he stopped.

The Beach Boys

3701 West 199th Street
Hawthorne, California

The site of the Wilson home, the childhood home of Brian, Dennis, and Carl Wilson (three of the original five Beach Boys) was once located at what would have been this address, which is now near the intersection of West 119th and Kornblum Avenue in Hawthorne. However, it was demolished for the construction of the 105 Freeway in Los Angeles County back in the mid-1980s, so it is impossible to stand in the precise site where the boys all grew up and first decided to start a musical career.

The Beatles

Davlen Studio
4162 Lankershim Boulevard
Universal City, California

In early 2003, an American Internet auction house claimed to have proof that the Beatles reunited in secret in the mid-1970s to record a final album. The website said the recordings had been made at a session in 1976 which ended in an argument between the members of the group. This created a huge controversy, utterly disputed by the remaining band members and management.

The tape label listed the songs "Happy Feeling," "Back Home, Rockin' Once Again," "People of the Third World," and "Little Girl." But, the tape itself was said to be "bulk erased" by the Beatles because the session ended in a disagreement. Larrabee Studios North currently occupies the building where this supposedly mysterious recording happened.

Berry, Chuck

2520 Goode Avenue
St. Louis, Missouri

Rocker Chuck Berry was born in San Jose, California on October 18, 1926. As an infant, Berry moved with his family to this modest house here in St. Louis where they lived for two years. However, Berry would eventually use the name of the street to christen his most famous character in song, Johnny B. Goode.

Bingenheimer, Rodney

7561 Sunset Boulevard
Hollywood, California

In the early 1970s, this was the center of glitter and glam rock and roll along Sunset Boulevard. Rodney Bingenheimer's English Disco was where David Bowie, Marc Bolan,

Led Zeppelin, Queen and dozens of others congregated to listen to live music and hang out. Bingenheimer himself was a local legend–a DJ and tastemaker who earned the unofficial title of "Mayor of Sunset Strip." While Bingenheimer is no longer the fashionable tastemaker he was back in the 1970s and early '80s (when he was instrumental in popularizing the punk rock and new wave genres), he's still on the radio in L.A. with a fervent fan base.

Boarding House

960 Bush Street
San Francisco, California

At one time the Boarding House was the premier rock and roll nightclub venue in the Bay Area. Among the many landmark events that took place at this legendary venue (founded by David Allen) include the recording of Steve Martin's classic comedy album *Let's Get Small*, plus the Bay Area debuts of Albert Brooks, Martin Mull, Robin Williams and George Carlin. Neil Young tested out all of 1978's *Rust Never Sleeps* here, among many other memorable concerts that took place at this site. The Boarding House is no longer in existence; condos now occupy the location.

The Boston Arena

St. Botolph Street
Boston, Massachusetts

Located on the campus of Northeastern University, Boston Arena (now called Matthews Arena) was built in 1910 and is currently home to both the men's and women's hockey teams at the school. But, it was once home to two famous musical events: The Big Beat Show and the Motown Revue.

The first took place on May 3, 1958, when a concert staged by legendary disc jockey Alan Freed resulted in a riot. Freed would soon be in trouble for all of the infamous "payola" scandals and many believe this concert riot was the beginning of his end. That concert was called "The Big Beat Show" and featured Buddy Holly & the Crickets, Chuck Berry, Jo-Anne Campbell and Jerry Lee Lewis.

Secondly, in 1962, the first ever Motown Revue was held here. The famous traveling show featured many acts including Mary Wells, Marvin Gaye and The Supremes.

Boston Tea Party

53 Berkeley Street
Boston, Massachusetts

This former synagogue once held a place as one of country's prime rock palaces. Opened in 1967 as the Boston Tea Party, this was where everyone from Led Zeppelin to the Velvet Underground played back in the late 1960's. In fact, it was here that Velvet Underground member John Cale played his last gig with the influential group, to be replaced by Boston local Doug Yule (who had chatted with the members backstage).

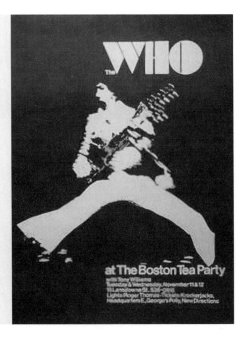

The venue was also a breeding ground for lots of local talent including Willie Alexander's The Lost and Peter Wolf's The Hallucinations (a band he was in before fronting J. Geils). In 1969, the Boston Tea Party moved to a location adjacent to Fenway Park, where it remains today as The Avalon.

The Carter Family Memorial Music Center

A.P. Carter Highway
Hiltons, Virginia
276-386-9480

The Carter family is the most influential group in country music history. Their influence of switching the emphasis from hillbilly instrumentals to vocals made many of their songs part of the standard country music canon, and made a style of guitar playing, "Carter-picking," the dominant technique for decades. Today, they celebrate their legacy in their own backyard.

Their center serves fans and supporters of old-time country and folk music through the presentation of weekly performances here at the Carter Family Fold. It also honors the memory of the first family of country music, the legendary Carter Family (A.P. Carter, Sara Carter, and Maybelle Carter), whose first recordings (in 1927) are credited with giving birth to the commercial country music industry. Here in this beautiful rural area, within several miles of each other, are several historic landmarks connected to the Carters.

One such site is A.P.'s birthplace, an old log cabin that is now an officially designated National Historic Site, which has been moved from an inaccessible, remote area unavailable to automobiles and visitors. It now is in the final stages of restoration and is permanently positioned right next door to The Carter Fold.

The two houses—A.P. and Sara's house, and Maybelle and Ezra's home—are still owned and occupied by family members so they're not open to the public, but they may be seen from the A.P. Carter Highway. The A.P. Carter Store, a general store owned and operated by A.P. Carter in the later years of his life, is now The Carter Family Museum. Located right next door to the Fold, it is open on Saturdays and during the festival each year. Tours at other times can be pre-arranged by calling 276-386-9480.

Charles, Ray

2107 West Washington Boulevard
Los Angeles, California

This building housed both the office and recording studios of the late legendary singer, Ray Charles. Since 1963, Charles had operated out of here and recorded, in addition to himself, Stevie Wonder, Billy Preston and Quincy Jones. Charles, who passed away in 2004, crafted a brilliant career as a singer, pianist, and composer.

His songs combined gospel, blues, pop, country, and jazz. Charles, who was blind since age seven, paved the way for such artists as Elvis Presley and Aretha Franklin among others. He won 12 Grammy Awards. His hits over the years include "Georgia on My Mind," "Drown in My Own Tears," and "I Got a Woman."

Coltrane, John

Birthplace

Hamlet Avenue at Bridges Street
Hamlet, North Carolina

A plaque here marks the birthplace of legendary jazz saxophonist and composer John Coltrane (1926-1967). Coltrane began playing tenor saxophone as a teen and worked with numerous big bands before coming into his own in the mid-1950s. He became a major stylist while playing as a sideman with Miles Davis. Coltrane made a number of influential recordings, among them the modal-jazz classics "My Favorite Things" (1961) and "A Love Supreme" (1964). On July 17, 1967 John Coltrane died due to complications arising from his years of alcohol and drug abuse.

Coltrane, John

Childhood Home

200 South Centennial Street
High Point, North Carolina

John Coltrane (1926–1967) grew up in North Carolina. The commemorative marker at the corner of Centennial Street and Commerce Avenue is located near his boyhood home on Underhill Street.

"Blue Train" House

1511 North 33rd Street
Philadelphia, Pennsylvania

In 1952, after returning home from the Navy and with funds provided by the GI Bill of Rights, John Coltrane, saxophonist, family man, and native of Hamlet, North Carolina purchased this three-story brick row house. The house was situated within the area known by locals as Strawberry Mansion, a working-class neighborhood populated at that time by families of diverse ethnic backgrounds. The 26-year-old Coltrane bought the house for himself, his mother, his aunt and his cousin and it is here where he composed the legendary "Blue Train" and several other tunes.

Crash, Darby

137 North Fuller Avenue
Hollywood, California

Darby Crash, lead singer of seminal Los Angles punk band The Germs died here on the morning of December 7, 1980. He and his girlfriend, Casey, both left suicide notes and took supposedly lethal doses of heroin. But while Darby died, Casey survived. The death was largely under-reported due to the fact that the very next day John Lennon was shot outside his New York City apartment.

Crosby, David

Medallion Plaza
6400 East Northwest Highway
Dallas, Texas

On April 12, 1982, back when it was a Cardi's nightclub, this was where singer/songwriter David Crosby was caught freebasing cocaine backstage. (The cops arresting Crosby also found he was in possession of a loaded .45 pistol.) He was arrested and eventually did time at a rehab center in New Jersey before skipping out and winding up in the Texas State Penitentiary.

Davis, Miles

312 West 77th Street
New York City, New York

This red townhouse is a former Russian Orthodox church and was jazzman Miles Davis's home from the early 1960s through the early 1980s. He recorded several classic albums while living here, including *Miles Smiles* and *Bitches Brew*. He left in the early 1980s after becoming involved with actress Cicely Tyson (whom he eventually married). Miles Davis continued to tour and per-

form regularly through the last years of his life, before passing away in September 1991 at the age of 65. Davis had entered St. John's Hospital in Santa Monica, California for what he described to his friends as a "tune-up." On the 28th of that month, he died from pneumonia and a respiratory failure.

The Doors

Aquarius Theater
6230 Sunset Boulevard
Hollywood, California

The Aquarius Theater opened in 1938 as the shimmering landmark, The Earl Carroll Theater, a nightclub/theater that was home to the "Most beautiful girls in the world." By

1968, it had become the Aquarius Theater, home of the production of *Hair*. It was also here that Elektra Records staged the comeback of one of their once biggest bands, The Doors. The shows were recorded for the album, *Live at the Aquarius Theater*. A rehearsal recorded here at the time of these legendary shows was also released commercially. Songs included "Touch Me," "Who Do You Love" and "Crystal Ship."

Dylan, Bob

Forest Hills Tennis Stadium
1 Tennis Place
Forest Hills, New York

As detailed in *James Dean Died Here,* Bob Dylan's 1965 performance at the Newport Folk Festival outraged folk purists who resented his new electric sound. A month later, Dylan played here (at a venue which had also recently hosted The Beatles). Dylan's first set was acoustic, which many loved. But then for Act II he trooped out a band that included Levon Helm and Robbie Robertson and, like in Newport, many people became outraged, this time throwing fruit and garbage at the stage before leaving.

Ellington, Duke

2129 Ward Place Northwest
Washington, D.C.

A plaque on the office building that's here marks it as the spot where the great Edward Kennedy "Duke" Ellington was born on April 29, 1899. The innovative composer, band-leader, and pianist would become recognized as one of the greatest jazz composers and performers in the world. Nicknamed "Duke" by a boyhood friend who admired his regal air, the name stuck and became forever associated with the finest creations in big band and vocal jazz.

His genius for instrumental combinations, improvisation, and arranging brought the world exquisite works like "Mood Indigo," "Sophisticated Lady," and the symphonic suites "Black, Brown, and Beige" (which he subtitled "a Tone Parallel to the History of the Negro in America") and "Harlem" (which he subtitled "a Tone Parallel to Harlem").

Eminem

8427 Timken Street
Warren, Michigan

This is the house that rapper Eminem grew up in—a three-bedroom, two-bath house that has been in his family for over 50 years (until his uncle sold it to two business men who put it up for auction on eBay—high bid, $11 million). The contro-versial rapper is one of the biggest-selling recording artists on the planet, with CDs such as *The Marshall Mathers LP* and *The Eminem Show.*

Thee Experience

7601 Sunset Boulevard
Hollywood, California

In the late 1960s, this famous building featured a huge painting of Jimi Hendrix's head on the front door–so to enter you had to walk through his mouth. Hendrix jammed here many times, as did Led Zeppelin and many others, including the Bonzo Dog Band, Messenger Service, The Blues Magoos, Alice Cooper and Bo Diddley. Today, the building still stands but it's an auction house.

Fender Guitars

Corner of Santa Fe and Pomona Streets
Fullerton, California

Guitar design-wiz Leo Fender once operated his factory on this site, where he mass-produced his breakthrough creations such as the Fender Broadcaster, the Telecaster and the Fender Precision Bass from 1945-1952. Though he never played guitar himself, Fender was inducted into the Rock and Roll Hall of Fame a few months after his death in 1991. Fender was born right here in Fullerton on August 10, 1909 and has displayed a certain genius for electrical engineering since his youth.

Fox Venice

620 Lincoln Avenue
Venice, California

In the mid-1970s, this theater was one of the most active creative hotspots in the greater Los Angeles area. Movies were screened here, there were Love-Ins, and lots of noted concerts, featuring bands such as Little Feat, Big Joe Turner and Bonnie Raitt. In fact, John Lee Hooker recorded a live album here with Canned Heat (*Live at the Fox Venice*). Today, it still stands, but it's an indoor swap meet.

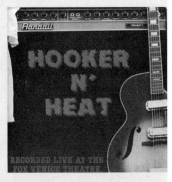

Franklin, Aretha

New Bethel Baptist Church
8450 C.L. Franklin Boulevard
Detroit, Michigan

In the 1950s, the Reverend C.L. Franklin preached and sang here (he was also a recording artist on Chess Records in Chicago). His three daughters performed here as well, one of whom was Aretha Franklin.

Gershwin, George

George Gershwin was born on September 26, 1898, in Brooklyn, New York. His original name was Jacob Gershwin and he became one of the most significant and popular American composers of all time. He wrote primarily for the Broadway musical theatre, but important as well are his orchestral and piano compositions in which he blended, in varying degrees, the techniques of classical music with the stylistic nuances and melodic styles of popular music and jazz. Here are some important sites related to his life:

Childhood Home

91 Second Avenue
New York City, New York

This red brick building with the storefront on the ground level is one of the early homes of the Gershwin family. In 1910, when George was 12 years old and his brother Ira was 14 years old, they resided here above a phonograph shop. One day a van appeared, unloaded a piano and hoisted it up to the Gershwin apartment. Mrs. Gershwin had bought it.

"No sooner had it come through the window and been backed up against the wall than I was at the keys," Gershwin later recalled. "I must have crowded out Ira very soon for the plan originally had been to start him off on the instrument." Gershwin learned to play it almost immediately without the benefit of lessons. Within six years he had published his first song.

Gershwin auditioned for various piano teachers for two years, then met Charles Hambitzer, who became his mentor. Hambitzer taught Gershwin conventional piano technique, introduced him to the European masters, and encouraged him to attend orchestral concerts (at home following such concerts, young Gershwin would attempt to reproduce at the keyboard the music he had heard).

Gershwin, George

First Songwriting Job

45 West 28th Street
New York City, New York

Located along "Tin Pan Alley," this is the former site of the Jerome Remick Music Co., where a teenaged George Gershwin worked as a "song plugger" from 1914–1917. While he worked there, the 15-year-old Gershwin began to experiment with his own compositions.

Two of his customers were Fred and Adele Astaire, then a teenage song-and-dance team in vaudeville, who later starred in two Gershwin Broadway musicals. It was also here where Gershwin met Irving Caesar, with whom he would go on to write the famous "Swanee." The young Gershwin worked here until 1917, when he left to write and publish his own songs.

"Rhapsody in Blue" Home

501 West 110th Street
New York City, New York

George Gershwin (along with his brother and lyricist, Ira) lived here from 1924–1929. It was in this apartment that Gershwin composed the seminal "Rhapsody in Blue." The song, the title of which was suggested by George's lyric-writing brother Ira, is for many Gershwin's most recognizable piece, a stunning blend of jazz and classical music that has been performed by the world's greatest orchestras (and used in countless films, television shows, and commercials).

Gershwin, George

First Performance of "Rhapsody in Blue"

Aeolian Hall
33 West 42nd Street
New York City, New York

Aeolian Hall is now part of City College of New York, but back in the 1920s it was a performance space. It was here on February 12, 1924 that George Gershwin first publicly performed "Rhapsody in Blue." He played it on piano as part of a program called the "First American Jazz Concert" that was presented by Paul Whiteman.

Hudson River Home

316 West 103rd Street
New York City, New York

George Gershwin also owned this small stone house near the Hudson River, where he lived with his family from 1925-1931. He purchased it in the hopes that it would give him a quieter place to work given how famous he was becoming, but to no avail—the house was regularly overrun with visitors and guests. A plaque on the side of the building details the Gershwin history there.

Last Residence

1019 North Roxbury Drive
Beverly Hills, California

This was the last residence of George Gershwin. While working on the score of *The Golden Follies* he collapsed into a coma and later died in Beverly Hills, California, on July 11, 1937, from a brain tumor. Gershwin was just 38 years old. The hospital where he died after his surgery was Cedars of Lebanon Hospital in Hollywood. Today, the blue-towered landmark houses the Church of Scientology.

Grateful Dead

The Château

838 Santa Cruz Avenue
Menlo Park, California

Back in the early 1960s, a rambling old house stood here, sort of a hostel for various musicians, artists and beatniks. Banjo player Jerry Garcia resided here with lyricist Robert Hunter. So, for many fans, this is the group's spiritual birthplace.

Magoo's Pizza Parlor

639 Santa Cruz Avenue
Menlo Park, California

When the Grateful Dead first started up as The Warlocks, they'd play a local pizza place, Magoo's Pizza Parlor, which had been located at 639 Santa Cruz Avenue in Menlo Park. Today, the site is a furniture store.

Lesh, Phil

1012 High Street
Palo Alto, California

The Warlocks met here at band member Phil Lesh's house in 1965 and decided a name change was in order. Thumbing through an encyclopedia, they came upon a reference to "the grateful dead" and settled on that as the new group name. Their first gig under that name took place in December, 1965.

Mars Hotel

192 Fourth Street
San Francisco, California

This run down, skid row flophouse was immortalized by the band on their 1974 album *From the Mars Hotel*.

The album included the soon-to-be Dead classics "U.S. Blues," "Scarlet Begonias" and "Ship of Fools."

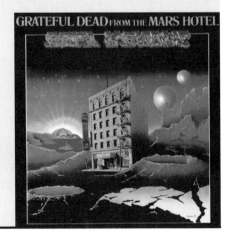

Grateful Dead

The Onion

9550 Haskell Avenue
Sepulveda, California

The odd-shaped Onion-dome Church can be rented today for many different kinds of events (and it is). But, in February, 1966, The Grateful Dead played here as part of the infamous Acid Test Series, organized by the LSD-touting group The Merry Pranksters, who

were "led" by author Ken Kesey. The Acid Tests were chronicled by author Tom Wolfe in his seminal work, *The Electric Kool-Aid Acid Test.* The Acid Test parties and Wolfe's book were catalysts for the "Love Generation" migration to San Francisco for the storied Summer of Love.

Royal Sonesta Hotel

300 Bourbon Street
New Orleans, Louisiana
504-586-0300

In the legendary Grateful Dead song, "Truckin'," the band sings of being "Busted, down on Bourbon Street." The lyric was based on a real incident that took place in room 2134 of this Big Easy hotel in January, 1970. Though marijuana and hashish was recovered in the room by undercover cops, charges against several band members were eventually dropped.

Soldier Field

425 East McFetridge Drive
Chicago, Illinois

The Grateful Dead played their last shows here in Chicago on July 8-9, 1995. Guitarist Jerry Garcia died later that year from drug complications, thus ending the band's tenure.

Great Lawn

Mid-Central Park from 79th to 85th Streets
New York City, New York

The Great Lawn is a 13-acre oval lawn with a carpet of lush Kentucky Bluegrass and eight ball-fields. This green area is famous for being a beautiful place for reading and contemplation, as well as for playing Frisbee and having a picnic among friends. It has also become a favorite for free concerts by the New York Philharmonic and the Metropolitan Opera. In addition, it has hosted famous concerts by Simon and Garfunkel (their reunion) and Diana Ross (in the rain). Adjacent to the Great Lawn is The Metropolitan Museum of Art, Turtle Pond, Belvedere Castle and the famed Delacorte Theater.

Green, Al

Full Gospel Tabernacle
787 Hale Road
Whitehaven, Tennessee

Just a few miles south of Graceland is a place where you can hear one of soul's sweetest voices at work. This is where the Reverend Al Green preaches (when he's not on the road). When he's there, he packs them in just as he did at concert halls in he 1970s. Green found faith in the 1970s after a girlfriend threw a hot pan of grits in his face.

Guns 'n' Roses

1114 North Clark Street
Hollywood, California

In the early 1980s, this apartment complex was where the band Guns 'n' Roses lived with their then-manager, Vicky Hamilton. The pad is located right near the famous Whiskey nightclub, where the band would often hang out.

Haley, Bill

Corner of Crosby and Fifth Streets
Chester, Pennsylvania

Located about 14 miles southwest of Philadelphia, a star embedded in the sidewalk here marks the former home (it burned down many years ago) of rocker Bill Haley of "Rock Around the Clock" fame.

Hendrix, Jimi

Garfield High School

400 23rd Avenue
Seattle, Washington

Jimi Hendrix attended high school here before dropping out to join the Army (he was later given an honorary diploma). Other famous attendees of this school were music great Quincy Jones and martial arts legend Bruce Lee. There is a bronze bust of Hendrix located in the library.

Hilton Hotel

720 South Michigan Avenue
Chicago, Illinois

The Plaster Casters were a bunch of 1960's groupies whose claim to fame was immortalizing their rock and roll conquests in the form of plastic molds. That's right—they'd actually make molds of the rock star's private parts. Jimi Hendrix became immortalized in February, 1968, in room 1628 of the Chicago Hilton. (And no, the hotel does not acknowledge what took place here.)

Hendrix, Jimi

Hotel Theresa

2090 Adam Clayton Powell Boulevard
New York City, New York

The office building you'll find here today was once one of Harlem's finest hotels. Many musicians and celebrities stayed here; it's even where Cuban President Fidel Castro stayed in 1960. When Jimi Hendrix first came to the Big Apple in January, 1964, he stayed here as well.

In fact, during that stay Hendrix won the Apollo Theater's weekly amateur contest. In May of 1965, Hendrix returned to the hotel, staying in room 416 while playing in Little Richard's band during an Apollo stand (under the name Maurice James).

Greenwood Memorial Park

4th Street and Monroe Avenue
Renton, Washington

This is the grave of Jimi Hendrix, who overdosed in London on September 18, 1970. Today, it's become a shrine for Hendrix fans all over the world. The graveyard is located in Renton, a suburb of Seattle, which was Jimi's birthplace. The site contains the graves of Hendrix, his half-brother Leon, half-sister Janie, father Al Hendrix and his wife Ayako. Hendrix's headstone reads: "Forever In Our Hearts–James M. "Jimi" Hendrix–1942-1970."

Holiday, Billie

First New York Apartment

108 West 109th Street
New York City, New York

When Billie Holiday first arrived in New York during the Depression she moved into this five-story apartment building with her mom. While living here, their place became a sort of crash pad for all kinds of hand-to-mouth musicians that the Holidays took pity on.

Also while living here, Holiday discovered that her future was not as a dancer, but as a singer. She failed a dance audition at a club called Pod's and Jerry's (at 168 West 132nd Street), but a piano player there asked if she could sing. Sing she did, and that's where she first started appearing before an audience.

Last New York Apartment

26 West 87th Street
New York City, New York

This was Billie Holliday's last New York apartment, where she lived during the final year of her life. By now she was a sad and lonely singer, whose career had all but dried up. Her health was poor, and on May 31, 1959 she collapsed and fell into a coma. She was rushed to the hospital and treated for drug addiction and alcoholism. While she was there, police found heroin in her room (many believe it was planted by a "well-wisher"). Her condition deteriorated and she died in the hospital on July 17th. The great "Lady Day" (as she is still called) remains one of the most revered jazz singers in history—a tortured soul who still manages to influence many singers the world over.

Holiday, Billie

Metropolitan Hospital

1901 First Avenue
New York City, New York

The great jazz singer Billie Holliday died here (under police guard) in room 6A-12 on Friday, July 17, 1959. She was just 44 years old. Holliday is buried in St. Raymond's Cemetery in the Bronx, right beside her mother.

Holly, Buddy

Childhood Home

1911 6th Street
Lubbock, Texas

This is the house where the Holley family lived at the time their fourth child, Charles Hardin Holley, was born on September 7, 1936. He would one day become "Buddy," and would also drop the "e" from his last name. A vacant lot sits where the house used to stand.

Fair Park Coliseum

Avenue A and 10th Street
Lubbock, Texas

Back in the mid-1950s, Buddy Holly and the Crickets played on the bottom part of tickets at concerts for both Elvis Presley and Bill Haley and the Comets here at this local arena (which still stands today). Holly's influence can still be felt all around his home town, especially at the Buddy Holly Center, located at 1801 Ave. G in Lubbock. One part museum, one part art center, it's a fittingly named place for a favorite local son.

Holly, Buddy

Hutchinson Junior High

3102 Canton Avenue
Lubbock, Texas

Buddy formed a duet here with his friend Bob Montgomery. Calling themselves "The Bob and Buddy Show," they'd regularly entertain at school functions.

Riverside Ballroom

115 Newhall Street
Green Bay, Wisconsin

On February 1, 1959, what would be Buddy Holly's final tour, The Winter Dance Party, became stranded en route to Appleton, Wisconsin. The bus had broken down with temperatures at 30 degrees below zero and no source of heat. Still, the tour somehow rolled on and Buddy and his crew (including Ritchie Valens) performed that night at the Riverside Ballroom here in Green Bay, Wisconsin (built in 1929).

It was their second to last performance (the last show was performed the next night in Clear Lake Iowa at the Surf Ballroom, all details of which appear in *James Dean Died Here*). However, outside the club is a touching memorial to the three fallen singers, commemorating their appearance here in Wisconsin.

Jackson Five

2300 Jackson Street
Gary, Indiana

This two-bedroom clapboard house is where Joe and Katherine Jackson lived with their nine children before striking it rich with the Jackson Five and moving to Southern California. Note: the street is not named for the family—it had already been named for President Jackson. Other notable stars hailing from Gary, Indiana include Tom Harmon; Hank Stram; actors Karl Malden, Alex Karras, Fred Williamson, and William Marshall; astronaut Frank Borman; and basketball's Dick Barnett.

Jackson Five

Garnett Elementary School
2131 Jackson Street
Gary, Indiana

One of Michael Jackson's first big performing moments happened here at the school that all of the Jackson Five attended. In 1963, the five-year old singer brought the house down with his version of "Climb Every Mountain" from *The Sound of Music*. Michael's first professional debut happened a year later at a club called Mr. Lucky's Lounge, which is still located at 1100 Grant Street in Gary.

Joplin, Janis

380 West Baltimore Avenue
Larkspur, California

This rustic, redwood-paneled home was Janis Joplin's last official residence. Situated up in the then-bohemian Marin County, one of her neighbors was Jerry Garcia. Joplin moved in here in December, 1969, and spent a reasonably peaceful last year of her life here before dying of a heroin overdose in Hollywood.

Laurel Canyon Country Store

2108 Laurel Canyon Boulevard
Los Angeles, California

Built in 1919, this casual market has served as a location for several films and is also a hangout for many Laurel Canyon artists, musician and actors. It feels like a small-town store—a cozy place where you just might run into Liam Neeson, Sophia Loren or Mick

Jagger. Back in the early 1970s, members of the Eagles, The Byrds, The Doors and other local rock and roll residents could always be found here. (A stone's throw from the market is a wood house where Jim Morrison used to live.)

Leadbelly

414 East 10th Street
New York City, New York

Famed bluesman Leadbelly (nee Huddie Ledbetter) lived in the building throughout the 1940s. While residing here, he entertained the likes of many legendary musicians including Woody Guthrie and Pete Seeger. Leadbelly had become a monumental figure in the history of folk music. He was "discovered" by the influential father-son team of folk-rock historians, John and Alan Lomax, in prison in Louisiana, where he was recorded on portable equipment.

It is claimed by Alan Lomax that the state govenor, O.K. Allen, pardoned him after Allen heard his recordings, which supposedly included an appeal by song directed to him. Leadbelly subsequently toured extensively but ended up back in prison in 1939, convicted of assault. (He served four separate prison terms for his violent behavior.) It was after this last prison term that Leadbelly moved to this apartment in 1940.

Lewis, Jerry Lee

1595 Malone Road
Nesbit, Mississippi
662-429-1290

Incredibly, you can take a personal tour at the home and ranch of the "Killer" himself, Jerry Lee Lewis. You can see the gold records, the pianos, the piano shaped swimming pool and tons of personal effects (plus the "Killer Kar Kollection," as Jerry Lee calls it). You may even see Jerry Lee himself if he's home. There are few (if any) other chances to witness a living legend in his own surroundings, and note, you have to call to book a tour reservation—don't just show up.

Also, if you want more Jerry Lee, visit the Jerry Lee Lewis Family Museum in Ferriday, Louisiana. Jerry's sister, Frankie Jean Lewis will personally guide you through the museum, which is located at 712 Louisiana Avenue in Ferriday. Call 318-757-2460 for tours. The museum (located in Jerry Lee's childhood home) is filled with pictures and "Killer" memorabilia.

Limp Bizkit

Peacock's Tattoo Studio
11233 Beach Boulevard
Jacksonville, Florida

This is where Fred Durst famously tattooed the band Korn while they were in town for a gig. He slipped them his Limp Bizkit demo tape while giving them their tattoos, thus launching the band's career. Their first album, *Three Dollar Bill Y'All$*, featured the singles "Counterfeit," "Faith" (a George Michael cover), and "Stuck," among others. The album went multi-platinum.

Madonna

234 East 4th Street
New York City, New York

When she first set out to conquer the music world, this is where Madonna lived. The year was 1978, back when both Madonna and the neighborhood were pretty poor. Trained as a dancer at the University of Michigan before moving to New York City, her albums *Madonna* (1983) and *Like a Virgin* (1984) secured her position as a universal pop icon.

Marley, Bob

First American Performance
Paul's Mall
733 Boylston
Boston, Massachusetts

Bob Marley and the Wailers made their U.S. live debut at the funky old jazz club called Paul's Mall. The set included the songs, "Lively Up Yourself," "Stir It Up," "Concrete Jungle" and "Get Up Stand Up." The club closed a long time ago but in its day featured the best jazz, blues and rock and roll artists of the day, including Muddy Waters, B.B. King and Bruce Springsteen.

Marley, Bob

Final Performance
Stanley Theater
719 Liberty Avenue
Pittsburgh, Pennsylvania

Bob Marley's last performance of his life was in Pittsburgh at the Stanley Theater, now called the Benedum Center. The show took place on September 23, 1980, and Marley had already become gravely ill with cancer. The set list included such classics as "No Woman, No Cry," "Jamming," "Exodus" and "Is This Love?" The great reggae legend died on May 11, 1981, at the Cedars of Lebanon Hospital in Miami, Florida. Bob Marley was just 36 years old.

McCartney, Paul

WKNR
15001 Michigan Avenue
Detroit, Michigan

Remember the infamous "Paul is dead" rumor that hinted that Beatle Paul McCartney had secretly died and was replaced by a look-alike? This is where it started. On October 12, 1969, WKNR-FM's popular DJ Russ Gibb opened the phone lines for his usual Sunday afternoon "rap" with his listeners. Then came the call that changed history.

Eastern Michigan University Student Tom Zarski called with questions about the supposed death of Paul, thus beginning so the tale that would immortalize both Russ and station WKNR-FM in Beatle lore. DJs, television news reporters, newspapers, and magazines picked up on the story (which had been rumored for a year or two after a supposed car accident McCartney had) and began to look for clues.

The rumor eventually became a full-fledged conspiracy theory as members of the media and Beatles fans searched album artwork and song lyrics for clues to the cover-up and McCartney's supposed death.

Believers had many theories, many of which revolved around the cover of the famed *Abbey Road* album. The cover photo was thought to be a funeral procession, with John

 Lennon leading the way while wearing white (symbolizing clergy) and Ringo Starr, dressed in black (playing the undertaker). Paul, the corpse, is out of step with the other Beatles, pictured barefoot and with his eyes closed. George Harrison is wearing work clothes, supposedly as the gravedigger.

Behind the band on the left side of the street is a Volkswagen Beetle with a license plate reading "28IF," suggesting that Paul would have been 28 years old if he were still alive. (Paul would actually have been just 27 when *Abbey Road* was released.) There's more: Believers eventually decided that McCartney had died in a car accident that happened at 5:00 A.M. on a Wednesday morning (the time and day, mentioned in the song "She's Leaving Home"), and that "he hadn't noticed that the lights had changed" ("A Day In The Life") because he was busy watching the pretty girl on the sidewalk ("Lovely Rita").

According to believers, McCartney had been replaced with the winner of a McCartney look-alike contest. The name of this look-alike has been recorded as either William Campbell or William Shears. Though all four members have denied it numerous times, many fans are convinced that the rumor was a hoax perpetrated deliberately by the Beatles as a joke. Today, the building that once housed WKNR is empty.

McCartney, Paul

The Truckee Hotel
10007 Bridge Street
Truckee, California
530-587-4444

In early 2003, regulars enjoying the Truckee Hotel's usual Thursday night jazz duo got a shock when Paul McCartney took to the small stage for an impromptu song he called "Truckee Blues." McCartney sang at about 10:30 P.M. Thursday after he and wife, Heather Mills, dined incognito at Moody's Bistro and Lounge in the Sierra ski town's historic hotel about 15 miles from Lake Tahoe.

Metallica

Tommy's Joynt
1101 Geary at Van Ness
San Francisco, California
415-775-4216

In September of 1986, Metallica bassist Cliff Burton was killed in a bus crash while the band was on tour in Sweden. After auditioning a slew of other bassists as potential candidates to replace Burton, they brought Jason Newsted here to this legendary San Francisco eatery (famous for its Beef Stew) to offer him the job.

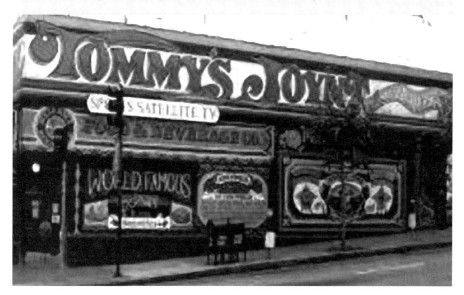

Nirvana

Maria's Hair Design

107 S. M Street
Aberdeen, Washington

Maria's Hair Design is the shop owned by Nirvana bassist Krist Novoselic's mom, and it's where Krist and Kurt Cobain practiced many a night during the early days of Nirvana.

Morrison Riverfront Park

Sargent Boulevard

Riverfront Park is the site of the much publicized fan vigil the night of Kurt Cobain's death.

Seafirst Bank Building

Market Street and Broadway

On July 23rd, 1985, Kurt Cobain was arrested for vandalism when he was caught writing "Ain'T goT no how waTchamacalliT" on the alley wall behind this bank (though today it's a Bank of America).

No Doubt

1173 Beacon Avenue
Anaheim, California

The members of the Southern California band No Doubt moved into this house, the former home of Eric and Gwen Stefani's grandparents. They built a recording studio in the garage which is where they cut their initial demos, not to mention a few of the songs that would wind up on their breakout 1996 album *Tragic Kingdom.* The album featured the songs "Don't Speak," "Just a Girl" and "Sunday Morning."

Orbison, Roy

City Hall
205 East Hendricks Boulevard
Wink, Texas

Singer Roy Orbison spent his youth in this tiny town, located about 54 miles west of Odessa. To honor their native son, a small museum and gift shop was created (with future plans for a plaque, statue, etc.). The influential musician died at the age of 52 on December 6, 1988, suffering a heart attack while visiting at his mother's home in Hendersonville, a suburb of Nashville, Tennessee. He actually was pronounced dead at the Hendersonville Hospital, located at 355 New Shackle Island Road in Hendersonville, Tennessee.

Parker, Charlie

Camarillo State Mental Hospital

California State University, Channel Islands
One University Drive
Camarillo, California

Until 1997, this was the Camarillo State Mental Hospital, where jazz legend Charlie Parker spent six months in 1947. The brilliant sax player had suffered a breakdown that, coupled with heroin and alcohol abuse, led to his confinement at the hospital. Parker was released from Camarillo in late January, 1947. He eventually died in New York City on March 12, 1955, at the age of just 36.

Parker, Charlie

Dewey Square

Adam Clayton Powell Boulevard and 118th Street
New York City, New York

This small, triangle-shaped park is where Charlie Parker sat and created a musical work called "Dewey Square." Today, the park is called A. Philip Randolph Triangle.

New York Home

151 Avenue B
New York City, New York

From 1950 to 1954 this was the home of the bop saxophonist Parker, his friend Chan, and their two sons. Parker is honored with a building plaque. He is also remembered with the Charlie Parker Jazz Festival held every summer in Tompkins Square Park.

Paul, Les

1514 Curson Avenue
Hollywood, California

This is the former site of where guitar genius and innovator Les Paul lived in the 1940s and 1950s with his wife, singer Mary Ford. In the garage that used to be located here, Paul developed his famous multi-track recording technique and the guitar that today bears his name.

Peppermint Lounge

128 West 45th (in the Knickerbocker Hotel)
New York City, New York

This became a hotspot in 1961 after the house band Joey Dee and the Starlighters released the record, *The Peppermint Twist.* The song became #1 in the nation and any-

one who was anyone flocked to the "Pep" to dance the dance in the club that made it famous. (The band followed the hit record by recording "Doin' the Twist at the Peppermint Lounge" live at the club—it was not nearly as popular.) The club no longer exists.

Presley, Elvis

Previous books *James Dean Died Here* and *Marilyn Monroe Dyed Here* documented several key Elvis-related sites, from his birthplace to where his first concert and last concert took place, among others. Here are some more that go even further, including the site that inspired the name of this book:

Arcade Restaurant

**540 South Main Street
Memphis, Tennessee
901-526-5757**

Here at the Arcade, you can sit in a booth (on the very same cushions no less) that a young Elvis sat on while sipping malts during his breaks as a driver for Crown Electric. After he became famous in the late 1950s, he still came, but he'd sit by the side door to avoid being recognized right away. There's even a small silver plaque that reads, "Elvis Presley's Booth Since 1953." The Arcade is the oldest restaurant in Memphis; it opened in 1919.

ARCADE RESTAURANT
MEMPHIS' OLDEST CAFE
HAS BEEN PLACED ON THE
NATIONAL REGISTER
OF HISTORIC PLACES
BY THE UNITED STATES
DEPARTMENT OF THE INTERIOR
Est. 1919

Presley, Elvis

Baptist Memorial Hospital

899 Madison Avenue
Memphis, Tennessee

Elvis has checked in and out of here for various ailments over the years but he was pronounced dead here in August 1977. (Lisa Marie Presley had been born here in February of 1968.)

Bloch Arena

Building 161 Bloch Arena
Pearl Harbor
Honolulu, Hawaii
808-422-0139

On March 25, 1961, Elvis Presley made his first post-Army appearance for the Navy. The King performed in a charity fund-raiser here at Bloch Arena to revitalize the flagging USS Arizona Memorial building fund. It is an event largely unremembered, even though Elvis essentially saved the day.

More than a thousand U.S. sailors were entombed in the battleship in Pearl Harbor when a bomb ripped apart the bow, splitting the hull. It sank in minutes and the bodies were never recovered. Dozens of plans were proposed to memorialize the crew of the Arizona, the U.S. Navy's single greatest loss of life, but for nearly 20 years military efforts at raising funds were fumbling and disorganized. There was also no agreement on the size and shape of the memorial.

Enter Elvis, who performed for charity to help pay for the memorial. (Minnie Pearl, a comedy "hillbilly" singer and star of "The Grand Ol' Opry" radio and TV show received "special guest" billing.) Elvis brought his complete road show and touring band. They included most of the original musicians and singers on Elvis's first records: D.J. Fontana on drums, Scotty Moore on guitar and the Jordanaires as backup singers. This was Elvis's last concert for almost a decade.

Presley, Elvis

De Neve Park

Beverly Glen Boulevard (one block north of Sunset Boulevard)
Los Angeles, California

Elvis Presley's Southern California life in the early to mid 1960s was a hectic tangle of recording, movies and television. To help unwind on the weekends, Elvis and his entourage would organize spirited touch football games in De Neve Park, not far from where he lived in Bel Air. Their favorite opponent was pop singer and television star Ricky Nelson and his band, although other celebrities—including Pat Boone and Max Baer, Jr.—also took part in the games.

Elvis-a-Rama Museum

3401 Industrial Road
Las Vegas, Nevada
702-309-7200

It started as a hobby for Chris Davidson, now it's the real deal—perhaps the most amazing Elvis museum on the planet. Davidson has amassed an incredible amount of Elvis stuff: his cars, the world famous '55 Concert Tour Limo, stage-worn jumpsuits, more than $500,000 in Elvis-worn jewelry, Hollywood movie clothing, personal documents and hand-written letters, even the King's personal speed boat. Elvis-a-Rama even boasts a theater for Elvis-style live shows, a gift shop and much more.

Elvis and Priscilla Honeymoon

1350 Ladera Circle
Palm Springs, California
760-322-1192

On September 16, 1966, Elvis leased this estate in Palm Springs, California for one year for $21,000. The futuristic house is famous today as being the place where, on May 1, 1967, Elvis and Priscilla Presley spent their wedding night. Recently restored, the estate is open for tours, not to mention weddings, corporate meetings, and, wouldn't you know, honeymoons.

Presley, Elvis

Elvis is Alive Museum

50's Café
Interstate 70, Wright City exit 199
Wright City, Missouri
636-745-3154

When Bill Beeny opened the 50's Café in 1981, his goal was to pull in travelers along Interstate 70 who would enjoy his extensive collection of 1950's celebrity photos and memorabilia. By 1991, the cafe was 99 percent Elvis. After fielding the question "Is Elvis alive?" one too many times, he decided to make the "museum" a reliquary of proof that the King is, in fact, still walking around. He displays government documents, pathology reports, DNA testing results, three thousand photographs, and transcripts of interviews with Elvis's relatives and former employees—all proving, according to Beeny, that Elvis lives.

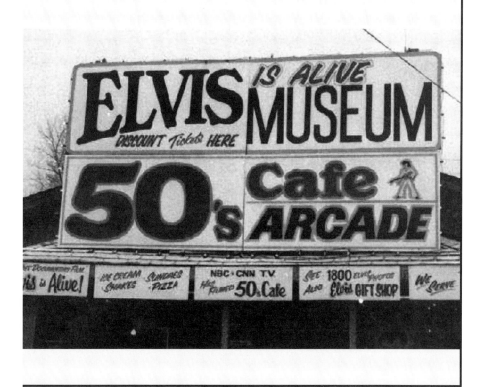

Presley, Elvis

Fool's Gold Loaf

4490 East Virginia Avenue
Glendale, Colorado

On the night of February 1, 1976, Elvis Presley was at Graceland hosting
Captain Jerry Kennedy, a member of the Denver police force, and Ron Pietrafeso, who
was in charge of Colorado's Strike Force Against Crime. Talking with the guys, Elvis
began to crave a Denver-area specialty he had indulged in before: the Fool's Gold Loaf.

He'd had it just once, when he'd visited a restaurant called the Colorado Gold Mine
Company Steakhouse in Glendale, a suburb of Denver. It was named this for its exorbi-
tant price—$49.95—and Elvis wanted one that night. They hopped into the King's
stretch Mercedes along with another couple of Elvis's buddies, drove to Memphis airport and hopped aboard Elvis's jet, the "Lisa Marie" (named after his daughter). Next
stop, Denver's Stapleton Airport!

The Colorado Gold Mine Company Steakhouse frantically prepared their specialty of the
house (22 orders of it, in fact) and had it waiting on the tarmac when the Lisa Marie
landed a couple of hours later. (A case of Perrier and a case of champagne went with
the sandwiches, as ordered.) Elvis and crew landed at 1:40 A.M. at Stapleton Airport and
taxied to a private hangar. The owner of the restaurant served them personally and for
two hours the entourage and Elvis feasted on the Fool's Gold.

And just what exactly is Fool's Gold Loaf? An entire loaf of bread is warmed and then
hollowed out. The loaf is then stuffed with peanut butter and jelly. Lastly, a pound of
lean bacon fills the belly of the loaf. Served hot, supposedly the serving size was one
loaf per person! Today, the restaurant at this site that prepared the Fool's Gold Loaf is
gone, replaced by a construction company, but the memory lingers on.

Forest Hill Cemetery

1661 Elvis Presley Boulevard
Memphis, Tennessee

In August 1977, Elvis was originally laid to rest here, right next to his mother, Gladys.
But several months later, both Elvis and his mom were moved to Graceland after
attempts were made to steal Elvis's body.

Presley, Elvis

The Frontier Hotel

3120 Las Vegas Boulevard South
Las Vegas, Nevada

In 1956, Elvis made his first appearance in Vegas at this hotel, opening for comedian Shecky Green in the Venus Room. He would go over much bigger when he came back 13 years later. (This is also where The Supremes performed their last show with Dina Ross on January 14, 1970.)

Graceland Too

200 East Gholson Avenue
Holly Springs, Mississippi
662-252-2515

Graceland Too attracts music fans seven days a week, 24 hours a day. Paul McLeod and his son, Elvis Presley McLeod, love to show off their tribute to "The King of Rock and Roll" that they have created at their home, just off the town square. Visitors from around the world have toured Graceland Too, many calling it the greatest tribute to Elvis they've ever seen. For a small admission you can tour Paul's home and see such items as Elvis' report card from 1951, a gold lame suit supposedly worn by Elvis during a 1957 concert, and a casket that plays "Return to Sender" in which McCleod plans to be buried.

Hampton Coliseum

1000 Coliseum Drive
Hampton, Virginia
757-838-5650

This famous arena has hosted everyone from The Rolling Stones to Metallica to Elvis Presley. But only Elvis has a special door. Not many know about the "Elvis Door," but it really exists. It was specially cut out of the Coliseum during one of the King's 1970's appearances so Elvis could go directly from his dressing room to his limo. Elvis's third and final visit to the Coliseum occurred on July 31 and August 1, 1976. Also, the documentary *Elvis On Tour* was filmed in the building during his 1972 appearances. Today, Elvis's shows here are commemorated on a bronze plaque located on the south concourse level of the Coliseum.

Presley, Elvis

Humes High School

**659 North Manassas Street
Memphis, Tennessee**

Elvis graduated from this high school in 1953. Today, there is a mini-Elvis museum, and the school auditorium is now dedicated to him.

Lansky Brothers Clothing Store

**126 Beale Street
Memphis, Tennessee**

This shop (which closed in 1990) billed itself as "Outfitter to the King" for years, as it is was where Elvis bought many on and offstage outfits. On the building's west wall is a mural dedicated to Memphis history, of which Elvis figures prominently.

Libertyland

**940 Early Maxwell Boulevard
Memphis, Tennessee**

After he became famous, Elvis would sometimes rent out this entire amusement park so he could throw parties and ride the Zippin' Pippin roller coaster. (Back then it was called the Fairgrounds Amusement Park.) The amusement park still holds promotions in honor of the King—events that, of course, feature The Zippin Pippin, his favorite ride in the world.

Elvis' Favorite Ride
The Zippin Pippin

The Zippin Pippin was Elvis Presley's favorite ride. The "King" rented Libertyland August 8, 1977 from 1:15 a.m. until 7 a.m. to entertain a group of about 10 guests. Decked in blue jumpsuit with a black leather belt, huge belt buckle with turquoise studs and gold chains, the "King" rode the Zippin Pippin repeatedly during a two-hour period. He lost his belt buckle on the ride that morning, and it was found and returned the next day. Elvis' Libertyland rental became his last public appearance. He died August 16.

Presley, Elvis

Poplar Tunes

308 Poplar Avenue
Memphis, Tennessee
901-525-6348

Still standing today is the Poplar Tunes record store. This is where Elvis Presley supposedly bought his first LP and also where his very own record was first sold. Of course, Elvis memorabilia hangs on the walls. Founded by John Novarese and Joe Cuoghi in 1946, Poplar Tunes has been credited with breaking records, boosting careers, and creating hit records through breakthrough promotions, in-store charting and research, and distribution of material to smaller markets throughout the Southeast. Today, the company still supplies product to hundreds of jukebox accounts, making it one of the top suppliers and warehouses of vinyl stock in the country.

Schwab Dry Goods

163 Beale Street
Memphis, Tennessee
901-523-9782

It's been in business since 1876, with the motto "If you can't find it at A. Schwab's, you're better off without it!" Elvis used to shop here, and today there are lots of Elvis souvenirs here.

Sierra Sid's Truck Stop Casino

200 North McCarran Boulevard
Sparks, Nevada

Sierra Sid's is home to the Guns of Elvis and other Elvis stuff. The memorabilia was all purchased from Elvis' daddy's (Vernon Presley) estate in 1981. In a wall of display cases next to the nickel slot machines you'll find jewelry (including a tiger-eye ring, watch and diamonds) that Elvis gave to his father. You'll also find four .45 handguns (one of which Elvis reportedly used to shoot out a TV set) and two complete sets of Elvis's 52 gold albums.

Presley, Elvis

These are some Elvis homes owned or rented during the years he lived at Graceland:

906 Oak Hill Drive
Killeen, TX
A home Elvis rented in 1958 during basic training at Ft. Hood, Texas.

10539 Bellagio Road
Bel Air, California
Elvis rented this home from November 1961 to January 1963.

1174 Hillcrest Avenue
Beverly Hills, California
Elvis and Priscilla bought this home in November 1967 for $400,000.

845 Chino Canyon Rd.
Palm Springs, California
Elvis and Priscilla bought this home in April 1970 paying $13,187.83 down and signing a mortgage for $85,000.

Prince

Paisley Park
Paisley Park Studios
7801 Audubon Road
Chanhassen, Minnesota

Though not open to the public, this is the nerve center/recording/production studio of the artist once again known as Prince. He's recorded most of his music here since 1987 (along with some other bands) and although the Purple One doesn't allow visitors, you can get a postcard view of the place from downtown Minneapolis. Since 1987, many of the world's top artists have worked at Paisley Park Studios to create chart-topping music, full-length feature films, commercials and music videos.

Ramone, Joey

11 East 9th Street
New York City, New York

This apartment building was the longtime home of Ramone's lead singer Joey Ramone, who passed away in 2001 from cancer at just 49 years old. Joey (real name Jeffrey Hyman) co-founded the Ramones, a pioneering punk band whose influence stretched all the way from the Sex Pistols and the Clash to U2 and Nirvana. The band recorded 21 albums and its hits included the punchy, three-chord classics "Blitzkrieg Bop," "Teenage Lobotomy" and "Rock 'n' Roll High School."

The Rat

528 Commonwealth Avenue
Boston, Massachusetts

For over 20 years, from the 1970s through the 1990s, The Rat (full name, The Rathskellar) was the premiere underground rock and roll club in Boston. The Cars started out here, and the cavern-like club also hosted Blondie, The Ramones, The Jam, Squeeze and many other cutting-edge bands back in the 1970s and 1980s. The Rat closed its doors for good in 1997, ending one of punk and new wave's most dominant venues. Today, there's a hotel at the location.

R.E.M.

The small city of Athens, located about 70 miles northeast of Atlanta, is home to the 30,000-plus students of the University of Georgia. It is also famous for being the fertile creative launching pad of R.E.M. (and also the B-52s). Here are a few R.E.M. landmarks:

The Church

394 Oconee Street
Athens, Georgia

Back in the late 1970s this church had been converted into cheapo student apartments. And it was here that guitarist Peter Buck and singer Michael Stipe lived and eventually formed the band R.E.M. In fact, it was here that a yet-to-be-named R.E.M. made its debut (at a friend's birthday party) on April 5, 1980.

A person in attendance who managed the local club called Tyrone's offered them a gig that May (paying $100) and the rest is history. Today, only the steeple of the church remains, and nearby is the railway trestle bridge that was pictured on the back of the album *Murmur*. A housing complex has also been built here at the site, making it hard to recognize the part of the steeple that remains.

Weaver D's Delicious Fine Foods

1016 East Broad Street
Athens, Georgia
706-353-7797

The slogan on the outside of this down-home café reads, Delicious Fine Foods–Automatic for the People. The slogan inspired the name of the 1992 smash album by R.E.M., and inspired Weaver D's (home of delicious southern fried chicken and vegetables served on molded Styrofoam plates).

R.E.M.

Wuxtry Records

197 East Clayton Street
Athens, Georgia
706-369-9428

It was at this legendary used (and new) record store that then store assistant Peter Buck met Michael Stipe and the two decided to try and form a band. Years later, Buck tried again to work here, but his success got in the way in that too many fans asked him to sign records. The store (and its sister store in Atlanta) remains a vital resource for music lovers (and they also have an upstairs area with tons of comics and other pop culture ephemera).

Rodgers, Jimmi

Hotel Taft
761 Seventh Avenue
New York City, New York

Singer Jimmie Rodgers, known as "The Singing Brakeman" and "America's Blue Yodeler" died here at the Hotel Taft. Also thought of as The Father of Country Music, the 35-year-old singer had suffered from complications due to TB when, numbed by morphine and alcohol, he succumbed to the disease on May 26, 1933. The list of those whom Rodgers influenced directly is very long and includes Gene Autry, Bill Monroe, Ernest Tubb, Hank Snow, Hank Williams, Johnny Cash, Merle Haggard and many others. While the hotel is long gone, a TGI Friday's restaurant occupies the site.

Rolling Stone Magazine

746 Brannan Street
San Francisco, California

It was in the loft here on November 9, 1967, that editor Jann Wenner (and staff) rolled out the very first issue of *Rolling Stone Magazine*. Several years later, Wenner moved his now hot publication to nicer offices. In 1975, he packed the entire enterprise up and moved it to New York City.

Rundgren, Todd

147 West 24th Street
New York City, New York

In the early 1970s, Todd Rundgren built a recording studio here in the top story loft of keyboardist Moogy Klingman. Dubbing it "The Secret Sound," The visionary musician and sought-after producer Rundgren recorded and produced several notable albums here. For himself, he recorded *A Wizard, A True Star* and *Todd* among others. In addition, he produced the Hall and Oates album *War Babies* here, and many others.

In the late 1970s, Rundgren left the city and headed north to Woodstock, New York where he would live and record for several years. Today, a candy company occupies the loft space where Rundgren worked.

The Scene

301 West 46th Street
New York City, New York

In the late 1960s this was arguably New York City's most popular rock and roll hangout. For several months in 1968, Jimi Hendrix was a constant attraction here, jamming with Clapton, Jeff Beck, Jim Morrison and others while recording *Electric Ladyland* at the Record Plant recording studio. The original building was torn down several years ago.

Shelly's Manne-Hole

1608 Cahuenga Boulevard
Hollywood, California

For 14 years (1960–1974), the famous Los Angeles jazz club Shelly's Manne-Hole was located here. Widely regarded as a most versatile and musical drummer, Manne (1920–1984) was a founding father of the West Coast jazz scene in the 1950s. Drummer Shelly Manne ran the place, which featured headliners such as Miles Davis, Bill Evans and John Coltrane. A manhole at the site commemorates the former club.

Soundgarden

7600 Sand Point Way
Seattle, Washington

The Seattle-based band Soundgarden formed in the mid-1980s, naming themselves after a statue called "The Sound Garden" which stands at the Lake Washington shore in Seattle. The statue makes odd, howling tones when the wind blows through its tuned pipes. The band was formed in 1984 by Chris Cornell (vocals) and Hiro Yamamoto (bass), who were later joined by Kim Thayil (guitar). The band's final album was 1996's *Down on the Upside*. Soundgarden announced its breakup in April 1997 and a greatest-hits compilation, *A-Sides*, was released a few months later.

Springsteen, Bruce

Freehold High School

Broadway at Robertsville Road
Freehold, New Jersey

It was while attending high school here in 1965 that Bruce Springsteen formed his first band, The Castilles. He graduated from the school two years later, but missed the graduation ceremony after teachers told him his hair was too long.

The Castilles played their first performance in 1965 at the Wood-haven Swim Club in Woodhaven, New Jersey. The group closed the show with Springsteen's arrangement of Glenn Miller's "In the Mood" and they earned $35. Today, the swim club has become the local YMCA and it's located at 470 East Freehold Road in Freehold.

First New Jersey Home

87 Randolph Street
Freehold, New Jersey

Today the site is a driveway for the St. Rose of Lima church, but until 1957 it was where Springsteen lived with his grandparents, mom and dad. In a 1987 song called "Walk Like a Man," Springsteen references the home with the line, "By Our Lady of the Roses, we lived in the shadow of the elms."

Second New Jersey Home

39½ Institute Street
Freehold, New Jersey

This was the Boss's household from 1958–1961. Interestingly, The Boss himself turned up here in the early 1980s and had his photo snapped leaning against the sycamore tree in the front yard—that shot became the underlay image of the *Born in the U.S.A.* album lyric sheet.

Springsteen, Bruce

Third New Jersey Home

68 South Street
Freehold, New Jersey

Bruce Springsteen and his family moved here in 1961, and it was on the roof of this home where he'd teach himself to play the guitar on summer nights. Later in the 1960s, Springsteen's parents left for California and left Freehold too.

Swingo's

1800 Euclid Avenue
Cleveland, Ohio

At one time, Swingo's may have been the country's ultimate rock and roll hotel. In the 1950s Elvis used to crash here, and the Rolling Stones were regulars in the 1960s (with dozens of other name bands).

But, it was Led Zeppelin that made a real mark on the place in the early 1970s, by tossing trays full of food out of their room and then calling the front desk to blame the chaos on another guest in the hotel—Elton John. Today, Swingo's still stands, but it has become a Comfort Inn.

"Take It Easy"

**The Northwest corner of Kinsley Avenue and Second Street
Winslow, Arizona**

Mention the name "Winslow, Arizona" and it's sure to trigger the song lyric, "Well I was standing on a corner in Winslow, Arizona," right? The lyrics from the popular Eagles song "Take It Easy," written by Jackson Browne and Glenn Frey, inspired the city to turn this very corner into a park right on historic Route 66.

A bronze sculpture of a young man wearing blue jeans with a guitar in hand sums up the hopes and musical dreams of a generation. It's called "Standin' on the Corner Park." The park features the artwork of muralist John Pugh and sculptor Ron Adamson. The song remains one of The Eagles's most popular, best-selling hits of all time, a classic cruising song that is a radio staple.

Tin Pan Alley

**28th Street between 6th Avenue and Broadway
New York City, New York**

Tin Pan Alley is where music publishers would peddle songs to artists and producers from the nearby theaters. This important stretch was the center of music publishing at the beginning of the 20th Century, when the music business was the sheet music business.

The publishers on the street all hired "pluggers" to play songs for prospective customers; the din from all their pianos playing at once gave the street its nickname. The street is now a center for clothing and accessories wholesalers.

Valley Music Center

20600 Ventura Boulevard
Woodland Hills, California

Today it's a Jehovah's Witness center, but it used to be a legendary California concert hall. Back in the 1960s the Valley Music Center was a vital haven for the fertile Southern California music scene including The Doors, Buffalo Springfield, The Byrds and Tina Turner.

Van Halen

Body Shop
8520 Sunset Boulevard
Hollywood, California

This strip club on the famous "Strip" was the site of a famous rock and roll presentation: in 1977 Warner Bros. executives gave Van Halen their first gold record here. The ceremony was hosted by the late comedy legend Milton Berle, who was the uncle of their then-manager.

Velvet Underground

Summit High School

125 Kent Place Boulevard
Summit, New Jersey

On December 11, 1965, The Velvet Underground made their performing debut in this high

school auditorium, playing a school dance. It was a triple bill with The Myddle Class as headliners and The Forty Fingers as co-support. This gig was arranged by the legendary journalist Al Aronowitz, who was also The Myddle Class manager. At this legendary show the band opened with "There She Goes Again," then played "Venus In Furs" and ended with their epic, "Heroin."

Velvet Underground

Café Bizarre

106 West 3rd Street
New York City, New York

This is the famed club where Andy Warhol discovered the Velvet Underground. He took them under his wing and made them "his" group. The Velvets had become a kind of house group until the famed artist plucked them from the obscure layers of the New York underground. Today, the site is occupied by a college dorm.

Electric Circus

23 St. Mark's Place
New York City, New York

The brainchild of William Morris agent Jerry Brandt, this former club played host to many crazy shows from 1967-1970, including those featuring The Exploding Plastic Inevitable, an explosive, shocking light/costume/sound revue featuring the Velvet Underground. Today, it's a rehabilitation center.

Velvet Underground

Reed-Morrison Loft

450 Grand Street
New York City, New York

Lou Reed and Velvet Underground band mate, the late Sterling Morrison lived in a fifth floor loft here in 1965. One wintry day in 1965, the Velvets were hanging out here when journalist Al Aronowitz popped in to check up on a claim Reed had made about being the fastest guitar player in the world.

Waiting out in Aronowitz's limo was Rolling Stone Brian Jones. Velvet guitarist John Cale rushed out to meet Jones, who was a hero of his. But too late—Jones supposedly had gone off to score acid in this rundown part of Little Italy. (Cale's apartment back then was at 56 Ludlow Street in New York.)

The Who

Cow Palace
Geneva Boulevard
Daly City (San Francisco), California

During a November 20, 1973 concert here, Who drummer Keith Moon collapsed onstage during the song "Won't Get Fooled Again." The roadies carried him backstage into the dressing room, where he was placed in a cold shower and brought to. After a 30-minute delay, Moon was unable to continue playing, and in fact was taken to a local hospital.

Who guitarist Pete Townsend took the microphone and said, "Hey, can anybody out there play drums? I mean good. Any takers come up here onstage." Scott Halpin, a 19-year-old, made his way to the stage and took over. Townsend introduced him, called for the song "Naked Eye," and they were off. The Who ran through two other songs, "Magic Bus" and "My Generation" before finishing the set with the substitute drummer.

Williams, Hank

Municipal Auditorium
Louis Armstrong Park, off North Rampart and St. Peter Streets
New Orleans, Louisiana

Country legend Hank Williams actually got married twice here on the same day in October, 1952, to Billie Jean Eshlimar. They sold tickets to the event ($1.50 per ticket) and the couple banked more than $25,000 that day.

Movies and TV

Alamo Square

Steiner Street (between Hayes and Fulton Streets)
San Francisco, California

Alamo Square is one of the most photographed locations in San Francisco. The famous "postcard row" at Hayes and Steiner Streets features an escalating formation of Victorian houses back-dropped by downtown skyscrapers–a stunning contrast.

No wonder it's been used for so many shows over the years including the opening credits for *Too Close For Comfort,* the opening credits for *Full House* and the films *The Woman in Red* (Gene Wilder lived in one of the houses) and *So I Married an Axe Murderer* (Mike Meyers breaks up with his girlfriend in the park located here).

The Amazing Colossal Man

25 East Fremont Street
Las Vegas, Nevada

This 1957 camp classic revolved around a man (Glen Langan) who grew 10 feet a day due to nuclear fallout and wreaked havoc throughout the Vegas Strip. In one memorable scene, he took on "Las Vegas Vic," the iconic, 40-foot high neon cowboy that towers here at the Pioneer Club. The neon statue is one of the most recognizable, garish pieces of architecture in Las Vegas.

American Pie

Millikan High School
2800 Snowden Ave
Long Beach, California

This was used as the exterior of the high school in the 1999 gross-out comedy, *American Pie*. The interior classroom scenes, hallway scenes, as well as the bathroom scene, were all shot a few miles from here at Long Beach Polytechnic High School, located at 1600 Atlan-tic Avenue in Long Beach. (The college scenes in *American Pie I* & *II* were shot on the campus of Cal State Long Beach, at 1250 N. Bellflower Boulevard.) Interestingly, this house is just around the corner from the house used in Ferris Bueller's Day Off.

American Pie

4153 Cedar Drive
Long Beach, California

This is the main house in the 1999 goofball comedy *American Pie* (home to Jim and his family, the character played by Jason Biggs). Fans will remember it fondly as the place where he sets up the camera to peep on Nadia (Shannon Elizabeth) while she is undressing. The same house also appears several times in the sequel, *American Pie II*.

Astoria Column

Coxcomb Hill
Astoria, Oregon

The one-of-a-kind Astoria Column has been seen in many films that have been shot in Astoria, including *Kindergarten Cop, Free Willy, Teenage Mutant Ninja Turtles III, Goonies* and *Short Circuit.* The tower is 125 feet tall and is located on top of 600-foot Coxcomb Hill. A 164-step spiral staircase ascends to a viewing deck, where visitors can enjoy a spectacular view of the lower Columbia region.

Patterned after the Trajan Column in Rome, the Astoria Column is the world's only large piece of memorial architecture made of reinforced concrete with a pictorial frieze in sgraffito technique. New York architect Electus D. Litchfield designed the column, patterning it after the Trajan Column erected in Rome by Emperor Trajan in 114 A.D.

Austin Powers

Imperial Palace Hotel
3535 Las Vegas Boulevard South
Las Vegas, Nevada

Mike Meyers's 1997 hip spy spoof *Austin Powers: International Man of Mystery* featured Vegas as prominently as any film ever. (Remember how pretty the glittering Strip looked in the scene where Burt Bacharach serenades Meyers and Elizabeth Hurley atop the red, double-decker bus?) The many casino interiors for *Austin Powers* were shot at the Riviera Hotel and Casino. They used the Oriental-themed Imperial Palace for Alotta Fagina's penthouse.

Battle of the Network Stars

Pepperdine University
Malibu, California

The 1970s featured one of the weirdest, cheesiest shows in TV history—*The Battle of the Network Stars*—a series of "specials" which pitted big time TV celebrities (Farrah Fawcett Majors, Scott Baio, Kristy McNichol, Melissa Gilbert, Gabe Kaplan, Robert Conrad and dozens more) against each other in odd (and often extremely competitive) athletic challenges.

Howard Cosell hosted the show (he was forced to offer things like commentary on Toni Tonille's football receiving skills or to berate Morgan Fairchild's tug-of-war abilities). They

were all shot here on the beautiful campus of Pepperdine University, which overlooks the Pacific Ocean in Malibu, California. It is one of the most picturesque colleges in the world, with postcard views in virtually all directions.

Benny, Jack

Clayton Street (near Sheridan Road)
Waukegan, Illinois

Comedian Jack Benny was born in Chicago as Benjamin Kubelsky, but he grew up in Waukegan. The town recently erected a statue of Benny in a plaza northwest of Clayton Street and Sheridan Road as part of a revitalization effort for the city's downtown. Benny became most famous after creating a radio (and then TV) program centered around a fictional version of himself: a successful comedian who was cheap, petty, and vain. The program introduced a stable of colorful characters who made Benny their foil, including Eddie Anderson, who played Benny's valet, "Rochester Van Jones," announcer Don Wilson, Mary Livingstone (Benny's real-life wife), bandleader Phil Harris, and tenor singer Dennis Day.

Beverly Hills Cop

Pasadena City Hall
100 North Garfield Avenue
Pasadena, California

It costs less to film in Pasadena than in Beverly Hills, which is what often brings film productions to this ornate building. Both *Beverly Hills Cop* and the sequel, *Beverly Hills Cop II* used this as Beverly Hills City Hall. It has also been used in other productions as Buckingham Palace, and as a French castle in the movie *Patton* starring George C. Scott.

Blockheads

201 West 8th Street
Los Angeles, California

The 1938 Laurel and Hardy classic, *Blockheads*, was shot throughout the greater Los Angeles area, but the film's great climax was filmed here. Billy Gilbert, toting a shotgun, chases our heroes down the alleyway at this address, located just south of MacArthur Park (an alley created by 8th Street and 807 South Westlake Avenue).

Blue Hawaii

Coco Palms Resort
241 Kuhio Highway
Kapaa, Hawaii (island of Kaui)

Who can forget Elvis Presley cavorting at the famed Coco Palms Resort in 1961's *Blue Hawaii*? Much of the film was shot at the resort, including a lengthy and lavish wedding sequence aboard a boat in the hotel's famous lagoons. The 396-room resort, with its distinctive Polynesian architecture, was among Hawaii's most elegant hotels in the 1950s and 1960s.

The film remains a favorite for many both for the music ("Blue Hawaii," "Can't Help Falling in Love With You") and the scenery, which harkens back to another time—full of vibrant, kitschy color in a gorgeous tropical setting.

Many traditions later emulated by other hotels, such as the nightly torch-lighting ceremony, started right here at the Coco Palms. The hotel was full on September 11, 1992, when Hurricane Iniki struck the island of Kauai. Afterwards, it was locked and never reopened. Today, there are plans afoot to refurbish it.

Blue Velvet

Wilmington, North Carolina

David Lynch's disturbing 1986 tale centered in "Lumbertown" was actually shot throughout Wilmington, North Carolina. Some of the more recognizable locations include the school Laura Dern attended, New Hanover High, located at 1307 Market Street, and the police station where Kyle McLachlan eyes the Man in Yellow—the Wilmington Police Headquarters, located at 115 Redcross Street. Also, Isabella Rossellini's Deep River apartment block is the Carolina Apartments, located at Market Street and Fifth Avenue.

Body Double

7776 Torreyson Drive
Los Angeles, California

Brian DePalma's twisting thriller featured many Los Angeles locations. However, none is more visually arresting or bizarre than the Chemosphere house, an octagonal, built-on-stilts spectacle located in the Hollywood Hills. The house was designed by famed architect John Lautner and remains one of the most interesting buildings in the Hollywood Hills.

The Brady Bunch

Kings Island
5688 Kings Island Drive
Kings Island, Ohio
513-754-5901

This popular Cincinnati-area amusement park will be familiar to *Brady Bunch* fans. The episode entitled *The Cincinnati Kids* from 1973 was featured as the family accompanied Mike to Cincinnati where he was to present plans for an addition to the Kings Island amusement park. While the kids enjoy the many rides, Mike is shocked to learn his plans have been lost in the park, and a frantic search ensues.

In the episode, the popular Racer rollercoaster was featured and this ride is often credited as the one that brought coasters back into the spotlight in the early 1970s. Note: the other memorable time the Brady's went on location was their ill-fated Hawaiian adventure when Greg discovered the "cursed" Tiki statue. In that episode, a luau takes place at the Royal Hawaiian Hotel on Waikiki Beach.

Butch Cassidy and the Sundance Kid

Durango and Silverton Narrow Gauge Railroad
479 Main Avenue
Durango, Colorado
970-259-0274

Remember in the movie *Butch Cassidy and the Sundance Kid*, when Butch and the gang attempt to blow open the train's safe and instead blow up the entire mail car, sending money all over the place? Supposedly, the force of the blast even caught the special-effect technicians, who went overboard with the gunpowder, by surprise. At this great historic railway station you can see the actual train they blew up, and even take a ride on it. About 10 miles east of Durango is a plaque commemorating where they shot the scene—ask at the station for directions.

Car Wash

Rampart Boulevard at Sixth Street (near Lafayette Park)
Los Angeles, California

1976's funky comedy hit was shot at the old De Luxe Car Wash here in downtown Los Angeles. *Car Wash* starred Richard Pryor, Sally Boyar and The Pointer Sisters, as well as the late J.J. Jackson (a disk jockey heard in the movie who later went on to be one of the original MTV Vee-Jays in the early 1980s). The car wash has since been torn down.

Casino

2955 Las Vegas Boulevard South
Las Vegas, Nevada

Martin Scorsese used the Strip to its full glossy effect in 1995's *Casino*. The production was largely shot in Vegas—in fact, that fictitious casino in Tangier was actually the Riviera Hotel and Casino. Do you remember the space-age-looking motel where Joe Pesci enjoyed a brief affair with Sharon Stone? It was at the La Concha, an odd-shaped hotel that was torn down as this entry was being written (2955 Las Vegas Boulevard South).

Chaplin, Charlie

Alexandria Hotel

501 South Spring Street
Los Angeles, California

Opened in 1906, for years the Alexandria Hotel was a magnet for celebrities and other notable guests. During its heyday, Winston Churchill, Enrico Caruso, King Edward VIII and American presidents such as Taft, Wilson and Roosevelt all stayed here. Charlie Chaplin lived here on and off in his early years in Los Angeles.

It was here, in 1919, that D.W. Griffith, Charlie Chaplin, Mary Pickford and Douglas Fairbanks made movie history by announcing the formation of their independent company, United Artists. The once grand hotel is today a low-rent flophouse.

City Lights

Wilshire Boulevard and Commonwealth Avenue
Los Angeles, California

Arguably Chaplin's greatest love story of all time, 1931's *City Lights* is the tale of Chaplin's heart-rending relationship with a blind flower girl. Shot at many locations throughout the Los Angeles area, this stretch of Wilshire Boulevard (at Commonwealth) is famous as the place where Chaplin walks arm in arm with the blind girl. Virtually unchanged today, the stroll took place alongside the Town House Hotel.

Chaplin, Charlie

The Kid

24 Olvera Street
Los Angeles, California

Who can forget Chaplin's 1921 tearjerker about the Tramp and the Kid, played by Jackie Coogan (who would one day gain more fame as Uncle Fester on *The Addams Family* TV show). The Kid, who is abandoned by his rich mother, inadvertently ends up in the care of Chaplin's sweet Tramp character, who becomes a father figure to the child.

This is the exact spot where they arrive and Chaplin reclaims the Kid near the film's dramatic climax, when Chpalin chases down the authorities who have taken the child away from him. Back then it was just an anonymous side street with an alley in downtown Los Angeles. Today, it's the tourist mecca known as Olvera Street, a celebration of Los Angeles's rich Mexican heritage, a place where shoppers can enjoy authentic Mexican restaurants and shops.

The Tramp

Truckee Hotel
10007 Bridge Street
Truckee, California
800-659-6921

For more than 125 years, this classic mountain-town hotel (located about 90 miles east of Sacramento) has served travelers. One important traveler in particular was Charlie Chaplin, who in 1925 stayed here at length while filming his classic *The Gold Rush* throughout the area. The historic hotel is still going strong; it's a charming retreat that's a throwback to the days when one of the film's greatest film legends called this his part-time home.

C.H.I.P.S.

777 West Washington Boulevard
Los Angeles, California

The exterior of this, the Central Los Angeles office of the California Highway Patrol, was used in the popular show *C.H.I.P.S*, starring Eric Estrada. The program ran from 1977–1983.

Cocoon

Sunny Shores Rest Home
125 56th Avenue South
St. Petersburg, Florida

This is the old folk's home featured in the 1985 charmer directed by Ron Howard, *Cocoon*. The film starred Don Ameche, Wilford Brimley and Hume Cronyn. Ameche won a Best Supporting Actor Academy Award for his part in the film, which blended themes of science fiction, immortality and everlasting love.

The Color of Money

6615 West Roosevelt Road
Berwyn, Illinois

Martine Scorsese's 1986 follow-up to the 1961's *The Hustler* starred Paul Newman reprising his role as Fast Eddie Felson. Shot at many different joints around Illinois, we first see Newman notice the up-and-comer played by Tom Cruise here at Fitzgerald's, as Cruise trounces John Turturro. Fitzgerald's, a classic pool hall built in 1915, was also featured in the film *A League of Their Own*.

Dark Shadows

100 Ochre Point Avenue
Seaview Terrace Estate
Newport, Rhode Island

Seaview Terrace is the house that was used for the exterior shots of Collinwood in the creepy 1960's TV soap opera *Dark Shadows*. *Dark Shadows* debuted on ABC on June 27, 1966, as the first Gothic daytime drama. It was created by producer Dan Curtis, who would later create the epic television mini-series *The Winds of War* and *War and Remem-brance*. In April 1967, famed Shakespearean actor Jonathan Frid joined the cast as Barnabas Collins, a 175-year-old vampire, who became one of the most popular characters on the show. Today, the house is a dormitory for Salve Regina University.

Dead Poets Society

St. Andrews School
Noxontown Pond Road
Middletown, Delaware

This school stood in as Welton Academy in the 1989 teacher-tearjerker starring Robin Williams. It's a private school that sits on two thousand acres.

Diamonds Are Forever

2175 Southridge Drive
Elrod/Lautner House
Palm Springs, California

The Elrod/Lautner home in the Southridge part of Palm Springs in the California desert is where the famous 1971 James Bond flick *Diamonds Are Forever* was filmed. It features a breathtaking panoramic view of the valley and can be rented today for about $20,000 per week. Built in 1968, it remains one of the most stunning homes in the world.

Dirty Dancing

Lake Lure Inn
US Highways 64/74A
Lake Lure, North Carolina
800-695-8284

In 1987's *Dirty Dancing*, Patrick Swayze and Jennifer Grey danced right here, in the blue waters of Lake Lure (near the Lake Lure Inn, also seen in the movie). This beautiful and rugged area of North Carolina stood in as New York State's Adirondack Mountains in this sleeper hit. Many fans make the pilgrimage here to see where *Dirty Dancing* was filmed.

Today, you can see the footbridge and the foundations of camp buildings used in exterior shots for the film. To reach the location by land, take Boys Camp Road and turn right on Chapel Point Road. However, the Lake Lure cabins that the staff lived in at "Kellerman's" were demolished not long after the movie was released and "Johnny's" cabin lasted just a year or so after filming wrapped. (The scene where Johnny attempts to teach Baby "the lift" in the water was just down the road from the Inn.)

Note: at the nearby Wicklow Inn Bed and Breakfast (877-625-4038) you'll find a remaining piece of the movie. When the movie set was dismantled, the former owners of this inn obtained the wallboards from one of the cottages featured in the movie. Later, when the inn was renovated, the boards were used to construct the outside wall of the Cottage Room, where they remain as a permanent piece of nostalgia from the movie.

It should be noted that another place was also used for the film—the Mountain Lake Hotel is located at 115 Hotel Circle, in Pembroke, Virginia (800-346-3334). This historic stone hotel is easily recognizable as the main lodge featured in the movie.

Dumb and Dumber

Union Pacific Railroad Department
Salt Lake City, Utah

Much of the hilarious 1994 comedy starring Jim Carrey and Jeff Daniels was shot in Utah and Colorado. One of the more memorable scenes was the Snowy Owl Benefit, filmed in this former train station, now a historic landmark building.

Evening Shade

2102 Louisiana Street
Evening Shade, Arkansas

The Colonial Revival home with a charming broad porch seen as the Newton home in the TV series *Evening Shade* (starring Burt Reynolds) is actually a private residence. Built in 1883, it's known as the Wilson-Mehaffy House (after its former owners William Wilson and Tom Mehaffy who owned the property from the turn of the century through the 1940s). The house is not open to the public. (Some of the program's exterior locations for the series were shot in the city of Evening Shade, Arkansas.)

Fabulous Baker Boys

Biltmore Hotel
506 South Grand Avenue
Los Angeles, California
213-624-1011

Shot throughout Seattle and Los Angeles, the most memorable scene in 1989's tale of two lounge piano players is no doubt

Michelle Pfeiffer's steamy rendition of *Makin' Whoopee*, performed atop a piano in the Crystal Ballroom here within one of Los Angeles's most elegant hotels.

The Biltmore hosted the Oscars in the 1930s and was also where Eddie Murphy fast-talked his way past the front desk in 1984's *Beverly Hills Cop.*

Ferris Bueller's Day Off

4160 Country Club Drive
Long Beach, California

In the 1987 smash comedy *Ferris Bueller's Day Off*, this is the Bueller's main home. It's featured at many times throughout the film, from the very first shot to the very end. It's right here where Ferris plays sick to get a day off school, where the school principal ends up in a confrontation with Ferris's sister (after coming over to try and bust Ferris), and where Ferris races back in the end. Interestingly, the rest of the movie was shot in Chicago.

Footloose

Lehi Roller Mills
833 East Main Street
Lehi, Utah
800-660-4346

In 1906, George G. Robinson founded Lehi Mill with a simple philosophy: "Only the best wheat makes the best flour." Wonder if he knew it would also be the site of a popular 1984 movie starring Kevin Bacon. After all, Lehi Roller Mills is where Kevin Bacon worked in the film *Footloose* and also where the famous dance at the end of the film took place.

Fried Green Tomatoes

Whistle Stop Café
Just off Highway 75
Juliette, Georgia

This café (along with the town and river) were the backdrop for the popular 1991 movie *Fried Green Tomatoes* (which was based on Fannie Flagg's novel). The film starred Kathy Bates, Jessica Tandy, Gailard Sartain and Mary Stuart Masterson, among others.

Ghost

104 Prince Street
New York City, New York

This was Demi Moore's impressive apartment in the 1990 comedy/thriller, *Ghost*. It's located in trendy Tribeca. Another site from the movie, where medium Whoopi Goldberg donates money to the nuns at the end of the film, was shot in front of Federal Hall (28 Wall Street). Whoopi Goldberg won a Supporting Actress Oscar for her "Ghost" performance in *Ghost*, which was a huge box office success.

Goodfellas

Copacabana
10 East 60th Street
New York City, New York

Martin Scorsese's gritty, graphic gangster film, 1990's *Goodfellas* was shot almost entirely on the streets of New York, like several other Scorcese classics. The film incorporated a lengthy tracking shot that purists drooled over for its timing and ingenuity. The scene was shot at the old (now-closed) Copacabana nightclub and the entrance today looks exactly as it did in the film.

Good Will Hunting

Woody's L Street Tavern
658 East 8th Street #A South
Boston, Massachusetts
617-268-4335

This is the unpretentious, local Irish bar made internationally famous after appearing in the Oscar-winning movie *Good Will Hunting*, which filmed several
scenes here. The movie's stars, Matt Damon and Ben
Affleck, are from nearby Cambridge, and they, along
with co-star Robin Williams, all hung out here quite a
bit during the filming. A sign on the wall outside the
pub denotes its place in movie history.

Hardcastle and McCormick

26800 Pacific Coast Highway
Malibu, California

This is where the late actor Brian Keith, playing Judge Milton C. Hardcastle, lived in the
popular series *Hardcastle and McCormick*, which ran from 1983-1986. The plot line was
this: Milton C. Hardcastle was a judge in Los Angeles. Mark McCormick was a racing
motorist, now convicted for robbery, and this was Hardcastle's last case. McCormick was
placed under supervision of Hardcastle and the pair start to inspect two hundred cases
that were never closed during Hardcastle's judgeship.

Hello, Dolly!

Located off Highway 9D, about 30 miles north of New York City
Garrison, New York

The small hamlet of Garrison—located just across the Hudson River from the West Pont
Military Academy—served as the primary shooting location for 1969's *Hello, Dolly!*, directed by Gene Kelly. Half a million dollars were invested to spruce up the historic town.

Today, you can still find traces of the film. The gazebo in Garrison's Waterfront Park is
still there, as is the barbershop façade. Horace Vandergelder's Grocery Store is actually the Golden Eagle Inn, a bed and breakfast.

Hill Street Blues

Maxwell Precinct Station
Corner of West 14th Place and South Morgan Street
Chicago, Illinois

The exterior of this classic-looking police station was used as the station for *Hill St. Blues,* the award-winning NBC show that aired from 1981–1987. This was the original prime time "ensemble drama," and it revolved around an overworked, understaffed police precinct in an inner city patterned after Chicago. This program opened the door for other successful ensemble dramas including *St. Elsewhere* and *L.A. Law.*

Johnie's Broiler

7447 Firestone Boulevard
Downy, California

Today it's a car dealership, but this diner's classic original structure remains intact, just as it was when Johnie's was used for many movies. Remember the fight scene in the restaurant between Ike and Tina Turner in the 1993 movie *What's Love Got To Do With It?* That was here.

Also, director Robert Altman came here to shoot part of 1994's *Short Cuts* (Lily Tomlin played a waitress who worked here). You may also recognize Johnie's from Diane Keaton's 1995 film *Unstrung Heroes* as well as 1994's *Reality Bites*, starring Winona Ryder and Ethan Hawke. On television, Johnie's Broiler was used as a bus station on a 1999 episode of The *X-Files*.

L.A. Confidential

Crossroads of the World
6671 Sunset Boulevard
Hollywood, California

Curtis Hanson's brilliantly stylistic cop movie from 1997 leaned heavily on many Los Angeles locations. Danny DeVito's office was located just beneath the classic revolving globe of one Hollywood's most classic visual landmarks, the Crossroads of the World. Designed in the 1930s to resemble an ocean liner, the one-time shopping mall has been seen in other movies as well, including *Indecent Proposal*.

Leaving Las Vegas

Various Las Vegas locales

Nicolas Cage won the Academy Award for Best Actor in 1995's *Leaving Las Vegas*. Though the casino interiors were shot 90 miles south of the Strip in Laughlin, there are still many key moments in the film that take place in Vegas.

Cage's character first met hooker Elisabeth Shue at a stoplight located just outside the Flamingo Hilton and Tower. Later, Shue found Cage in front of Bally's Casino Resort at 3645 South Las Vegas Boulevard. They had a discussion in front of Circus Circus's giant lit-up clown. Then, Shue got picked up by the college jocks on the aerial walkway in front of the turrets of Excalibur, located at 3850 Las Vegas Boulevard South.

Legally Blonde

Rose City High School
325 South Oak Knoll Avenue
Pasadena, California

Legally Blonde may have been based in Boston, but all but a few scenes of the 2001 Reese Witherspoon hit were shot in Southern California, primarily the Pasadena area. The interior of the Law School classroom scenes were shot in this high school. Also, the University of Southern California at 3535 South Figueroa Street stood in for Harvard and the law school library scenes were shot at the Pasadena Central Library, located at 285 East Walnut Street, in Pasadena.

Lost in America

Desert Inn
3145 Las Vegas Boulevard
Las Vegas, Nevada

In 1985's hilarious *Lost in America*, ad-exec-utive Albert Brooks watched in horror as his wife (Julie Haggerty) blew the family nest egg at The Desert Inn. He then tried (unsuc-cessfully) to convince the pit boss (Garry Marshall) to give it back. The Desert Inn has since been torn down, replaced by a Steve Wynn-owned hotel.

Love Story

119 Oxford Street
Cambridge, Massachusetts

This 1970's textbook tearjerker starring Ali McGraw and Ryan O'Neal is centered at Harvard, where McGraw is a working-class student (Ryan is the rich kid who turns his back on family riches to be with her). This house in Cambridge is the modest place where they set up their life together before she gets ill. It was on this very doorstep that McGraw speaks the classic line, "Love means never having to say you're sorry."

MacGyver

150 North Larchmont Boulevard
Los Angeles, California

During the first two seasons of the show *MacGyver* (from 1985–86), this is where

Richard Dean Anderson lived, in a loft above a pharmacy. Today, the pharma-cy is a bagel shop. If you look careful-ly down this pretty street near upscale Hancock Park, you may recognize the area from many of the old, silent Keystone Kop comedies that were filmed along here many years ago.

Mean Streets

264 Mulberry Street
New York City, New York

1973's personal tale of Italian Americans living in Little Italy, New York put both Martin Scorcese and Robert De Niro firmly on the map. A tale of punks and "mooks," most of the film was shot in New York (though Harvey Kietel's apartment was on Hollywood Boulevard). One of the most pivotal locations in the film was here at Old St. Patrick's Cathedral in Little Italy, where De Niro and Keitel have an important chat together. (The church was also used in *The Godfather*.)

Men in Black

54 MacDougal Street
New York City, New York

This is the site of The Rosenberg Jewelry Store, which gets famously blown up in 1997's *Men in Black*, a breakout hit for Will Smith, Tommy Lee Jones and director Barry Sonnenfeld. As the film's advertising copy told us, they were "Protecting the earth from the scum of the universe. They were more secretive than the C.I.A. More powerful than the F.B.I. And they're looking for a few good men. They are the Men in Black."

Mystic Pizza

56 West Main Street
Mystic, Connecticut
860-536-3700

The small Mystic Pizza restaurant caught the attention of screenwriter Amy Jones, who

was vacationing in the seaport town of Mystic, Connecticut. Jones chose the pizzeria as the focus and setting for her story of the lives and loves of three young waitresses.

The film *Mystic Pizza* was shot on location in 1988 in Mystic and other neighboring towns, but a set was built for the interiors, as the actual Mystic Pizza restaurant was too small and could not close for months of filming. Today, they've opened a second location in the nearby town of North Stonington.

Napoleon Dynamite

59 South 2nd East Street
Preston, Idaho

2004's quirky hit comedy about a gawky, underdog teen named Napoleon Dynamite brilliantly tapped into the awkward alienation many kids feel. Napoleon's oddball home life, his best friend Pedro, his hopelessly out of date Uncle Rio and the cranky llama, Tina (among others), struck a chord with both youth and adult audiences, spawning many oft-quoted one liners from the movie.

Shot in the co-writer/director Jarred Hess's hometown (a speck on the map known as Preston, Idaho), *Napoleon Dynamite* seems destined to influence at least several generations to come (and a few that have already passed). This particular address is the home of Pedro Sanchez. Other hotspots in town include Napoleon's house (1447 East 800 North Street), Rex Kwon Do studios (12 ½ North State Street), Preston High School (150 East 2nd Street), the Desert Industries Thrift Store (36 South State Street) and the playground (behind the schools at 525 S. 4th Street East). For die-hard fans who found Kip and LaFawnduh's wedding at the very end of the DVD, that took place at the Lamont Reservoir on the outskirts of town.

National Velvet

4515 Park Estrada
Calabasas, California

Much of the 1944 classic where Elizabeth Taylor and Mickey Rooney train on a horse that goes on to win the Grand National was shot here at the site that used to be the old Warner Bros. Ranch. Today it's the Calabasas Golf Club, and on the edge of the course you can still see several old barn buildings from the movie. This film made a star of 12-year-old Elizabeth Taylor, who played the role of the spunky Velvet Brown, Noted film critic Pauline Kael called it "One of the most likeable movies of all time."

Newhart, Bob

430 North Michigan Avenue
Chicago, Illinois

In 2004, a statue was erected in Chicago to commemorate Bob Newhart's role as psychologist Bob Hartley on the 1970's *The Bob Newhart Show*. The life-size statue is in front of the office building seen in the opening credits of the excellent show, which also starred Suzanne Pleshette, Peter Bonerz, Bill Daily and Jack Riley.

Placed by the cable network TV Land, it's another in a series of statues placed by them including: Andy Taylor (Andy Griffith) and his son, Opie (Ron Howard), of *The Andy Griffith Show* in Raleigh, N.C.; Ralph Kramden (Jackie Gleason) of *The Honeymooners* at New York's Port Authority bus terminal; and Mary Richards (Mary Tyler Moore) of the *Mary Tyler Moore Show* in Minneapolis.

Ocean's Eleven

3600 South Las Vegas Boulevard
Las Vegas, Nevada

Steven Soderbergh's 2002 splashy, entertaining remake of 1960's *Ocean's Eleven* was heavily centered here at the elegant Bellagio—in fact one of the movie's focal points was the hotel's famous fountain, light and music show. Set on the eight-acre lake out front, the fountains can shoot water up to 240 feet in the air.

The Outsiders

Admiral Twin Drive-In Theatre
7355 East Easton Street
Tulsa, Oklahoma
918-835-5181

This classic drive-in was the setting for Francis Ford Coppola's 1982 movie *The Outsiders.* The film, adapted from the SE Hinton book, starred many young actors who would go on to various degrees of stardom including C. Thomas Howell, Matt Dillon, Ralph Macchio, Patrick Swayze, Rob Lowe, Emilio Estevez and Tom Cruise. The Tastee-Freez that also played a pivotal part in the movie was located on the Northeast corner of Main and 86th Street North in Tulsa, but has since been torn down.

Pal Joey

Spreckles Mansion
2080 Washington Street
San Francisco, California

1957's *Pal Joey* starred Frank Sinatra as a smooth nightclub entertainer. It also starred Rita Hayworth, Kim Novak and the great music of Rodgers and Hart. The Chez Joey nightclub seen in the film is the classic structure, the Spreckles Mansion, located in Pacific Heights.

Peyton Place

Camden, Maine

In 1957, the steamy, racy and controversial New England novel *Peyton Place* was made into a movie (starring Lee Philips, Lana Turner and Diane Varsi), and it was filmed here in Camden, Maine. Among the many recognizable locations from this quaint, coastal New England town is the White Hall Inn (52 High Street in Camden, 207-236-3391).

Perfect Day

3120 Vera Avenue
Los Angeles, California

The legendary comedy team of Laurel and Hardy made many classic films with director Hal Roach in this area adjacent to Culver City (where Roach had his studio). Several loca-

tions today remain virtually unchanged from way back when. This house from 1929's *Perfect Day* is a good example. The boys memorably get a flat tire in front of the house, which looks much the way it did when the crew shot here in the summer of that year.

The Player

The Argyle
8358 Sunset Boulevard
Hollywood, California

Formerly the St. James Club and Hotel, this historic and grand 13-story building was the first high-rise built on Sunset Strip. Today it's called The Argyle hotel, and over the years it's played host to many stars. It was also a choice spot of Howard Hughes, who kept a number of suites here for his various girlfriends.

Clark Gable, Jean Harlow, Marilyn Monroe and John Wayne all stayed here over the years, too (Wayne is said to have kept a cow on the balcony outside his penthouse suite for fresh milk). And this is where Tim Robbins comes one night and hears a poolside pitch (and also gets a cryptic note inviting him to come meet "Joe Gilles"), in Robert Altman's cameo-studded insiders flick, 1992's *The Player*.

Pretty Woman

Rex II Ristorante
617 South Olive Street
Los Angeles, California

The formal dining room in this former upscale Italian ristorante was the site of the famous snail-flipping scene in the film *Pretty Woman* starring Julia Roberts and Richard Gere. Rex II Ristorante, located in what was once a 1920s-era haberdashery, has since closed, but has been replaced by a new restaurant—Cicada.

Remember the Titans

Druid Hills High School
1798 Haygood Drive
Atlanta, Georgia
678-874-6300

Disney's inspirational film from 2000 starring Denzel Washington was based on real events that took place in Alexandria, Virginia, in 1971. The story deals with the challenges surrounding the integration of black and white students at T. C. Williams High School, in particular within the football team (Washington played the coach).

The school that was primarily used in the film is Druid Hills. However, the school has no stadium or football field, so the football scenes were shot at Berry College, located at 2277 Martha Berry Highway NW, in Mount Berry, Georgia.

The Sandlot

Main Street
Midvale, Utah

1993's excellent movie *The Sandlot* is ranked by many purists as one of the best movies ever made about baseball. The story is about a young boy who moves to a new town and wants to learn about baseball from the local group of players. Several key scenes were shot along Main Street here in the community of Midvale, Utah. The field shots were filmed in Bountiful, Utah and Rose Park, Utah. (Bountiful is just north of Salt Lake City and Rose Park is actually within Salt Lake City.)

Scarecrow and Mrs. King

4247 Warner Boulevard
Burbank, California

This was the Cape Cod house used as Kate Jackson and Beverly Garland's home in the series *Scarecrow and Mrs. King*, which ran from 1983-1987. The show revolved around Secret Agent Lee "Scarecrow" Stetson, who enlists the aid of divorced housewife Amanda King.

Scarface

728 Ocean Drive
Miami, Florida

Al Pacino's brutal 1983 turn as two-bit thug Tony Montana (as directed by Brian De Palma) was set in Miami and Bolivia (though most of the actual locations were divided up between Florida and California). Now a hamburger joint, this was the site of the "Sun Ray Apartments," where Montana's brother was cut up by a chainsaw. (The two garish estates in the movie were actually located in the tiny town of Montecito, located just a few miles east of Santa Barbara, California.)

7th Heaven

4390 Colfax Avenue
Studio City, California

In the family drama *7th Heaven*, the Reverend Eric Camden (Stephen Collins) is not only father of seven, but also pastor at Glen Oak Community Church. And, services are not held on a set, but at a real church also known as the First Christian Church in Studio City. First Christian Church is no stranger to television. Its credits include *Hart to Hart* and the TV movie *A Walton Easter*.

Sex and the City

Various locations around New York City

The feisty, racy and very popular HBO series starring Sara Jessica Parker featured many real locations around New York City. Remember these?

Art Gallery

141 Price Street

The Louis K. Meisel Gallery is where the filming was done for the gallery where Charlotte worked.

Cupcake Bakery

401 Bleeker Street

Magnolia Bakery is where Carrie and Miranda memorably devoured cupcakes.

Jimmy Choo

645 Fifth Avenue (in the Olympic Tower)

This fashionable boutique is one of Carrie's favorite shoe stores.

O'Neal's Speakeasy

174 Grand Street

O'Neal's Speakeasy is where scenes from Scout, the show's popular bar, were shot.

Shaft

55 Jane Street
New York City, New York

This is the apartment of John Shaft, the iconic black detective played by Richard Roundtree in 1971's *Shaft*. The popular "blaxploitation" film inspired two sequels and a TV series, and of course the definitive song by Isaac Hayes. The movie was remade in 2000, with Samuel L. Jackson in the starring role.

Shampoo

1120 Wallace Ridge
Beverly Hills, California

The famous party scenes from Warren Beatty's 1975 hit *Shampoo* were shot here in this beautiful home north of Sunset Boulevard. Though in the film it was supposed to be the Beverly Hills mansion of Jack Warden, in reality this was Warren Beatty's actual home at the time. Another famous location from the movie was where Julie Christie finds herself under a table with Warren Beatty. This was shot at the old Bistro Garden in Beverly Hills, home today to Spago (176 North Canon Drive).

Sideways

The Hitching Post II
406 East Highway 246
Buellton, California
805-688-0676

2004's surprise critical smash *Sideways* is built around a Santa Ynez Valley wine-country road trip. In addition to featuring several vineyards from this scenic area just north of Santa Barbara, this central California coast restaurant plays a pivotal role in the film. Aside from being the favorite dining establishment and watering hole for the film's main character, Miles (Paul Giamatti), it is also the place where he meets his soulmate and fellow oenophile, Maya (Virginia Madsen), who works there as a waitress. Famous both for its fine wines and authentic Santa Maria barbecue, it was also here at the Hitching Post II's bar that *Sideways* writer Rex Pickett hung out as he was researching the area for his novel, from which the movie was based.

Silence of the Lambs

Carnegie Museum of Natural History
4400 Forbes Avenue
Pittsburgh, Pennsylvania

In this 1991 thriller, Jodie Foster's character, Clarice Starling, meets the notorious entomologist Hannibal Lecter (played by Anthony Hopkins) here. (Parts of *Flashdance* were also filmed here.) The place where Lecter escapes from his holding cell is the Allegheny County Soldiers and Sailors Memorial Hall, located at 4141 Fifth Avenue in Pittsburgh.

Simon & Simon

802 Fifth Street (at F Street)
San Diego, California

The mismatched detectives in *Simon & Simon*, brothers A.J. and Rick Simon (played by Jameson Parker and Gerald McRaney), worked in a third-floor office of this building in San Diego's historic Gaslamp Quarter. Simon & Simon ran for eight seasons, from 1981–1988.

Six Degrees of Separation

860 Fifth Avenue
New York City, New York

It's perhaps best known for inspiring a Kevin Bacon game, but this critically acclaimed play also made for a pretty good film. The 1993 effort, starring Will Smith as a charismatic con man, featured this apartment as the home of Donald Sutherland, one of Smith's primary victims. However, only the outside of the building was used in the film. The interiors were shot in a building at 1049 Fifth Avenue. The film also starred Ian McKellan, Mary Beth Hurt, Richard Masur and Stockard Channing.

Six Feet Under

2302 W. 25th Street
Los Angeles, California

A featured site on the eccentric HBO series *Six Feet Under* is the family home and mortuary, the Fisher & Sons Funeral Home. The house that's used in the show can be found near Gramercy Park in L.A., and no, it's not a mortuary—just a house.

Slapshot

Cambria County War Memorial
326 Napoleon Street
Johnstown, Pennsylvania

The story of a thuggish hockey team (the Chiefs), 1976's *Slapshot* (starring Paul Newman) was based in part on a real pro hockey team, the Johnstown Jets, from Johnstown, Pennsylvania. And, in fact, the movie was shot here in Johnstown. The local arena was used for all of the game sequences.

Today, the local team is called the Chiefs and they still play in this historic arena that dates back to 1950. The place offers some of the best and closest seats of any arena in professional ice hockey. (Note: 1983's *All the Right Moves* starring Tom Cruise was also shot here in gritty Johnstown.)

The Sopranos

The wildly popular HBO show about gangland New Jersey features many places located in and around the Garden State:

Bada Bing

Satin Dolls
230 State Highway Number 17
Lodi, New Jersey
201-845-6494

Satin Dolls is the real name of the club used for scenes that take place at the Bada Bing strip club in *The Sopranos*. Satin Dolls is a gentleman's club located in Lodi, New Jersey on Route 17. Some of the girls that dance at the club are the same girls that are in *The Sopranos*.

Joe's Bake Shop

Ridge Road (corner of Juancey Street)
North Arlington, New Jersey

In episode eight of the first season, Christopher Moltisanti (Michael Imperioli) replicates a *Goodfellas* scene by shooting a baker in the foot. The scene takes place at Joe's Bake Shop in North Arlington.

The Sopranos

Pizzaland

260 Belleville Turnpike
North Arlington, New Jersey

You can see Pizzaland on *The Sopranos* during every
opening scene as Tony Soprano drives home.

Satriale's Pork Store

101 Kearny Avenue
Kearny, New Jersey

In the pilot episode of *The Sopranos,* the pork store scenes were shot at Centanni's in
Elizabeth, New Jersey. For subsequent episodes, location scouts found this former auto
parts store in Kearny, and transformed it into the exterior of Satriale's. HBO holds the
lease on this formerly abandoned building.

Some sites seen during the Sopranos' opening credits:

The ceiling of the Lincoln Tunnel heading west to New Jersey. Tony is driving north and
drives up the helix to Route 3 West.

The New Jersey Turnpike sign at Secaucus . . .

The "Cash-Only" lane entrance to NJ Turnpike at 16W is clearly visible. (Note: this view
is no longer the same since the state converted to the automated Easy Pass system.)
Tony Soprano (played by actor James Gandolfini), takes a ticket.

The Goethals bridge, viewed from northbound truck lane side of the New Jersey
Turnpike.

View looking east from the New Jersey Turnpike extension (between exits 14 and 14C
in Jersey City) going eastbound towards the Holland Tunnel to New York

The Carteret tank farms as viewed from the southbound New Jersey Turnpike between
exits 13A and exit 12.

Sacred Heart Basilica Cathedral, Newark, New Jersey (the Pope spoke here during a
visit to the United States).

South Pacific

**Lumahai Beach
Kauai, Hawaii**

Hawaii sparkles in this 1958 classic musical starring Mitzi Gaynor and Juanita Hall. Gaynor washes her hair here at this famous beach, which is included in several movie tours of the island. Just to the north on the picturesque Na Pali Coast is Makahoa Point, which became the enchanted island of Bali Hai. This is one of the most visited film sites on all of the Hawaiian Islands.

Spartacus

**Hearst Castle
San Simeon, California**

Stanley Kubrick's epic from 1960 (starring Kirk Douglas, Jean Simmons and Tony Curtis among others) saw much of its action shot on the Universal Lot in Hollywood (with the major battles being shot in Spain). However, part of the historic residence of William Randolph Hearst (the white marble swimming pool, to be specific) became the outside of Cassuss's magnificent villa.

Strangers on a Train

**120 White Street
Danbury, Connecticut
203-778-8337**

Today, it's the Danbury Railway Museum, but back in 1951 it was still a working station on the New Haven Railroad and also where director Alfred Hitchcock shot his classic *Strangers on a Train*. (The station served as the setting for the fictional town of Metcalf.)

Swingers

Hills Coffee Shop
6145 Franklin Avenue
Hollywood, California

Until recently, the Hills Coffee Shop was located here in this nondescript Best Western Hotel right by the Hollywood Freeway. It was seen in 1996's *Swingers* as the place where the swingers would meet up for their heart-to-heart chats. (Much of the actual script was also written there, as it was a popular, downscale Hollywood hangout.)

Until recently, the restaurant lived on at 1745 North Vermont Avenue, about two blocks south of Franklin. They had also changed their name to the Hollywood Hills Restaurant.

The hipster tale centered around a character named Mike (played by Jon Favreau) who left his girl in New York when he came to L.A. to be a star. It also featured Vince Vaughn and Ron Livingston.

Tarentino, Quentin

Video Archives
1822 Sepulveda Boulevard
Manhattan Beach, California

Video Archives opened here in the early 1980s. Designed with the cinephile in mind, it was here where a 22-year-old Quentin Tarentino went to work. He and co-workers Roger Avary and Jerry Martinez would spend their time watching, discussing and recommending videos to customers.

Tarentino made his first (unfinished) film in 1986, *My Best Friend's Birthday*, written with his acting class friend Craig Hamann. He followed by writing his first script, *True Romance,* a year later. By 1988, Tarantino had written his second script, *Natural Born Killers* and in 1990 he sold the script for *True Romance* for $30,000.

He decided to use the money to make his third script *Reservoir Dogs* on 16mm and in black and white with his friends in the leading roles. It was at about this point Tarantino left the video store, which no longer stands on this site.

That Thing You Do

Watson's Drug Store & Soda Fountain
Orange, California

In 1996, Tom Hanks used this nostalgic drugstore as a setting in his 1950's era movie *That Thing You Do*. In fact, the drugstore has been used for many productions given its small town, locked-In-a-1940's, time-warp feel. Established in 1899, Watson's Drug Store & Soda Fountain is the oldest continuously operated business in the city, and the oldest drugstore in Orange County.

Once inside, you'll be transported back in time, thanks to the smell of hamburgers and fries, old-time ads hanging on the walls and waitresses wearing traditional black-and-white uniforms.

There's Something About Mary

Cardozo Hotel
1300 Ocean Drive
Miami, Florida

1998's comedy smash *There's Something About Mary*, starring Ben Stiller, Matt Dillon and Cameron Diaz was shot at many locations around Florida and Rhode Island. This popular Miami Hotel is where the wince-provoking pipe cleaning scene was shot.

Thirtysomething

1710 Bushnell Avenue
South Pasadena, California

The facade of this 1902 Craftsman Bungalow-style house was used as the home of Ken Olin and Mel Harris on the celebration of yuppieddom, TV's *Thirtysomething*. (It was also Jeff Daniels's house in 1990's *Welcome Home, Roxy Carmichael*.)

Tootsie

Old Route 209
Hurley Mountain Inn
Hurley, New York
845-331-1780

The historic Hurley Mountain Inn, located in New York's Hudson Valley, is where Dustin Hoffman (Tootsie) sits after being outed as a man in Sydney Pollack's 1982 comedy classic about a temperamental actor who disguises himself as a woman to get more work.

True Grit

123 North Lena Street
Ridgeway, Colorado

In 1969, John Wayne teamed with Glen Campbell and Kim Darby to make one of his most famous films, *True Grit*. The tale told of a drunken, hard-nosed U.S. Marshal and a Texas Ranger who help a stubborn young woman hunt down her father's murderer in Indian territory. The town of Ridgeway becomes Fort Smith in the movie, and nearby is the ranch where Wayne jumps his horse over a river. Ridgeway still has a *True Grit* Cafe, full of John Wayne memorabilia, located at 123 North Lena, 970-626-5739.

Walker, Texas Ranger

Tarrant County Courthouse
100 East Weatherford Street
Fort Worth, Texas

Though they would eventually build a replica of the interior of the Tarrant County Courthouse, originally the show starring Chuck Norris was shot right here. The program was an action-drama centered on modern-day Texas Ranger Cordell Walker, whose independent crime-solving methods had their roots in the rugged traditions of the Old West.

Wall Street

222 Broadway
New York City, New York

Oliver Stone's 1987 tale of '80's high-power greed was centered here at this downtown Manhattan office building, which was used both for Charlie Sheen's office and those of the slimy powerbroker, Gordon Gekko, played by Michael Douglas. The film is perhaps the ultimate yuppie tale of greed and downfall in the 1980's.

The Waltons

Route 617
Schuyler, Virginia
434-831-2000

The Walton's Mountain Museum, established in 1992, is located in the old Schuyler Elementary School across the street from the boyhood home of Earl Hamner (the real-life "John-Boy" who created the popular TV series). In fact, Schuyler Elementary is where Hamner actually graduated from in 1940 in a class of 12 students.

The charming museum houses replicas of sets from *The Waltons*, including John-Boy's bedroom, the Waltons' kitchen and living room and Ike Godsey's store, which also serves as the museum's gift shop. As for the actual Hamner home, today it is a private residence still belonging to the Hamner family. You are permitted to take pictures of the house, but it is not open to public.

The Way We Were

Plaza Hotel
New York City, New York

Sydney Pollack's 1973 tearjerker starring Barbara Streisand and Robert Redford saw the final meeting of the two stars take place at this historic New York hotel, just outside the famous Fifth Avenue entrance. (The made-up Wentworth College, where the two met, is actually Union College in Schenectady, upstate New York.) As of this writing the future of the classic hotel is unclear and it may in fact soon become condominiums.

The Witch's House

516 North Walden Drive
Beverly Hills, California

Officially, it's known as "The Spadena House," though tourists from around the world have come to know it as simply The Witch's House. Originally built in 1921 for Irving Willat's

movie studio in Culver City (and used in several silent films), this strange, dramatic creation was then moved to Beverly Hills in 1926, where today it is now a private home (and undergoing renovation as of this writing). The house is a popular stop for tour buses and tourists as it stands out like a sore thumb among some of the most glamorous homes in Beverly Hills.

Young Frankenstein

Hoffman Hall
University of Southern California
Los Angeles, California

Mel Brooks's 1974 classic black and white comedy starring Gene Wilder, Teri Garr, Peter Boyle and Marty Feldman actually used props and lab equipment from the original *Frankenstein* film, which this lovingly parodied. In the movie, we see Wilder teaching his students from here at Hoffman Hall, part of the University of Southern California. *Young Frankenstein* also starred Madeline Kahn, Cloris Leachman, Teri Garr and Kenneth Mars. It remains one of Mel Brooks's most popular films, a timeless comedy that also manages to poke a lot of intelligent fun at the entire horror genre.

Art and Literature

American Gothic

Burton and Gothic Streets
Eldon, Iowa
319-335-3916

In August of 1930, artist Grant Wood was visiting this small town in the southern part of Iowa when he stumbled upon a house that would eventually make him famous. Grant Wood imagined a farmer and his spinster daughter standing in front of the 1880's, five-room house built in a style known as "Carpenter Gothic." He sketched his idea on brown paper and had someone take a photograph of the house so that he could work out his vision when he returned home.

The now-famous painting, which glorified and satirized rural Americans, may be the most parodied work of art ever. The model for the farmer's daughter in the picture was Grant's sister, Nan Wood Graham. The model for the farmer was Dr. B.H. McKeeby, the family dentist. Although not open to the public, visitors are welcome to view the house from the outside as Grant Wood did in 1930 when its unusual Gothic window inspired him.

The State Historical Society of Iowa owns and preserves the American Gothic house. It is listed on the National Register of Historic Places. Grant Wood had been born on a farm near Anamosa, Iowa and grew up in Cedar Rapids. Though he lived and worked around the world, he always maintained a strong bond to Eastern Iowa. He died in February 1942.

Arbus, Diane

155 Bank Street
New York City, New York

This block-long complex was once the Bell Telephone/Western Electric Laboratories, where some of the most important inventions of the 20th Century were created. These include the vacuum tube (1912), radar (1919), sound movies (1923) and the digital computer (1937). In 1927, one of the first demonstrations of television transmission occurred here. This was also the original home of the NBC radio network.

However, in 1969 it was converted to an artists' colony and it was here where photographer Diane Arbus committed suicide on July 28, 1971. (Arbus lived at 120 East 10th Street from 1968–1970.) Arbus's death brought even more attention to her name and photographs, which had earned her an international reputation as one of the pioneers of the "new" documentary style. Today, the Bank Street Theatre is located here.

Audubon, John James

Mill Grove
Audubon, Pennsylvania
610-666-5593
Directions: Take I-76 West to King of Prussia to Route 422 North/West. Continue to Audubon exit. At the first light turn left onto Audubon Road, which dead ends at the entrance to the sanctuary.

Mill Grove was the first American home of John James Audubon, artist, author, and naturalist. Located in Audubon, Pennsylvania, it is now a wildlife sanctuary and is the only true Audubon home still standing in America. The mansion house was built in 1762 and Captain Jean Audubon, John James's father, acquired the property in 1789. That year,  he sent his son John to oversee the estate, which included a working lead mine.

Audubon lived here for little more than two years, but it was at Mill Grove that he gained his first impressions of American birds and wildlife while journeying into the adjoining forested country. Today the mansion serves as a unique gallery displaying the major works published by the talented John James Audubon. Mill Grove has also been designated a National Historic Landmark.

Basquiat, Jean-Michel

57 Great Jones Street
New York City, New York

Influenced by Andy Warhol, Basquiat was a rebellious high school dropout who started out as a graffiti artist, making images and writing slogans on the walls of buildings. He also produced painted T-shirts, found-object assemblages, and paintings.

In the early 1980s he was "discovered" by the art establishment, and his works in paint and crayon on unprimed canvas, featuring crude, angry, and raw, powerful figures and graffiti-like written messages, were much sought after by collectors. He died of a heroin overdose at the age of 27. He lived and worked in this building, then owned by Andy Warhol.

Burgess, Thornton W.

4 Water Street (Route 130)
Sandwich, Massachusetts
508-888-4668

The Thornton W. Burgess Museum is located on the beautiful Shawme Pond here in the historic center of Cape Cod's oldest town, Sandwich. Visitors today will get to experience the life, works, and spirit of famed children's author and naturalist Thornton Burgess (*Mother West Wind's Children, Billy Mink, Lightfoot the Deer*, etc.). This 18th century house (which is the museum) exhibits artifacts, art, writings and other personal and professional memorabilia that relate to Burgess's life and work. Also on the grounds is a lovely "tussie mussie" herb garden overlooking the pond. As well, the museum gift shop offers many unique items in addition to a full selection of Burgess books.

Children's Literature

Charles M. Schulz Museum

2301 Hardies Lane
Santa Rosa, California
707-579-4452

Based in the area where *Peanuts* creator Charles M. Schulz worked for so many years, the charming Charles M. Schulz Museum (opened in 2002) features Schulz's business and personal papers, original comic strips and drawings, a library with a large collection of Peanuts books in several languages, many photographs, memorabilia and special exhibits related to the great artist and thinker. Schulz was first published by Robert Ripley in his *Ripley's Believe It or Not!*

The St. Paul Pioneer Press published his first regular comic strip, *Li'l Folks*, in 1947. (It was in this strip that Charlie Brown first appeared, as well as a dog that resembled Snoopy). In 1950, he approached the United Features Syndicate with his best strips from *Li'l Folks* and *Peanuts* made its first appearance on October 2, 1950. This strip became one of the most popular comic strips of all time.

Peanuts ran for nearly 50 years without interruption and had appeared in over 2,600 newspapers in 75 countries. In November, 1999, Schulz suffered a stroke, and later it was discovered that he had terminal colon cancer. Schulz announced his retirement on December 14, 1999, at the age of 77. The last original strip ran on February 13, 2000. Schulz had died at 9:45 P.M. the night before in Santa Rosa, California of a heart attack.

As part of his will, Schulz had requested that the *Peanuts* characters remain as authentic as possible and that no new comic strips based on them be drawn. To date his wishes have been honored, although reruns of the strip are still being syndicated to newspapers.

The Dr. Seuss National Memorial Sculpture Garden

The Quadrangle (State and Chestnut Streets)
Springfield, Massachusetts

You'll find the Dr. Seuss National Memorial Sculpture Garden at the Quadrangle in Springfield, Massachusetts, the city where Theodore Seuss Geisel was born and which many believe inspired much of his magical work from *The Lorax* to *The Cat in the Hat.*

Children's Literature

Goodnight Moon
Main Street
Greenville, South Carolina

If you have kids, odds are you've read the classic, simple, charming book *Goodnight Moon* (probably over and over again). Here in Greenville, the book is uniquely celebrated thanks to a local high school student who wanted to do something good for the community. A bronzed sculpture of the book and one mouse are mounted on the fountain in front of the Hyatt Regency hotel and the other eight mice are installed along a nine-block stretch of Main Street between the Hyatt & the Westin Poinsett hotels. The artist who created the work is Zan Wells, and by finding the mice, you also get a chance to explore Greenville's Main Street.

The Little Red Lighthouse
178th Street and the Hudson River
New York City, New York
212-304-2365
Directions: From Lafayette Place at West 181st Street, take steps, footpath and footbridge over the highway, down to the park and south to the Lighthouse.

The Jeffrey's Hook lighthouse, erected in 1880 and moved to its current site under the George Washington Bridge in 1921, has become famous as the children's literary landmark, *The Little Red Lighthouse*.

The story of the lighthouse in Fort Washington Park was popularized by the children's book *The Little Red Lighthouse* and the *Great Gray Bridge*, written by Hildegarde H. Swift with illustrations by Lynd Ward, published in 1942. In this fictional account of Jeffrey's Hook lighthouse, the structure was presented as a symbol of the significance of a small thing in a big world.

Children's Literature

Make Way for Ducklings

Public Garden
Boston, Massachusetts
Directions: The Public Garden is bordered by Arlington, Boylston, Charles and Beacon Streets. The ducklings are on the northeast corner of the park.

In Robert McCloskey's 1941 classic children's book *Make Way for Ducklings* Mr. & Mrs. Mallard are looking for a place to live. Every time Mr. Mallard finds a place, Mrs. Mallard says it is not a good place to raise a family. They finally decide on a place in Boston along the Charles River. Mrs. Mallard has eight ducklings and decides to leave the Charles River site and settle in the Boston Commons. Today in the lovely and historic Public Garden, you'll find bronze statues of the ducklings, depicting them just as they are in the book. (They were created in 1985.)

There is another tribute to the book like this one in a park in Moscow, Russia—a gift from the children of the United Stated to the children of Russia.

Children's Literature

Mary Had a Little Lamb

72 Wayside Inn Road
Sudbury, Massachusetts

This is the original Redstone School, used to teach the children of District Number Two on Redstone Hill in Sterling from 1798 to 1856. When the building was moved here to Sudbury, where it sits today near Longfellow's Wayside Inn, it was used in their public school system to teach grades one through four from 1927 to 1951. It is now a small museum, and is used to demonstrate early American rural schooling traditions.

But, it holds an even more important place in American history. This is the building where Mary Tyler (1806-1889) went to school followed by her little lamb. Here are the first 12 lines of the famous verse, which are said to be written by John Roulstone:

Mary had a little lamb,
Its fleece was as white as snow,
And every were that Mary went,
The lamb was sure to go.

It followed her to school one day;
That was against the rule;
It made the children laugh and play;
To see the lamb at school.

And so the teacher turned it out;
but still it lingered near;
And waited patiently about;
Till Mary did appear.

The schoolhouse is located adjacent to the historic Wayside Inn in Sudbury, and just down the road from a famous farmhouse where Babe Ruth lived back when he played for the Boston Red Sox.

Children's Literature

Mother Goose

Granary Burial Ground
Park and Tremont Streets
Boston, Massachusetts

The author of *Mother Goose's Rhymes* is said to lie in a grave here marked "Elizabeth Foster Goose." She lived in colonial times here in Boston and entertained her grandchildren with rhymes and chants that she remembered from her own childhood. It is said that Thomas Fleet, her son-in-law, made a collection of these rhymes and put them in a book called "Songs for the Nursery" or "Mother Goose's Melodies." The Granary Burying Ground is also the site of the graves of Paul Revere and John Hancock. It is one of the most historic burial grounds in all of the United States and a must-visit when in Boston.

Concord Museum

200 Lexington Road
Concord, Massachusetts
978-369-9763

The Concord Museum was founded in 1886 and maintains collections of memorabilia from two of the United States' most influential authors, Ralph Waldo Emerson and Henry David Thoreau. The Thoreau memorabilia includes a desk, bed, and chair that he is said to have used in his cabin at Walden Pond. Additionally, you'll see Thoreau's writings, his flute, a photograph, and many other items.

Also on display are items that belonged to poet and essayist Ralph Waldo Emerson. A desk and chair that he is said to have used to write many of his influential essays are on display along with other memorabilia. As Thoreau and Emerson were friends, you may also read some of the correspondence between the two authors as you tour the exhibits.

Crane, Stephen

165 West 23rd Street
New York City, New York

 Author Stephen Crane (*The Red Badge of Courage*) was a down-on-his-luck, 24-year old when he took over the large room at the top of this five-story, red building in 1896. While here, he spent his time writing newspaper and magazine articles. Painter John Sloan (1904–11) also lived on the top floor here and the view is featured in many of Sloan's paintings.

cummings, e.e.

4 Patchin Place (between Sixth Avenue off West 10th Street)
New York City, New York

In 1923, poet e.e. cummings returned from Europe and moved into a studio on the top floor here. cummings and his third wife, Marion Morehouse, eventually bought the entire house and he lived there for the rest of his life until his death in 1962.

Over the years, many other writers and people in the arts have lived here at Patchin Place. Avant-garde writer Djuna Barnes lived here from 1940 until her death in 1982 at the age of 90 and actor Marlon Brando shared an apartment here with his sister, Frances, in 1943 and 1944.

de Kooning, Willem

88 East 10th Street
New York City, New York

The famous painter Willem de Kooning lived here and painted here in his home studio with his wife Elaine from the late 1940s through the mid-1950s. De Kooning, born in 1904 in Rotterdam, started his first series of *Women* in 1938, which would become a major recurrent theme. During the 1940s, he participated in group shows with other artists who would form the New York School and become known as Abstract Expressionists.

De Kooning's first solo show, which took place at the Egan Gallery in New York in 1948, established his reputation as a major artist; it included a number of the allover black-and-white abstractions he had initiated in 1946. The *Women* of the early 1950s were followed by abstract urban landscapes, parkways, rural landscapes, and, in the 1960s, a new group of *Women*. Willem de Kooning died in 1997 in East Hampton, New York.

Dickens, Charles

Eagle Hotel
21 North 2nd Street
Harrisburg, Pennsylvania

A plaque here reads: "A three-story brick hotel, maintained by the Buehler family, 1811–64, stood on this site. Many State officials and legislators of the time took quarters here. Charles Dickens, a guest in 1842, praised his host in 'American Notes.'" Charles Dickens (1812-1870) wrote such classics as: *A Christmas Carol, Oliver Twist, David Copperfield, A Tale Of Two Cities, Great Expectations*, and many others.

Dvorak, Antonin

327 East 17th Street
New York City, New York

The renowned Czech composer, Antonin Dvorak, lived here with his family from 1892 until 1895. He was appointed the head of the city's National Conservatory of Music in 1892. Dvorak wrote the famous symphony *From the New World* in 1893 while he was here. Overcome by homesickness, he returned to Prague in 1895. He was director of the conservatoire from 1901 until his death in 1904.

Emerson, Ralph Waldo

27 Summer Street
Boston, Massachusetts

The essayist and great American thinker Ralph Waldo Emerson was born in a house that stood on this site on May 25, 1803. In October, 1817, at the age of 14, Emerson went to Harvard University and was appointed "President's Freshman," a position that gave him a room free of charge.

After graduating, Emerson made his living for several years as a schoolmaster, eventually studying divinity himself, and emerging as a Unitarian minister. A dispute with church officials over the administration of the Communion service led to his resignation. About the same time, his young wife and one true love, Miss Elena Louisa Tucker, died in February 1831.

In 1836, Emerson and other like-minded intellectuals founded *The Dial*, a periodical that served as a vehicle for the transcendental movement, although the first issue did not appear until July 1840. Meanwhile, Emerson published his first book, *Nature*, in September, 1836. Other major works included *Compensation, Self-Reliance, Circles* and *The Transcendentalist*. Emerson died in 1882.

Faulkner, William

Rowan Oak
Old Taylor Road
Oxford, Mississippi
662-234-3284

In 1930, Nobel Prize-winning novelist William Faulkner purchased "The Bailey Place" and soon named the beautiful, pre-Civil War manor, "Rowan Oak." It was the Faulkner's family home until 1962, the year of William Faulkner's death. Included in the furnishings of Rowan Oak today are paintings by Faulkner's mother and a bust of Don Quixote, given to Faulkner in 1961 by the president of Venezuela.

In addition, the handwritten plot outline of *A Fable* can be seen on the walls of Faulkner's office, which he built after being awarded a Nobel Prize in 1949. A portable typewriter sits on the table, a bottle of horse liniment and a carpenter's pencil nearby, just as they were on the day Faulkner died on July 6, 1962. Behind the house is a stable, and a cook's house and kitchen, used by Faulkner as a smokehouse. Many tourists also enjoy walking from Rowan Oak into town, as Faulkner did almost everyday. Both the grounds and home are open to visitors.

Foster, Stephen

38 Canal Street
New York City, New York

Back in the mid-1800s, this address was the site of the New England Hotel. The fleabag residence was where the composer Stephen Foster had a fatal accident on January 10, 1864. The composer of "Oh! Susanna," "Old Folks at Home" and "Beautiful Dreamer" had become an out-of-control alcoholic and died with a paltry 38 cents in his pocket. At the time of his death, Foster had composed some 285 songs and arrangements, many of them established as true American folk songs that are still enjoyed by millions today.

Grandma Moses Schoolhouse

Bennington Museum
75 Main Street
Bennington, Vermont
802-447-1571

This historic schoolhouse, actually attended by Grandma Moses and other members of her family in Eagle Bridge, New York, was moved to the grounds of the excellent Bennington Museum in 1972. Today, the schoolhouse features exhibitions recording the life and achievements of the artist Anna Mary Robertson Moses (1860–1961), who became known to the world as Grandma Moses, one of America's most noted folk artists.

Artifacts and documents discuss her life, the universal fame she gained, and more. Today, visitors can even watch Moses herself paint and hear her discuss her extraordi-

nary life by viewing a classic 1955 Edward R. Murrow interview with Moses for his legendary CBS television show *See It Now*. At age 100, she illustrated an edition of *The Night Before Christmas* and the book was published after her death. Grandma Moses died on December 13, 1961. She lived to be 101 and in the last year of her life, incredibly, she painted 25 pictures.

Hammett, Dashiell

15 East 23rd Street
New York City, New York

In 1928, this was the Hotel Kenmore, where, from 1927–1929, writer Nathaniel West was the night manager. Back then, he'd allow friends and fellow writers free board and food–these people included Edmund Wilson, Erskine Caldwell, S.J. Perelman and William Maxwell. Most importantly, Dashiell Hammett finished his famed novel *The Maltese Falcon* here in this building. Hammett remains the first master of classic, hard-boiled detective fiction.

His crisp writing, cynical characters and layered plots helped define the private eye genre in movies, radio and television and his influence is still felt today.

Hawthorne, Nathaniel

The Wayside Inn
399 Lexington Road
Concord, Massachusetts
978-369-6975

Located inside the Minute Man National Park was the home of the muster master, or roll caller, of the Concord Minute Men. It was later the home of Bronson and Louisa May Alcott, the Nathaniel Hawthorne family, and Margaret Sidney, an author of children's books during the late 19th century. Here, Louisa May Alcott and her sisters lived much of the childhood described in *Little Women.*

Now part of Minute Man National Historical Park, The Wayside was preserved by children's author Margaret Sidney, creator of the *Five Little Peppers*, and her daughter, Margaret. The Wayside is the only National Historic Landmark lived in by three literary families, and collectively their works span more than three centuries.

Hemingway, Ernest

Birthplace

339 North Oak Park Avenue
Oak Park, Illinois

Ernest Miller Hemingway was born at 8:00 A.M. on July 21, 1899, here in the family home built by his widowed grandfather, Ernest Hall. Hemingway was the second of Dr. Clarence and Grace Hall Hemingway's six children. He had four sisters and one brother. He was named after his maternal grandfather Ernest Hall and his great uncle Miller Hall.

Today at the home you can explore displays featuring rare photographs of Hemingway, his childhood diary, letters, early writings and other memorabilia. Exhibits and videos at the Museum focus on his first 20 years in Oak Park, and its impact on his later works. There is also a great gift shop.

A Farewell to Arms

1021 West Cherry Street
Piggott, Arkansas (about 90 miles northwest of Memphis, Tennessee)
870-598-3487

Hemingway visited here many times between 1927 and 1940. After all, he was at that time married to Pauline Pfeiffer, daughter of Piggott residents Paul and Mary. They actually owned this house and the red barn in the back, which they converted into a

writing studio so Hemingway had a place to write. It was here that he composed *A Farewell to Arms* and most likely fragments of the seven other books he wrote while married to Pauline.

Recently, the property came under the administration of Arkansas State University at Jonesboro. The Red Barn is now a Hemingway Museum and the Pfeiffer House is a literary conference center so that visiting scholars can study Hemingway in a place where he lived and wrote. Both the home and the barn studio were named to the National Historic Register in 1982.

On a cinematic note, Piggott is also where famed director Elia Kazan shot much of his dark, 1957 classic *A Face in the Crowd*, starring Andy Griffith and Patricia Neal.

Hemingway, Ernest

For Whom the Bell Tolls

Sun Valley Lodge
Sun Valley, Idaho

Ernest Hemingway wrote part of *For Whom the Bell Tolls* in Room 206 at this classic four-story lodge in the village center. He first visited this area in the fall in 1939, joined by writer Martha Gellhorn who would become his third wife. He nicknamed his suite here "Glamour House," and had a temporary bar and bookshelves installed. (Hemingway even mentions Sun Valley in Chapter 13 of *For Whom the Bell Tolls*.)

L.C. Bates Museum

Good Will-Hinckley School, Route 201
Hinckley, Maine
207-453-4894

It's something no true fan of Ernest Hemingway should miss—a blue marlin caught by the author when he was in the midst of writing *The Old Man and the Sea*. That item is one of many ephemeral treasures within this small, offbeat museum located on the campus of a school for disadvantaged children. Closed in the 1950s and recently re-opened as is, this dusty, musty archive also includes minerals, stuffed birds, assorted fossils and many other obscure items.

Jeffers, Robinson

Tor House
26304 Ocean View Avenue
Carmel, California

This was the home of the great poet, Robinson Jeffers and his wife, Una. The pair arrived here along the beautiful Monterey-area coast in 1914 and began building the cliffside house in 1918. Using granite boulders gathered from the rocky shore of Carmel Bay (along with lava from Hawaii, a headstone from Ireland, even a portion of the Great Wall of China), Jeffers built Tor House and Hawk Tower as a home and refuge for himself and his family. (A craggy hill is also called a "Tor," which inspired the name of the house.)

It was here that he crafted all of his major poetical works: the long narratives of "this coast crying out for tragedy," the shorter meditative lyrics and dramas on classical themes, culminating in 1947 with the critically acclaimed adaptation of *Medea* for the Broadway stage, with Dame Judith Anderson in the title role. Over the years, many lumi-  naries visited Jeffers here including Sinclair Lewis, Edna St. Vincent Millay, Langston Hughes, Charles Lindbergh, George Gershwin and Charlie Chaplin.

Today, visitors can experience the scene just as Jeffers did, relaxing in the poet's furniture while listening to poems written about and within those stone walls. Docent-led tours of Tor House, Hawk Tower and the old-world gardens are conducted hourly every Friday and Saturday. The first tour begins at 10 :00 A.M. and the final tour is at 3:00 A.M. Each tour is limited to a maximum of six people. For safety reasons, children under 12 years of age are not allowed.

Johns, Jasper

Corner of Houston and Essex Streets (Greenwich Village)
New York City, New York

In the old bank building here, artist Jasper Johns created many of his masterworks from 1967-1988. Johns was born in South Carolina during the Depression and moved to New York in the early 1950s to work as a commercial artist. In 1954, Johns created his first painting of the American flag. That painting became the first of a series that took commonplace objects and elevated them to pieces of art.

Using the ancient technique of encaustic (which blends pigment with a binder of hot wax), Johns formed highly textural surfaces that characterize much of his work. Jasper Johns also formed an important, influential friendship with artist Robert Rauschenberg early in his career. Together, these two artists became heavily identified with Pop Art and Minimalism.

Kerouac, Jack

501 East 11th Street
New York City, New York

At one time a tenement apartment stood on this lot, and writer Jack Kerouac stayed here in the summer of 1953. It is believed that the building inspired the setting for Kerouac's classic novel, *The Subterraneans*. Additionally, poet Alan Ginsberg dubbed the building "Paradise Alley."

The Kiss

Times Square
New York City, New York

For millions of Americans, Alfred Eisenstaedt's 1945 *Life* magazine photograph of a sailor planting a kiss on a nurse symbolized the cathartic joy of V-J Day. After a celebrated five-decade career, Alfred (who died in the mid-1990s) called *V-J Day, Times Square* his most memorable photograph. Widely considered the father of photojournalism, he began creating photo essays in Berlin during the 1920s and early 1930s. He immigrated to the U. S. in 1935 and joined the original photography staff at *Life* magazine in 1936.

Lewis, Sinclair

810 Sinclair Lewis Avenue
Sauk Centre, Minnesota
320-352-5201

This is the boyhood home of America's first winner of Nobel Prize for literature in 1930, Sinclair Lewis. The award reflected his groundbreaking work in the 1920s on books such as *Main Street* (1920), *Babbitt* (1922), and *Arrowsmith* (1925). He was also awarded the Pulitzer Prize for *Arrowsmith*, but declined it because he believed that the Pulitzer was meant for books that celebrated American wholesomeness and that his novels, which were quite critical, should not be awarded the prize.

Today, narrated, guided tours are approximately 25 minutes long and take you through the restored, turn-of-the-century home where Sinclair Lewis lived with his parents and brothers. Alcohol would play a dominant role in his life and he died of the effects of advanced alcoholism in Rome, Italy, in 1951. In 2001, his book *Main Street* was named one of the 100 best English-language novels of the 20th century by the editorial board of the American Modern Library.

Longfellow's Wayside Inn

72 Wayside Inn Road
Sudbury, Massachusetts
978-443-1776

This charming inn (which also boasts a restaurant and beautifully historic grounds) was originally known as Howe's Tavern from 1716 to 1861. In the late 1890s, Edward Rivers Lemon, an admirer of antiquities, purchased the inn as "a retreat for literary pilgrims," capitalizing on the interest generated by a widely read book of poems published in 1863 by Henry Longfellow called *Tales of a Wayside Inn*.

Longfellow visited the Howe Tavern in 1862, and based his book on a group of fictitious characters that regularly gathered at the old Sudbury tavern. Lyman Howe was the character featured in *The Landlord's Tale*, where Longfellow penned the immortal phrase "Listen my children and you shall hear, of the midnight ride of Paul Revere." Lemon renamed the old Howe Tavern "Longfellow's Wayside Inn" and operated it with his wife, Cora, until his death in 1919.

In 1923, Cora Lemon sold the Inn to automobile manufacturer Henry Ford, who would eventually have the most visual impact on the Wayside Inn site. He moved the one-room Redstone School (of *Mary Had a Little Lamb* fame) to the grounds in 1925; built the Grist Mill in 1929 and the Martha-Mary Chapel in 1940; and acquired some 3,000 acres around the Inn. He also developed a trade school for boys, which operated from 1928 to 1947.

Many believe he intended to build the "village site" that he eventually created in Dearborn, Michigan, right here in Sudbury. While he stopped short of that goal, he did

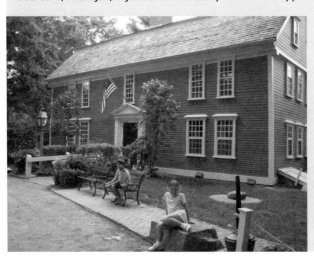

create the non-profit status that the inn operates under today. Henry Ford was the last private owner of the Wayside Inn. Today, this is one of the most popular historic inns in the New England area, renowned for both its beauty and history.

Mailer, Norman

41 First Avenue
New York City, New York

Norman Mailer's first novel, *The Deer Park*, was written while he lived here from 1951–1952. Interestingly, Mailer used to meet Dan Wolf on the roof of the building—together, they founded *The Village Voice* in 1955. Mailer's many important literary works include *The Naked and the Dead* (1948), *The Armies of the Night* (1968; Pulitzer Prize), and *Oswald's Tale* (1995), a study of the life of President Kennedy's assassin, Lee Harvey Oswald. Mailer is recognized today as the main innovator of what's called the "nonfiction novel." In the 1960s and 1970s he developed this form of journalism which combines actual events, autobiography, and political commentary with the richness of the novel form.

Mapplethorpe, Robert

24 Bond Street
New York City, New York

Controversial photographer Robert Mapplethorpe lived and worked here through much of the 1980s. Known for his expressive black-and-white studies of male and female nudes, flowers, and celebrity portraits, some of his work was considered graphic and controversial. In 1990, a Cincinnati jury found that city's Contemporary Arts Center and its director not guilty of obscenity for exhibiting Mapplethorpe's photographs. Robert Mapplethorpe died from complications arising from AIDS in 1989.

Mencken, H.L.

1524 Hollins Street
Baltimore, Maryland

A National Historic Landmark, this brick, Italianate row house was the residence of noted *Baltimore Sun* journalist and curmudgeon author Henry Louis Mencken from 1883 until his death in 1956. A crusty, acidic personality, Mencken gained national recognition as one of the most influential critics of American culture, politics, education and life, coining the word "booboisie" to describe the American public. Once part of the Baltimore City Life Museums, the house is currently not open to the public.

Mitchell, Joan

60 St. Mark's Place
New York City, New York

Before her triumphant move to France in the late 1950s, expressionist painter Joan Mitchell lived and worked here for about six years. Mitchell was one of the finest painters of the second generation of Abstract Expressionism. In Manhattan during the 1950s, Mitchell encountered "action painting," developing friendships with such artists as Willem de Kooning and Franz Kline.

In 1959, Mitchell settled in France where, rejecting the movements that dominated art from the 1960s on, she continued to paint in an abstract expressionist style. Usually very large, sometimes in multi-panel format, her paintings incorporate both turbulence and control and are frequently inspired by landscapes and poetry.

Muir, John

4202 Alhambra Avenue
Martinez, California
925-228-8860

This is the 14-room mansion where naturalist John Muir lived from 1890 to his death in 1914. While living here in the coastal town of Martinez, Muir accomplished many things: he battled to prevent Yosemite National Park's Hetch Hetchy Valley from being dammed, served as the first president and one of the founders of the Sierra Club, played a prominent role in the creation of several national parks, and wrote hundreds of newspaper and magazine articles and several books expounding on the virtues of conservation and the natural world. Muir's work laid the foundations for the creation of the National Park Service in 1916. In 1964, the Muir house and historic Martinez adobe became part of the National Park Service.

O'Henry

409 East 5th Street
Austin, Texas

This small Queen Anne cottage is the home of the O'Henry Museum, which honors William Sydney Porter, the short story writer better known as O'Henry, who lived in Austin in the second half of the 19th century. In 1887, O'Henry married Athol Estes, whose family owned the house. It served as the couple's home from 1893 to 1895.

O'Henry published a weekly paper entitled The Rolling Stone for one year before the venture failed in 1895, which precipitated his move to Houston to work for The Houston Post. While in Houston he was convicted of embezzlement, purported to have occurred during his earlier vocation as a bank teller in Austin. Seeking to avoid prison he fled to Honduras.

He returned to the U. S., and to Austin, only when he learned that his wife was dying. He eventually served a three-year prison sentence in Ohio, during which time he honed his

skills as a writer of the short story. The original address of the abode was 308 East 4th Street, but it was moved multiple times until it found a final resting place on 5th Street.

O'Henry

28 West 26th Street
New York City, New York

At one time this building was the Hotel Caledonia, where writer O'Henry lived from 1906–1907, before moving to the Chelsea Hotel. However, he kept a room here for writing and it was here where he collapsed on June 3, 1910. He would die two days later.

O'Keeffe, Georgia

Georgia O'Keeffe Museum

217 Johnson Street
Santa Fe, New Mexico
505-946-1000

The Georgia O'Keeffe Museum in Santa Fe, New Mexico, opened to the public in July 1997, 11 years after the death of O'Keeffe. Since then, the museum has welcomed more than 1,300,000 visitors from all over the world. The museum's permanent collection of O'Keeffe paintings, drawings, and sculpture is the largest in the world. Throughout the year, visitors can see a changing selection of at least 50 of these works. In addition, the museum presents special exhibitions that are either devoted entirely to O'Keeffe's work or that combine examples of her art with works by her American modernist contemporaries.

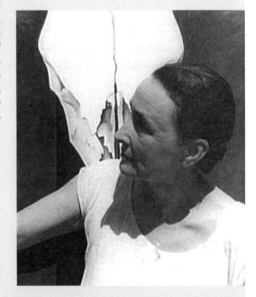

Home and Studio

County Road 164
Abiquiu, New Mexico
505-685-4539

The home and studio of the artist Georgia O'Keeffe (1887–1986) in Abiquiu, New Mexico (approximately 50 miles northwest of Santa Fe), is one of the most important artistic sites in the southwestern United. States. Georgia O'Keeffe's stark paintings of cattle skulls bleached by the desert sun are familiar to all. From 1949 until her death in 1984, O'Keeffe lived and worked here at Abiquiu.

The buildings and their surroundings, along with the views they command, inspired many of her paintings and continue to provide great insight into her vision. The home and studio are maintained by the Georgia O'Keeffe Foundation, and are open to the public. Tours are available of O'Keeffe's home in Abiquiu for groups of 16 or less, by appointment only. The Georgia O'Keefe Foundation recommends making reservations at least six months in advance and requests a $20 per person donation.

O'Keeffe, Georgia

Lawrence Tree

Kiowa Ranch
20 miles north of Taos, New Mexico (off of Route 522 near San Cristobal)
505-776-2245

"The big pine tree in front of the house, standing still and unconcerned and alive...the overshadowing tree whose green top one never looks at...One goes out of the door and the tree-trunk is there, like a guardian angel. The tree-trunk, the long work table and the fence!"—D. H. Lawrence. Under this mammoth pine tree, author D.H. Lawrence (*Women in Love* and *Lady Chatterley's Lover*) would spend his mornings writing at a small table.

In 1929, artist Georgia O'Keeffe came to Taos and during her visit spent several weeks here at the beautiful and remote Kiowa Ranch. While here, she painted the stately pine,

which still stands today. O'Keeffe wrote that she would lie on the long weathered carpenter's bench under the tall tree staring up past the trunk, up into the branches and into the night sky.

That image is captured in her now world-famous oil painting, *The Lawrence Tree*, which is currently owned by the Wadsworth Antheneum in Hartford, Connecticut. Today, visitors can see the tree and the rest of what remains of the ranch, including a shrine where D.H. Lawrence's ashes are interred. Note: this is an isolated area with no facilities to speak of; the shrine and its environs are open during daylight hours.

Old Manse

269 Monument Street
Concord, Massachusetts
978-369-3909

Located just a stone's throw from the Old North Bridge in historic Concord, the Old Manse has one of the richest histories anywhere. It has witnessed the lives of many Native Americans who used it for temporary camps, the beginnings of the American Revolution on April 19, 1775 and the lives of great 19th-century American writers (who helped usher in transcendentalism). The home was built in 1770 by the grandfather of Ralph Waldo Emerson, who spent some of his boyhood at the home.

Nathaniel Hawthorne occupied the house from 1842-1845 and gave the house its name (his *Mosses from an Old Manse* was written in the study). Among the furnishings you'll see here during the excellent tour is the desk at which Nathaniel Hawthorne wrote. Also at the Manse is a re-creation of the vegetable garden that Henry David Thoreau planted for the Hawthornes before they arrived; the garden is based on the journals of Hawthorne and George Bradford.

O'Neill, Eugene

West 43rd Street in Times Square
New York City, New York

The southeast corner of the block was the site of the Barrett House Hotel, where playwright Eugene O'Neill was born on October 16, 1888, while his father was in town starring in *The Count of Monte Cristo*. O'Neill went on to become a Nobel and Pulitzer Prize-winning playwright whose plays portray tormented families and people torn between wealth and the noblest of ideals. Some of his classics include *Beyond the Horizon* (1920), *Anna Christie* (1921), *Strange Interlude* (1928) and the semi-autobiographical *Long Day's Journey Into Night* (1956). O'Neill died in 1957.

Poe, Edgar Allan

3321 Monument Avenue
Richmond, Virginia

This house/museum is the oldest known dwelling within the original city of Richmond, dating back to before the Revolutionary War. Edgar Allan Poe lived nearby in the early in his career, and the Poe Museum features the life and work of the great writer by documenting his accomplishments with pictures, relics, and more, all focusing on his many years in Richmond. Established in 1921, the Poe museum is only blocks away from Poe's first Richmond home and his first place of employment, the *Southern Literary Messenger*.

Poe, Edgar Allan

100 Broadway
Baltimore, Maryland

The circumstances surrounding Edgar Allan Poe's death remain a mystery even today. What's known is this: after a visit to Norfolk and Richmond for lectures, Poe was found drunk and wearing tatters outside a Baltimore tavern (reports vary on exactly where the tavern was located—many believe it was Ryan's Saloon on Lombard Street). How he arrived in that condition is not known. Had he been robbed? Had he simply gone on a bender? Was he experiencing some form of mental attack? It may never be clear. However, Poe

was in fact taken unconscious here, to Washington College Hospital where he died on Sunday, October 7, 1849, several days after arriving. He was just 39 years old.

The original building that once held the hospital is completely intact, but it has been converted into apartments. Two markers have been placed in memory of the great writer. Poe is buried not far from here in the yard of Westminster Presbyterian Church, located at Fayette and Greene Streets in West Baltimore. His gravesite has regularly been visited by someone who has left a half a bottle of cognac and roses since 1949. Another nearby Poe landmark in Baltimore is the Poe House located at 203 Amity Street. Poe lived here for several years in the early 1830s with his aunt, among others. It was during this time in Poe's life that he decided to write short stories instead of poetry.

Pollock, Jackson

46 East 8th Street
New York City, New York

The famed artist's first painting studio was located nearby at 51 East 9th Street, but this is where Pollock moved in 1936. From 1943-1945, he shared the home with his wife Lee Krasner. The couple eventually moved out to Long Island (where Pollock was killed in a 1956 car crash).

Rauschenberg, Robert

381 Lafayette Street
New York City, New York

After exploding onto the art scene in the 1960s, artist Robert Rauschenberg built an impressive home and studio by fusing this loft with the church that can be glimpsed in the rear. Rauschenberg's enormously inventive paintings incorporated everyday images and objects in a style that would go on to influence hundreds of other artists. Over the years, Rauschenberg has also collaborated with composer John Cage and choreographer Merce Cunningham.

Red Lion Inn

30 Main Street
Stockbridge, Massachusetts
413-298-5545

The Red Lion Inn is one of the few remaining American inns in continuous use since the 18th century. It's been providing food and lodging since 1773, and it was even immortalized in Norman Rockwell's painting *Main Street, Stockbridge*. The Red Lion Inn has 109 guest rooms and suites, both formal and casual dining, and it is a great place take a step back in time in one of the prettiest parts of New England.

Rockwell, Norman

9 Glendale Road
Stockbridge, Massachusetts
413-298-4100

The Norman Rockwell Museum houses the world's largest and most significant collection of original Rockwell art. Highlights include enduring favorites from Rockwell's *Saturday Evening Post* covers, the powerful *Four Freedoms*, and the nostalgic *Stockbridge Main Street at Christmas*. The Norman Rockwell Archive contains more than 100,000 photographs, letters, and other rare mementos. The great artist lived in Stockbridge for the last 25 years of his life and many of his world-renowned images were drawn from the surrounding community and its residents.

Rogers, Will

From his birthplace home in Oklahoma to his Santa Monica Ranch in Pacific Palisades, California, philosopher and American icon Will Rogers left a memorable trail of landmarks. Rogers, a natural born performer and charmer, used cowboy-roping tricks in his comedic performances and eventually started calling himself a "Poet Lariat." His satirical outlook on life won him millions of fans and he left a deep legacy as a comedian, philosopher, movie star, newspaper columnist, and author.

In 1922, at the age of 43, Will Rogers began his writing career working for no less than *The New York Times*. His daily column, "Will Rogers Says," was soon syndicated which brought him a national audience for his sharp-witted takes on politics, the economy, government, and everyday life. Tragically, Rogers died in an airplane crash off the coast of Alaska in 1935.

Dog Iron Ranch and Birthplace Home

Route 2
Oologah, Oklahoma
918-275-4201

Will Rogers was born in this attractive Greek Revival-style house in 1879, four years after the house was built. He spent his first 11 years in this house known as "The White House on the Verdigris." In 1890, after his mom died, Will and his dad moved to Claremore, Oklahoma. Today, visitors to this site can actually see the room where Will was born.

Rogers, Will

Shrine of the Sun

4250 Cheyenne Mountain Zoo Road
Colorado Springs, Colorado
719-578-5367

In 1935, the year Will Rogers was killed in an airplane crash, a friend of his named Spencer Penrose was in the midst of building a scenic mountain drive to allow a majestic view of Colorado Springs, Colorado. Upon hearing of his friend's untimely death, Penrose dedicated the shrine located at the top of the mountain drive in honor of Rogers. Visitors today will discover a photographic timeline of the life of Will Rogers.

The Will Rogers Memorial

1720 West Will Rogers Boulevard
Claremore, Oklahoma
800-324-9455

This 16,652 square-foot building was destined to become Will Rogers's retirement home, not a museum. However, after he was killed, plans changed and in 1938, it opened as a shrine to the gifted philosopher. Today, visitors get to experience the great American "Who never met a man he didn't like." There are nine galleries here containing thousands of artifacts and memorabilia dedicated to Rogers.

The Will Rogers Museum maintains an extensive research library dedicated to Rogers's life and time. An archive, which is not open for general tours, contains photographs, manuscripts, personal letters, and other Rogers memorabilia.

Will Rogers State Historic Park

1501 Will Rogers State Park Road
Pacific Palisades, California
310-454-8212

Will Rogers lived on this 186-acre ranch from 1924-1935 with his wife Betty and their three kids. Living here, Rogers entertained hundreds of notable Americans including

movie stars and politicians. Today, the home is open to the public, and so are the woody grounds, which are perfect for picnicking and hiking.

Stieglitz Gallery

291 Fifth Avenue
New York City, New York

This is site of what was almost certainly America's most important art gallery. Renowned photographer and owner Alfred Steiglitz's first gallery is where painters such as Georgia O'Keeffe and Picasso had their first shows, and where photographers such as Paul Strand, Steicher and Stieglitz exhibited. Stieglitz championed the emerging American modernist artists—such as Arthur Dove, Marsden Hartley and John Marin—supporting them monetarily and showing their work at his gallery called "291," named for its address on Fifth Avenue (today it's a bank).

Stieglitz's gallery was the first venue in the country to actively exhibit avant-garde American and European art, including artists Matisse and Duchamp. Stieglitz exhibited Georgia O'Keeffe's West Texas watercolors in 1917, which was his last gallery exhibition, and the two became lovers and married in 1924.

Stuart, Gilbert

815 Gilbert Stuart Road
Saunderstown, Rhode Island

The artist Gilbert Stuart was born here on December 3, 1755. He grew to become a renowned portraitist. In fact, in his five-decade career, of the 1100 pictures he produced, less than 10 were not likenesses. Of these portraits, nearly one-tenth are images of George Washington, to whom he was introduced by their mutual friend Chief Justice John Jay.

Perhaps most famous is the Washington portrait of Stuart's that appears on the dollar bill. (In addition to Washington, Stuart also painted President Adams, President Jefferson, President Madison and President Monroe.) Stuart died on July 9, 1828 at the age of 72. He is buried with many other influential Americans in the Old South Burial Ground in Boston. The historically significant birthplace includes Stuart's former home, a restored gristmill, and the millpond and grounds.

To Kill a Mockingbird

Monroe County Courthouse
31 North Alabama Avenue
Monroeville, Alabama
251-575-7433

Harper Lee's best-selling, Pulitzer Prize-winning novel *To Kill a Mockingbird*–with its memorable characters Atticus Finch, Scout, Jem, Dill and Boo Radley–was inspired by Lee's hometown of Monroeville, Alabama. Many literary scholars and local residents will attest to their belief that some of Ms. Lee's childhood acquaintances served as models for the colorful personalities in the revered book concerning the struggle against racial injustice in the South during the 1930s. One of her playmates was Truman Capote, who spent early years and summers in Monroeville with his cousins and aunts; Harper Lee revealed that the character Dill is derived from Capote.

The beautiful old Courthouse on the town square, which now houses the Monroe County Heritage Museums, was the model for the famed courtroom scene from the book. After movie rights were acquired, the director, film crew and Gregory Peck (who played Atticus in the movie) traveled to Monroeville in the early 1960s in hopes of filming here, but the town had changed too much. Today, however, more than 20,000 people a year come to visit the museum, many of whom are there because of their interest in *To Kill A Mockingbird*. Admission is free.

Trotsky, Leon

77 St. Marks Place
New York City, New York

When the noted Bolshevik leader Leon Trotsky was exiled from Russia in 1917, he ended up here in the East Village. In the basement of this building, Trotsky worked on the dissident newspaper called *Novy Mir* (The New World). The Russian Communist revolutionary was one of the principal leaders in the establishment of the U.S.S.R.

Twain, Mark

21 Fifth Avenue at East 9th Street
New York City, New York

It's no longer here, but where this apartment building stands is where writer Mark Twain's house was located between 1904 and 1908. A 65-year-old man when he moved here, Twain left New York forever in 1908, after the death of his daughter, Jean. She had long experienced epileptic attacks and died while taking a bath the day before Christmas. In 1954, the house was razed along with the famous Breevort Hotel, which stood on the same block.

Warhol, Andy

Andy Warhol Museum

117 Sandusky Street
Pittsburgh, Pennsylvania
412-237-8300

There's no place else like it—more than 3,000 objects and ephemera from Andy Warhol's extensive personal archive are on display for the first time in the U.S. The museum is housed in a renovated, seven-floor warehouse building and features more than 500 works of art, drawn from its extensive collections of works by Andy Warhol in all media, as well as from its huge archives and a collection of works by other artists. Warhol's films are screened continuously at the museum, and of course, the gift shop is phenomenal.

Residence

57 East 66th Street
New York City, New York

In 1974, Warhol purchased this six-story townhouse for $310,000. Warhol paid the full amount upfront so he wouldn't have to deal with a mortgage. He lived here for the rest of his life and a plaque on the side of the pretty home states that it was the home of "famous pop artist Andy Warhol." In 1988, the Warhol Estate auctioned off some ten thousand items belonging to the artist, and it netted a record $30 million dollars—the single largest collection ever handled by Sotheby's.

Warhol, Andy

Andy Warhol Preserve

Off Route 27 (a half mile east of the intersection with East Lake Drive)
Eastern Tip of Montauk, Long Island, New York

In 1972, Warhol bought a home here on the farthest reaches of Montauk with his friend, film director Paul Morrissey. Between 1972 and 1987, Warhol entertained everyone from Liz Taylor, John Lennon, and Liza Minnelli out here. The Rolling Stones rehearsed for their 1975 tour of the America's here, and on August 6, 1977, the artist celebrated his 49th birthday here. After Warhol's death in 1987, Morrissey donated 15 acres of the property to The Nature Conservancy to create the Andy Warhol Preserve in honor of the artist.

The Factory(s)

Much of Warhol's myth, mystique and style was developed over the years at the various "Factory(s)" he presided over in New York City—the studio/hangouts that served as a magnet for the glittering underground in New York, and that would influence so much of Warhol's work. These are the various locations where the Factory(s) existed:

Factory I

231 East 47th Street
New York City, New York

The Factory started here in 1964 on the fifth floor of a building beneath an antiques store called "The Connoisseur's Corner." A photographer by the name of Billy Name who crashed at the Factory painted the Mid-Hudson with an industrial silver paint that ultimately became the trademark of the Factory look.

Factory II

33 Union Square West
New York City, New York

After a couple of years, Factory I was torn down and so Warhol moved his colorful circus here to Union Square. It was at this location that Warhol began shooting films. In 1968, a woman named Valerie Solanas shot and almost killed Warhol here. While working at this Factory, Warhol also came up with the idea to make celebrity portraits his mainstay.

Warhol, Andy

Factory III

860 Broadway
New York City, New York

The Factory moved here in 1974, just around the corner from Factory II. From here, Warhol continued to paint and produce celebrity portraits. By now, he was also very busy in running *Interview* magazine. Today, there is a Petco store on the site.

Factory IV

158 Madison Avenue
New York City, New York

Ten years later, 1984 saw the last incarnation of the Factory here at an old Con-Edison substation between 32nd and 33rd Streets. Warhol had just several years to live at this point.

New York Hospital-Cornell Medical Center

525 East 68th Street
New York City, New York

Andy Warhol checked into this hospital on Friday, February 20, 1987 under the alias "Bob Robert." Routine gall bladder surgery was performed on February 21st, and then the artist was taken to a private room located on the 12th floor of Baker Pavilion. At 4:00 A.M. the next day, Warhol's blood pressure was recorded as "stable," but at 5:45 A.M. Warhol turned blue and his pulse became very weak before ceasing. Though the hospital staff tried for 45 minutes to resuscitate him, Andy Warhol was pronounced dead at 6:21 A.M. on February 22, 1987. He was just 58 years old. Andy Warhol is laid to rest at St. John Divine Cemetery in Bethel Park, Pennsylvania.

Weir, J. Alden

735 Nod Hill Road
Wilton, Connecticut
203-834-1896

This beloved Connecticut farm inspired American Impressionist painter J. Alden Weir (1852-1919) to explore his artistic impressions of nature. Over the course of 37 years, Weir and visiting friends such as Childe Hassam and John Twachtman painted the gentle rolling hills, rocky pastures, people, and animals of the 153-acre farm. After Weir's death in 1919, the creativity continued.

Weir's daughter Dorothy married sculptor Mahonri Young, who built a second studio on the property. After Young's death, the farm was sold to artist couple Sperry and Doris Andrews. Each generation enjoyed artistic inspiration at Weir Farm. Each generation also honored and preserved the historic integrity of the landscape.

Today, park visitors can still see this American Impressionist landscape and are free to wander and explore. Artists should know that the park's partner, the Weir Farm Trust, also provides professional artists with opportunities such as its artist-in-residency program.

Wharton, Edith

14 West 23rd Street
New York City, New York

Novelist Edith Wharton was born here January 24, 1862. When she was four, the family moved to Europe for six years but they returned in 1872 and Edith lived on this street until her marriage in 1885. Wharton's career spanned over 40 years and included the publication of more than 40 books, including *The Age of Innocence, Ethan Fromme*, and *The House of Mirth.* Considered by many to be one of the major American novelists and short story writers of the 20th century, Edith Wharton died in France in 1937.

Wilde, Oscar

Chickering Hall
Fifth Avenue at 18th Street
New York City, New York

On December 24, 1881, the legendary writer Oscar Wilde (*The Picture of Dorian Gray*) embarked on a voyage to America. Sponsored by the London theatre manager D'Oyly Carte, he was to spend one year lecturing across North America and Canada (his subject was to be the Aesthetic Movement in Britain).

Wilde would eventually visit many cities from January through October, 1882, but this is where he gave his very first lecture on January 9, 1882 (the hall is no longer here). The years following this triumphant tour were not kind to Wilde. In 1895 he would be convict-

ed of gross indecency and sentenced to serve two years hard labor in a prison just outside London, England.

He was released on May 19, 1897 and spent his last years penniless, in self-inflicted exile from society and artistic circles. He went under the assumed name of "Sebastian Melmoth," after the central character of the gothic novel *Melmoth the Wanderer*. After his release, he wrote the famous poem *The Ballad of Reading Gaol* ("For he who lives more lives than one, more deaths than one must die"). Oscar Wilde died of cerebral meningitis on November 30, 1900 in a Paris hotel.

Williams, Tennessee

Birthplace Home and Welcome Center

Corner of Main and Third Street, South
Columbus, Mississippi
504-561-5858

Built in 1875, this two-story, Victorian house was the birthplace home of the great playwright Thomas Lanier (Tennessee) Williams. Moved to its present location in 1995, this home now serves as a State Welcome Center. Williams lived in this home, then the Rectory for St. Paul's Episcopal Church, for three years. Walter Dankin, William's grandfather, served as the church's Rector. The home, built of wood native to Mississippi, has been restored to its 1911 condition.

Only the first floor is open to visitors, and tourists are welcome to come and go at their leisure. Visitors will also enjoy the newspaper and magazine articles about Williams that are displayed. Additionally, many tourists enjoy walking just one block north to see the stately St. Paul's Episcopal Church where the young Williams was baptized.

Williams, Tennessee

Hotel Elysee

60 East 54th Street
New York City, New York
212-753-1066

On February 24, 1983, 72-year-old Tennessee Williams choked to death on a bottle cap at his New York City residence at the Hotel Elysee (it was the lid of one of his pill bottles). He is buried at the Calvary Cemetery at 5239 West Florissant Avenue in St. Louis, Missouri (314-381-1313). Also buried there are Dred Scott and Civil War General William Tecumseh Sherman.

A Streetcar Named Desire I

La Concha Hotel
430 Duval Street
Key West, Florida
305-296-2991

Royalty and Presidents have both graced this classy, art deco-flavored hotel. After Tennessee Williams starting hitting it big with *The Glass Menagerie* in 1944, he rented a two-room suite that he shared with his grandfather. Today, these suites, rooms 563 and 663 are named the Tennessee Williams suite and Ernest Hemingway suites (Hemingway also stayed here). It was here where Williams started the play *The Poker Night*, which became *A Streetcar Named Desire* (a 1948 Pulitzer Prize-winner).

A Streetcar Named Desire II

Hotel Maison de Ville
727 Rue Toulouse
New Orleans, Louisiana
800-695-8284

Before he purchased his own house in the French Quarter, Tennessee Williams would often stay in room number nine of this gorgeous, historic hotel, where he completed *A Streetcar Named Desire* and drank Sazerac in the hotel courtyard. The room, which opens onto the patio, was also the setting for Dick Cavett's famous 1974 interview with Williams. Today, guests can sleep in the same room where Tennessee Williams wrote one of the world's most famous plays.

Additionally, the seven Audubon Cottages, about a block and a half away on Dauphine Street, were named for the illustrious naturalist and painter John James Audubon. In 1821, he produced a portion of his *Birds of America* series while residing in what is now called Cottage Number One. (This is also part of the Hotel Maison de Ville.)

Wood, Grant

The Grant Wood Studio and Visitor Center
810 Second Avenue SE
Cedar Rapids, Iowa
319-366-7503

Grant Wood's home and studio was located here from 1924 to 1934. Near downtown Cedar Rapids, the Studio is owned and operated by the Cedar Rapids Museum of Art, which houses the world's largest collection of works by Grant Wood. Wood was a prominent member of the Regionalist movement. His most famous painting, *American Gothic*, which is now at the Art Institute of Chicago, was painted in this studio in 1930.

The highly acclaimed artist was born in Anamosa in 1891 and died in 1942 following a very successful career. Tours of this fascinating studio/museum are available. The Grant Wood Studio is a founding member of the Historic Artists Homes and Studios affiliates program of the National Trust for Historic Preservation.

Wright, Frank Lloyd

12621 North Frank Lloyd Wright Boulevard
Scottsdale, Arizona
480-860-2700

Famed architect Frank Lloyd Wright started creating this complex, called "Taliesin West," in 1937 to serve as his home, studio and architectural laboratory. Today, a National Historic Landmark, Taliesin West (pronounced Tally EHS´sen) is now a small community of about 70 students, architects, and administrators who study and perpetuate Wright's daring architectural concepts. Located 13 miles north of old Scottsdale, the facilities include theaters for film and the performing arts, architectural offices, pools, gardens, and terraces, as well as the living quarters of the residents and a workshop and studios of the Frank Lloyd Wright School of Architecture and the Taliesin Fellowship.

Pop Culture Landmarks by State

Alabama
To Kill a Mockingbird – 315
Tuskegee Institute – 135

Arizona
Boyer, Charles – 167
Depp, Johnny – 171
Dillinger, John – 148
Douglas, Michael – 171
Miles, Sarah – 177
Miranda, Ernesto – 153
Ross, Diana – 182
Simmons, Richard – 184
Swayze, Patrick – 188
Take It Easy – 242
Williams, Ted – 192
Wright, Frank Lloyd – 322

Arkansas
Evening Shade – 260
Hemingway, Ernest – 298
Wal-Mart – 96

California
A&W – 89
Abdul, Paula – 163
Adams, Nick – 163
Alamo Square – 247
American Pie – 248
Battle of the Network Stars – 250
Beach Boys – 194
Beatles – 194
Begelman, David – 164
Bennifer – 165, 166
Beverly Hills Cop – 251
Bingenheimer, Rodney – 195
Biggest Parking Lot – 18
Blockheads – 251
Boarding House – 195
Bob's Big Boy – 90
Body Double – 253

Bow, Clara – 167
Boysenberry – 66
Bronstein, Phil – 168
Bubble Gum Alley – 19
Buckley, Tim – 169
C.H.I.P.S. – 257
Cabazon – 20
Car Wash – 254
Chaplin, Charlie – 255–256
Charles M. Schulz – 288
Charles, Ray – 198
Cheeseburger III – 67
Chess – 21
Chez Jay – 22
Ciro's – 22
Crash, Darby – 200
Diamonds Are Forever – 258
Fabulous Baker Boys – 260
Fender Guitars – 203
Ferris Bueller's Day Off – 261
Formosa Café – 23
Fox Venice – 204
French Dip Sandwich – 72
Gershwin, Gorge – 207
Guns 'n' Roses – 210
Hardcastle and McCormick – 263
IHOP – 90
Jack in the Box – 91
Jackson, Michael – 173
Janes House – 23
Jeffers, Robinson – 300
Johnie's Broiler – 264
Joplin, Janis – 216
Keith, Brian – 174
L.A. Confidential – 265
Lamarr, Heddy – 175
Laurel Canyon Country Store – 217
Legally Blonde – 265
Liberty Bell Slot Machine – 41
Lugosi, Bela – 176
MADD – 126

Acknowledgments

Acknowledgments

Writing a book like this (and the others before it) would be tough without the assistance, support and generosity of others.

Thanks to my publisher/editor/friend, Jeffrey Goldman; his wife, Kimberly; their son, Nathaniel; and their newest bundle of joy due to be published soon. Also to Amy Inouye and Ken Niles for their excellent work in designing and producing this book.

I also want to acknowledge Hampton Inn Hotels, for allowing me to be part of the award-winning Save-A-Landmark program, specifically Hidden Landmarks. To know that a corporation does so much in the way of preservation and historic education is impressive. To be a part of it is a privilege. I encourage you to visit www.hamptonlandmarks.com to experience all that Hampton Inn is doing. Specifically, thank you to (at Hampton Inn and Hilton Hotels Corp.): Judy Christa-Cathey, Kendra Walker and Tori Walsh. It is such a pleasure to work with you. Same goes to my friends at Cohn/Wolfe, Los Angeles: Jeremy Baka, Dawn Verhulst, Allison Schwartz, Katie Wittenburg and Dawn Wells. (And a special thanks as well to Melissa O'Brien.)

Thanks also to David McAleer, Larry Helton, The Wayside Inn, Scott Michaels at www.findadeath.com, Adrianne Robinson, Michael Esslinger, Donna McCrohan Rosenthal, Pauline Frommer, Danielle Pedersen (and the great staff at Westways Magazine), the Cisco Chamber of Commerce, Hillary L. Geronemus, Lita Weissman at Borders, and Mark Sedenquist and Megan Edwards at www.RoadTripAmerica.com for their ideas, support and resources.

A big nod to Professor Robert Saldarini from Bergen Community College (and to the gang at Alpha Epsilon Phi—long live Griswold!) and to the Phi Theta Kappa International Honor Society. I am now a proud honorary member of PTK, and their On The Road program last year and this (which utilized my books as pop culture tools) made me feel honored. Thank you, fellow Kappans.

Thanks to the National Park Service and the Library of Congress for their terrific resources. Also, to the many Chambers of Commerce that helped me with my research. Thanks to OnPoint designs for tending to www.chrisepting.com. (Thanks Oscar!) To my old friend, John Mungo, thanks for being there—even 30 years later! To my new friend, Kenny Foderaro, thank you for helping the world see things better.

To my wife, Jean; son, Charlie; daughter, Claire; and my mom—thank you as always. I love you. (And Charlie, you are the index king!)

To you holding this book right now, thank you so much for the support. There are many books out there to choose from and I appreciate that, at least for this moment, you have this one in your hands. I hope you enjoy it.

Chris Epting

Photo Credits

America's Stonehenge, p. 15
Crown Point Chamber of Commerce, p. 27
The James Dean Gallery, p. 29
www.buckysdome.org, p. 33
Pikeville Tourism, p. 38
Jean Epting, p. 43
Berkeley Plantation, p.51
Tony Packo's Café, p. 52
Winchester Mystery House, p. 55
Courtesy of News/Talk 1020 KDKA, Pittsburgh; Infinity Broadcasting Corporation, p. 62 (top)
Ed Jackson, p. 68
Cozy Dog, p. 70
Dr. Pepper Museum, p. 71
Jell-O Museum, p. 73
Judy Garland Birthplace, p. 80
Cisco Chamber of Commerce, p. 81
Lawrence Berkeley National Laboratory, p. 85
Boscobel Hotel, p. 87
Subway, p. 93 (top)
John Kane, p. 100 (bottom)
Larry Helton, p. 146, p. 182
Indiana Historical Bureau, State of Indiana., p. 159
Scott Michaels, p. 163, p. 174, p. 176
David McAleer, p. 170, p. 200 (top), p. 244 (bottom), p. 262 (bottom)
Mike Oldham, p. 191
Arcade Restaurant, p. 226
Poplar tunes, p. 233 (top)
Schwab Dry Goods, p. 233 (bottom)
Wuxtry Records, p. 237
Adrianne Robinson, p. 269 (bottom), p. 134 (bottom)
Grant Wood Tourism Center and Gallery, p. 322

All remaining photos were either shot by the author or culled from the author's personal collection. Any omissions or errors are deeply regretted and will be rectified upon reprint. Additionally, all appropriate lengths were taken to secure proper photo credit and permissions.

Like Elvis? You'll *Love* Marilyn Monroe!

Marilyn Monroe Dyed Here
More Locations of America's Pop Culture Landmarks
by Chris Epting

In 1945, a watershed moment in pop culture history occurred when Norma Jeane Baker walked into a beauty salon at 6513 Hollywood Boulevard and changed her hair from brunette to blonde. With *Marilyn Monroe Dyed Here*, Chris Epting follows-up his critically acclaimed *James Dean Died Here* with another collection of the locations where the most significant events in American popular culture took place. This fully illustrated encyclopedic look at the most famous and infamous pop culture events includes historical information on over 600 landmarks—as well as their exact locations. *Marilyn Monroe Dyed Here* is an amazing portrait of the bizarre, shocking, weird and wonderful moments that have come to define American popular culture.

Chapters and Sample Entries

Americana: The Weird and the Wonderful
- *Saturday Night Live*'s "Cheeseburger!" restaurant
- Elvis Presley gets a haircut

History and Tragedy
- Little Rock, Arkansas high school integration
- The Great White concert fire

Crime, Murder, and Assassination
- Elizabeth Smart kidnapping
- Central Park jogger

Celebrities: The Tragic and the Ugly
- Frank Sinatra landmarks
- Marilyn Monroe's America

Let's Go to the Movies
- Woody Allen's New York
- Alfred Hitchcock's California

Rock 'n' Roll, R&B, and the Blues
- A Bob Dylan walking tour
- Rolling Stones landmarks

Channel Surfing
- *Laverne & Shirley*'s brewery
- *Welcome Back Kotter*'s high school

The Write Stuff
- Steinbeck writes *Grapes of Wrath*
- Ernest Hemingway commits suicide

$16.95 • ISBN 1-891661-39-6 • Trade Paper • 312 pages
6 × 9 • Hundreds of Photos • Travel / Popular Culture

Call 1-800-784-9553 to Order

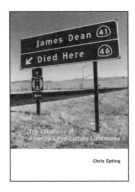

Books Available from Santa Monica Press

**Atomic Wedgies, Wet Willies
& Other Acts of Roguery**
by Greg Tananbaum and
Dan Martin
128 pages $11.95

Blues for Bird
by Martin Gray
288 pages $16.95

The Butt Hello
*and other ways my cats
drive me crazy*
by Ted Meyer
96 pages $9.95

Café Nation
*Coffee Folklore, Magick,
and Divination*
by Sandra Mizumoto Posey
224 pages $9.95

Calculated Risk
*The Extraordinary Life of
Jimmy Doolittle*
by Jonna Doolittle Hoppes
360 pages $24.95

Can a Dead Man Strike Out?
*Offbeat Baseball Questions
and Their Improbable
Answers*
by Mark S. Halfon
192 pages $11.95

Cats Around the World
by Ted Meyer
96 pages $9.95

Childish Things
by Davis & Davis
96 pages $19.95

The Dog Ate My Resumé
by Zack Arnstein and
Larry Arnstein
192 pages $11.95

Dogme Uncut
*Lars von Trier, Thomas
Vinterberg and the Gang
That Took on Hollywood*
by Jack Stevenson
312 pages $16.95

Elvis Presley Passed Here
*Even More Locations of
America's Pop Culture
Landmarks*
by Chris Epting
336 pages $16.95

**Exotic Travel Destinations
for Families**
by Jennifer M. Nichols and
Bill Nichols
360 pages $16.95

Footsteps in the Fog
*Alfred Hitchcock's
San Francisco*
by Jeff Kraft and
Aaron Leventhal
240 pages $24.95

How to Speak Shakespeare
by Cal Pritner and
Louis Colaianni
144 pages $16.95

**How to Win Lotteries,
Sweepstakes, and Contests in
the 21st Century**
by Steve "America's
Sweepstakes King" Ledoux
224 pages $14.95

**Jackson Pollock:
Memories Arrested in Space**
by Martin Gray
216 pages $14.95

James Dean Died Here
*The Locations of America's
Pop Culture Landmarks*
by Chris Epting
312 pages $16.95

The Keystone Kid
Tales of Early Hollywood
by Coy Watson, Jr.
312 pages $24.95

Letter Writing Made Easy!
*Featuring Sample Letters for
Hundreds of Common
Occasions*
by Margaret McCarthy
224 pages $12.95

**Letter Writing Made Easy!
Volume 2**
*Featuring More Sample
Letters for Hundreds of
Common Occasions*
by Margaret McCarthy
224 pages $12.95

Life is Short. Eat Biscuits!
by Amy Jordan Smith
96 pages $9.95

Marilyn Monroe Dyed Here
*More Locations of America's
Pop Culture Landmarks*
by Chris Epting
312 pages $16.95

Movie Star Homes
by Judy Artunian and
Mike Oldham
312 pages $16.95

Offbeat Food
*Adventures in an
Omnivorous World*
by Alan Ridenour
240 pages $19.95

Offbeat Marijuana
*The Life and Times of the
World's Grooviest Plant*
by Saul Rubin
240 pages $19.95

Offbeat Museums
*The Collections and Curators
of America's Most Unusual
Museums*
by Saul Rubin
240 pages $19.95

A Prayer for Burma
by Kenneth Wong
216 pages $14.95

Quack!
*Tales of Medical Fraud from
the Museum of Questionable
Medical Devices*
by Bob McCoy
240 pages $19.95

Redneck Haiku
by Mary K. Witte
112 pages $9.95

**School Sense: How to Help
Your Child Succeed in
Elementary School**
by Tiffani Chin, Ph.D.
408 pages $16.95

Silent Echoes
*Discovering Early Hollywood
Through the Films of
Buster Keaton*
by John Bengtson
240 pages $24.95

Tiki Road Trip
*A Guide to Tiki Culture
in North America*
by James Teitelbaum
288 pages $16.95

	Quantity	Amount
Atomic Wedgies, Wet Willies & Other Acts of Roguery ($11.95)	_____	_____
American Hydrant ($24.95)	_____	_____
The Butt Hello . . . and Other Ways My Cats Drive Me Crazy ($9.95)	_____	_____
Calculated Risk ($24.95)	_____	_____
Can a Dead Man Strike Out? ($11.95)	_____	_____
Childish Things ($19.95)	_____	_____
The Dog Ate My Resumé ($11.95)	_____	_____
Dogme Uncut ($16.95)	_____	_____
Elvis Presley Passed Here ($16.95)	_____	_____
Exotic Travel Destinations for Families ($16.95)	_____	_____
Footsteps in the Fog: Alfred Hitchcock's San Francisco ($24.95)	_____	_____
A House Rabbit Primer ($14.95)	_____	_____
How to Speak Shakespeare ($16.95)	_____	_____
How to Win Lotteries, Sweepstakes, and Contests . . . ($14.95)	_____	_____
Jackson Pollock: Memories Arrested in Space ($14.95)	_____	_____
James Dean Died Here: America's Pop Culture Landmarks ($16.95)	_____	_____
The Keystone Kid: Tales of Early Hollywood ($24.95)	_____	_____
The Largest U.S. Cities Named after a Food ($16.95)	_____	_____
Letter Writing Made Easy! ($12.95)	_____	_____
Letter Writing Made Easy! Volume 2 ($12.95)	_____	_____
Life is Short. Eat Biscuits! ($9.95)	_____	_____
Loving Through Bars ($21.95)	_____	_____
Marilyn Monroe Dyed Here ($16.95)	_____	_____
Movie Star Homes ($16.95)	_____	_____
Offbeat Museums ($19.95)	_____	_____
A Prayer for Burma ($14.95)	_____	_____
Quack! Tales of Medical Fraud ($19.95)	_____	_____
Redneck Haiku ($9.95)	_____	_____
School Sense ($16.95)	_____	_____
Silent Echoes: Early Hollywood Through Buster Keaton ($24.95)	_____	_____
Tiki Road Trip ($16.95)	_____	_____
	_____	_____
	_____	_____

Shipping & Handling:		
1 book	$3.00	
Each additional book is	$ .50	

	Subtotal	_____
CA residents add 8.25% sales tax		_____
Shipping and Handling (see left)		_____
	TOTAL	_____

Name _____

Address _____

City _____ State _____ Zip _____

☐ Visa ☐ MasterCard Card No.:_____

Exp. Date _____ Signature _____

☐ **Enclosed is my check or money order payable to:**

Santa Monica Press LLC
P.O. Box 1076
Santa Monica, CA 90406